Brand Choice

Brand Choice

Revealing Customers' Unconscious-Automatic and Strategic Thinking Processes

Randolph J. Trappey III and Arch G. Woodside

First published 2005 by
PALGRAVE MACMILLAN
Houndmills, Basingstoke, Hampshire RG21 6XS and
175 Fifth Avenue, New York, N. Y. 10010
Companies and representatives throughout the world

PALGRAVE MACMILLAN is the global academic imprint of the Palgrave Macmillan division of St. Martin's Press, LLC and of Palgrave Macmillan Ltd. Macmillan® is a registered trademark in the United States, United Kingdom and other countries. Palgrave is a registered trademark in the European Union and other countries.

ISBN 1–4039–4641–8 hardback

This book is printed on paper suitable for recycling and made from fully managed and sustained forest sources.

A catalogue record for this book is available from the British Library.

A catalog record for this book can be obtained from the Library of Congress.

10   9   8   7   6   5   4   3   2   1
14   13   12   11   10   09   08   07   06   05

Printed and bound in Great Britain by
Antony Rowe Ltd, Chippenham and Eastbourne

Contents

List of Tables

List of Figures

1
Customer Thinking and Brand Choice

Introduction: learning what evokes the brand or store in customers' minds

Research on consumer automatic-unconscious and strategic-cognitive processes in associating brands with evaluative attributes (i.e., best quality; best value; slowest service) offer valuable tools for marketers wanting to understand the primary associations (i.e., the drivers) a brand owns in the minds of customers. A few such drivers connect to the brand that the consumer identifies as her primary choice. With the research methods described in this book, advertising and marketing strategists also learn which, if any, consumers retrieve their brand automatically-unconsciously in connection for important evaluative attributes.

Marketing strategists may make the mistake of advertising an attribute and benefit consequence that their brand cannot possibly possess. This failure-to-connect may be the case because a competing brand dominates the market with respect to this particular attribute or benefit. Strategists may also err in advertising a quality or benefit that has little or nothing to do with their brand's ability to attract and maintain primary customers. Given that consumers can easily summon up a brand as first coming to mind for a specific attribute, a handful of such automatic associates are demonstrably valuable in predicting brand choice behaviour.

Because most automatic brand associations are likely grounded in reality, this research offers a valuable tool for improving product and service offerings to consumers. Furthermore, research on attitude-accessibility connecting brands with evaluative beliefs is particularly essential for building paramorphic models of consumer unconscious and cognitive processes – especially unconscious processes involving bottom-up agendas. The empirical models demonstrated in this text fit well with Howard's (1989) proposal for limited problem-solving situations. Research presented herein also provides circumstantial evidence in support of the associate-to-cue proposition and choice sequence proposed by Holden (1993, p. 387): "By placing cues known to facilitate retrieval in the choice situation, the probability of brand evocation is increased, and thereby increases the probability of choice of the brand – without evocation, the probability of choice is zero."

This monograph is the product of applied and theoretical studies conducted and reported in part by the authors. The work reflects generally the authors' philosophical partiality for working with commercial enterprises in preference to relying upon government and social funding bodies for monies when conducting business related research. Consequently, much of the work included herein tests and expands existing marketing and consumer psychology theories in an applied commercial framework. Notwithstanding this, parts of the research – Chapter 7 in particular, is research conducted entirely on an experimental basis funded primarily by the authors with the aim of commercial marketing applications at a later date.

Each chapter is a separate self-contained research study. Taken in their entirety, the chapters present a common theme of research pertaining to some aspect of cognitive processing models of brand choice behaviour. What follows is a brief outline of the text organisation and a synopsis of the contents of each of the chapters.

Understanding why customers buy your brand

Chapter 2 explores automatic-unconscious processing of information associated with brand recall. In this chapter evidence is presented that a consumer's top-of-mind brand name associations with a few traces of information are robustly correlated to brand choice behaviour. The evidence demonstrates that consumers can quickly retrieve a brand name from their long-term memories when asked an unaided recall question for specific attributes – such as, for automobiles, "most reliable" and "best styling." Not only are these unaided brand name responses useful for understanding primary brand choice behaviour but also for learning why a brand appeals to some customers and not to others.

This chapter further explores how when shopping, a customer is likely to refer to a limited number of evaluative attributes and select the brand automatically associated with these attributes. The chapter reviews the relevant psychological and consumer research literature on automatic-unconscious processing. The details of the method and results of a field study to test the hypotheses are described. It culminates with a discussion and conclusions important for advertising research and marketing strategy formulation.

Customer portfolio analysis

Chapter 3 examines how customer portfolio analysis may be of use for improving retailers' efforts effectively to position their stores in the minds of consumers. In this chapter a customer portfolio for a store is demonstrated to include new-primary, loyal-primary, and defector (formerly primary) customers, as well as intermittent customers who shop chiefly at competing stores. Customers' attitude-accessibility with regard to first-linking a specified store with evaluative attributes can offer valuable information on the shopping behaviour of customers in a store's portfolio.

Several hypotheses related to customer portfolio analysis and store attitude-accessibility are examined. The principal hypothesis is that the attitude-accessibility of the major supermarkets competing in the same metropolitan area will differ substantially among loyal, new, competitors' customers, and defector customer segments for each store. More specifically, for a given store, greater shares of loyal and new customers will exhibit positive, store attitude-accessibility profiles compared to non-customers and defectors.

The results of a cross-sectional telephone survey of 317 supermarket shoppers are described, and the findings support the hypotheses. The chapter concludes with recommendations for planning changes in retailing positioning strategies and for monitoring success of implementing these strategies.

Understanding near and distant customers

Holden and Lutz (1992) propose that the reason consumers evoke different brands from long term memory into working memory is that different associates (e.g., benefits, attributes) have stronger links to some brands than others. This proposition is examined further in Chapter 4 for associate-to-store evocations for supermarket shopping, in a market environment where several competing supermarkets are readily accessible for shopping.

Chapter 4 expands on the central proposition of Holden and Lutz (1992) by offering additional related hypotheses: (H1) each competing store has a unique constellation of a few (3 to 7) associates that evoke the store's name among its primary customers; (H2) in associate-to-store retrievals, substantial differences occur in the proportions of a store's primary consumers evoking the store's name for a benefit among those consumers living closest to their primary store versus consumers living closest to competing stores; (H3) consumers are able to retrieve one or more competing stores (versus their primary store) for being "worst" on one or more benefits – for example, when asked to name the supermarket having the highest overall food prices.

The chapter reviews the relevant psychological and consumer research literature on automatic-unconscious processing and concludes with an application of the theory to store choice. The research in this chapter is of use to retailing strategists who seek an understanding of the causes for the gains and losses between competing stores.

Modelling bank loyalty

Keller (1993) demonstrates that raising awareness of a brand increases the probability that the brand will be a member of a set of brands that receive serious purchase consideration. In Chapter 3 it was demonstrated that a brand's attribute-to-brand evocations would vary amongst the brand's portfolio of customers – ranging from new, loyal, defector and competitor. Chapter 5 examines in detail to what extent these evocations differ between various levels of brand consciousness along with how they may interact with switching behaviour, loyalty, commitment and perceptions of risk.

More and more, financial services institutions recognise that customer ownership is a notion that can no longer be treated casually. Customer retention is regarded as a critical component of long-term profitability and survival. Competition has caused institutions to introduce permanent measures aimed at both maintaining and retaining profitable customer relationships. Much of the revolution is technology driven, with Internet banking playing a key role in a plethora of new products, services and brands aimed simultaneously at wooing new customers and retaining existing ones. Consequently, insight into brand switching behaviour amongst financial services customers is central to understanding how retention can be affected in the new knowledge economy.

Past research (Mittal and Lee, 1989; Goldsmith et al., 1991) reports a positive relationship between customer involvement and commitment. The research suggests further that commitment is a part of brand loyalty. However, little work has been done to explore the correlation between a customer's involvement and/or commitment with the financial services institution and the propensity to switch between institutions. Moreover, an examination of the role Internet banking may play in brand switching behaviour is absent.

Colgate and Stewart (1998) demonstrate significant variations pertaining to how remotely the customer wishes to deal with his or her bank. Nevertheless, little effort has been directed towards investigating whether or not the individual customer's perception of switching costs has an impact on the type of relationship he or she has with the financial services institution. With regard to this, Chapter 5 examines to what extent perceived switching costs affect a customer's propensity to switch financial services institutions. Furthermore, we examine the role Internet banking may have in changing the present situation.

Prospect theory (Kahnemann and Tversky, 1979) is a descriptive model of decision-making under risk. This concept is examined generally in relation to brand switching behaviour amongst financial services customers and in particular amongst holders of Internet accessible bank accounts. Chapter 5 also examines what is usually considered an intervening variable between customer loyalty and customer retention – the action control paradigm. Attentive to this theory, the research reported herein evaluates how it may be linked to customer switching behaviour amongst financial institutions.

Changing customer expectations requires marketers to interact differently and in most cases in an anticipatory manner. Because financial institutions will seek to offer increased convenience to bank customers by encouraging them to engage in virtual interactions, branding and customer loyalty issues will become particularly important in testing the validity and extending the theory of the previously mentioned constructs. Chapter 5 examines how concomitant higher levels of satisfaction and control connected with the virtual bank account may or may not increase customer loyalty.

Finally, will the perception and reality of lower switching costs associated with Internet accessible online bank accounts lessen the perceived risk customers' associate with changing banks? If so, will this increase the propensity of customers to switch financial institutions? To date, very little research has addressed this issue (Hermanns and Sauter, 1999). Chapter 5 concludes with an examination of this issue and proposes specific recommendations for marketers of financial services and products.

Knowledge and experience

How does a customer's knowledge and experience with a product or service interact with and/or increase net returns on advertising? Chapter 6 examines this issue through the lens of a quasi-experiment in advertising research. Quasi-experiments are tests of the effects of changing levels of outcome variables (e.g., sales levels) caused by treatment variables (e.g., advertising and linkage-advertising) when random assignment has not been used to create equivalent comparison groups from which treatment-caused change is inferred (Cook and Campbell, 1979, p. 6). Research presented in this chapter utilises nonequivalent but comparable groups to examine causal relationships between linkage-advertising and multiple dependent customer variables such as knowledge and experience. Linkage-advertising is the literature and related materials given to customers who respond to advertisers' offers of these materials (Woodside, 1994). Linkage-advertising "links the up-front advertising to the sale with additional arguments and benefits which the up-front advertising [i.e., the print or broadcast advertisement that includes the linkage offer] didn't have space or time to include" (Rapp and Collins, 1987).

Chapter 6 describes a large-scale field study of tourists frequenting Prince Edward Island, Canada. The study is an application of a quasi-experiment to determine the impact of linkage-advertising on several dependent variables. The method and results presented support the use of quasi-experiment designs in advertising research and the general proposition that linkage-advertising likely causes substantial changes in multiple consumer variables such as knowledge and experience. Chapter 6 also describes how the results from the field study can be used to estimate the return on investment of the linkage-advertising program.

First, we illustrate two quasi-experimental designs: a one-group post-test-only design and a quasi-experimental design with predicted higher order interaction effects. The first is used widely in assessing the effects of linkage-advertising but is not recommended. Next we depict the application of the method and results to data from the large-scale field study. Lastly, we examine the net revenues of the linkage-advertising program and the role consumer variables such as knowledge and experience may play. Recommendations are made for using quasi-experiments in advertising research.

The role of cognitive ability (g)

Though Fazio and colleagues (1989) established linkages between response latency (RTs), attitude and behaviour towards the brand, research in the consumer behaviour and marketing disciplines continues to ignore the role that human cognitive ability may play in the process. Are measures of response latency to unaided brand recall questions just proxy measures of reaction times to elementary cognitive tasks (ECT)? If this is the case, then what role if any does human cognitive ability as measured by g (general intelligence) play both in brand recall and in directing consumer attitudes, behaviours and decisions towards the brand?

ECTs are typically dissimilar to conventional cognitive ability tests in that test items require no reasoning or problem solving actions by the subject. Since ECTs are unlike IQ tests, which incorporate test items based on previously acquired knowledge, psychometric g can be systematically and independently studied. ECTs are designed to generate data from which individual differences in discrete processes such as stimulus apprehension, discrimination, choice, visual search, and information retrieval from short-term memory scan (STM) and long-term memory (LTM) can be ascertained. The tasks are typically so uncomplicated that each person in the study can execute them effortlessly with few if any errors. Test errors, if any, should not be the result of a lack of understanding of the task requirements by the subject in the study.

While unaided brand recall tests the strength of the brand, the study of its dependence on human factors such as cognitive ability may provide marketing managers with new knowledge about customers. An experiment was conducted first among children to understand the relationship between general intelligence (g) test scores and varied measures of response latency to tasks of unaided brand recall (TOMA) for high involvement and low involvement products. The research was then repeated as a large-scale study of adults living and residing in the London metropolitan area. Results from both the pilot study of children and the large-scale study of adults are reported herein.

Even though research by the authors and others have demonstrated that attitude-to-brand accessibility is an automatic-unconscious process, no previous research in this area has explored to what degree unaided brand recall could be affected by the speed of human information processing and by implication working memory (WM) capacity. Could it be that consumers with higher levels of g, who are demonstrably more capable of processing information at faster speeds, are able automatically to access and retrieve more brand information in a unit of time? If so, this would imply that consumers with higher levels of cognitive ability are likely to have more information available to them in the strategic processing phase of decision-making.

The hypotheses that this chapter explores propose that a subject's ability automatically access to brand names in memory and recall them in a timed unaided brand recall test is governed in part by the subjects information processing ability as reflected by g. It is further hypothesised that at a fundamental level, the recognition of advertising stimuli, the retrieval of information, the provision of a heuristic for brand evaluation, and the ultimate relevance decision that determines further higher-level processing, are all ultimately governed by human cognitive ability or general intelligence (g).

The purpose of the research is to offer preliminary evidence to the effect that "human variables" controlling for consumer behaviour necessarily include, together with age and gender, human cognitive abilities as well.

Conclusion

This chapter provides a review of the main findings for each of the chapters in this monograph. A brief discussion of the strategic and practical implications for marketers is included on a chapter-by-chapter basis. The final chapter includes also a to the point examination of the limitations that encompass the whole of the research, as well as avenues for future research. Future research should advance the research in Chapter 7 with respect to the role human cognitive ability may play in consumer brand recall, choice and other behaviours.

References

Colgate, M. and Stewart, K. "The challenge of relationships in services," *International Journal of Service Industry Management*, 9, 5 (1998).

Cook, T. D. and Campbell, D. T. *Quasi-experimentation*. Chicago: Rand McNally, 1979.

Fazio, R. H., Powell, M. C. and Williams, C. J. "The Role of Attitude Accessibility in the Attitude-to-Behaviour Process." *Journal of Consumer Research*, 16, 4 (1989): 280–88.

Goldsmith, R. E., Emmert, J. and Hofacker, C. "A causal model of consumer involvement: replication and extension" *Proceedings Winter Educators" Conference* (1991).

Hermanns, A. and Sauter, M. *Management-Handbuch Electronic Commerce*. Frankfurt: Verlag Vahlen, 1999.

Holden, S. J. S. "Understanding Brand Awareness: Let Me Give You a C(l)ue!" in *Advances in Consumer Research*, Volume 20, Provo, UT: Association for Consumer Research (1993): 383–388.

Holden, S. J. S. and Lutz, R. J. "Ask Not What the Brand Can Evoke: Ask What Can Evoke the Brand?" *Advances in Consumer Research*, 19, (eds) J. F. Sherry, Jr. and B. Sternthal, Provo, UT: Association for Consumer Research (1992): 101–107.

Howard, J. A. *Consumer Behaviour in Marketing Strategy*. Englewood Cliffs, NJ: Prentice-Hall, 1989.

Kahnemann, D. and Tversky, A. "Prospect Theory: An Analysis of Decision under Risk," *Econometrica*, 47 (March 1979).

Keller, K. "Conceptualising, Measuring, and Managing Customer-Based Brand Equity," *Journal of Marketing*, 57, 1 (1993).

Mittal, B. and Lee, M. S. "A causal model of consumer involvement," *Journal of Economic Psychology*, 10 (1989).

Rapp, S. and Collins, T. *Maximarketing*. New York: McGraw-Hill, 1987.

Woodside, A. G. "Modeling linkage-advertising: Going beyond better media comparisons." *Journal of Advertising Research*, 34 (July/August), (1994): 22–31.

2
Automatic-Unconscious Process Models of Primary Choice

Three realities

In the globally integrated consumer oriented societies of 21st Century, there are three realities all marketers must eventually come to terms with when advertising and marketing a brand:

- Customers have very limited attention spans;
- They devote little time or effort to processing information about brands or stores; and
- They have access, desire, or ability to retrieve easily only a few bits of information about brands or stores included in their long-term memories (see Olshavsky and Granbois, 1979; Kassarjian, 1981).

This chapter offers evidence that a consumer's top-of-mind brand or store-name associations with a few bits of information, such as "most reliable" and "lowest overall prices," relate strongly to the consumer's shopping and buying behaviour. For brand and store choice, Tigert (1983) refers to these few associate-to-brand or store retrievals as "hot buttons." These hot buttons are a brand's "determinant attributes" (cf. Alpert, 1971). Thus, this chapter argues and demonstrates empirically that the following view about customers is overstated and misleading:

> Subjects just do not care much about products; they are unimportant to them. Although issues such as racial equality, wars, and the draft may stir them up, products do not. Hence, the emerging conclusion must be that true attitudes about these items most likely do not exist for many subjects. Bicycles, colas, and toothpaste generally do not have attitudes associated with them. To claim that attitudes about these products do exist is to claim that subjects "give a damn" about them. [Most] subjects do not. (Kassarjian, 1981)

The evidence here is that customers can quickly name a brand or a store (i.e., retrieve a name from their long-term memories) when asked what brand (or store) first comes-to-mind for specific bits of information, such as, for automobiles, "most reliable" and "best styling" and, for grocery stores, "most convenient for you" and "lowest overall food prices"; and that these top-of-mind brand (or store) name responses are robustly correlated with customers' primary brand and/or store choices.

Discovery of such information is useful for learning why some brands are appealing to some customers and unappealing to other. Furthermore, research in this chapter demonstrates that customers should not be asked for the thoughts that first come-to-mind for a given brand or store. Rather, it is recommended that marketers work backwards by asking customers to name the brand or store that first comes-to-mind for each of a limited number of bits of information – possible determinant attributes.

Listed below are two principal reasons marketers and advertisers should work backwards when seeking to discover the underlying nature of their brand. First, a customer is able automatically to evoke only a few brands or stores from long-term memory. This process is analogous to a customer going to a file drawer in her or his head and retrieving a folder containing some names and evaluations. The customer must then process and select the most representative name to answer the questions (see Grunert, 1988; 1990). Consequently, when shopping, a customer is likely to refer to a limited number of evaluative attributes – hot buttons – and select the brand or store automatically associated with these hot buttons. Second, when marketers work forwards by asking a customer what thoughts first come to mind about a given brand or store, three assumptions are made: (1) the brand or store mentioned is in the customer's long-term memory, (2) she or he can retrieve that particular name, and (3) that name will be retrieved easily. Often all three of these assumptions are incorrect.

This chapter first presents a review of relevant psychological and consumer research literature on automatic-unconscious processing. Then formal hypotheses follow from the literature review. The third section and the appendix describe details of the method of a field study to test the hypotheses. The chapter then closes with a discussion and conclusions relevant for advertising research and marketing strategy.

Literature review and theoretical foundations

In consumer research, Grunert (1988; 1990) emphasises that two kinds of cognitive processes can be distinguished, namely automatic and strategic processes.

1. Automatic processes are mostly unconscious. These processes are learned. They change very slowly, and are not subject to the capacity limitations of working memory.

2. Strategic processes are also known as conscious thinking. They are subject to capacity limitations, but they can be easily adapted to situational circumstances.

The vast majority of consumer decisions are in fact not based on a large degree of conscious thinking. A lot of information processing is unconscious. To name just a few examples: the cognition of outside stimuli and the decision to select them for conscious attention are unconscious processes. The integration of new information with information already stored in memory is an unconscious process. Retrieval of information from long-term memory into working memory is unconscious as well. The basic pattern is clear: unconscious information processing sets the limits within which conscious information processing can occur (Grunert, 1988).

Defining automatic-unconscious processing

Shiffrin and Dumais (1981) provide a practical definition of automatic-unconscious processing: the activation of some concept or response whenever a given set of external initiating stimuli are presented, regardless of a subject's attempt to ignore or bypass the distraction. Based on the concept of automatic-unconscious processing, Fazio (1986) and his colleagues (Fazio, Powell, and Herr, 1983; Fazio, Powell, and Williams, 1989) propose and empirically support a model of the process by which attitudes guide behaviour. According to Fazio's attitude-accessibility model, attitudes guide appraisals of objects (such as brands and possibly retail stores) only if they have been activated from memory upon observation of the object. The model includes the view that behaviour in any given situation is a function of the individual's immediate perceptions of the attitude object in the context of the situation in which the object is encountered. "Hence, the accessibility of the attitude from memory is postulated to act as a critical determinant of whether the attitude-to-behaviour process is initiated" (Fazio et al., 1989).

Measuring attitude-accessibility

How can attitude-accessibility be measured? Two methods demonstrate high inter-method reliabilities (Pearson r's above .80): the subject's top-of-mind brand order mention in response to requests to name her or his most preferred brand; and the speed of responding (a latency measure) to the question of whether or not the subject likes or dislikes a brand when the brand's name is observed or mentioned (cf. Fazio, 1986).

In a related but separate stream of studies from the marketing and consumer research literature predating the more recent work in social psychology (Fazio et al., 1983; Fazio et al., 1989), several researchers (using other expressions of the same concept) hypothesise automatic-unconscious processing as a moderating link between the relation of attitude and behaviour (cf. Axelrod, 1968; Cohen, 1966; Gruber, 1969; Haley and Case, 1979; MacLachlan, 1977; MacLachlan and LaBarbera, 1979; MacLachlan, Czepiel, and LaBarbera, 1979; Aaker, Bagozzi, Carman, and MacLachlan, 1980). Cohen (1966) is most specific in providing a theoretical rationale for a "level of consciousness concept" as an important determinant of "the amount of brand strength".

Total [unaided] recall of a brand relates to brand attitudes, which range from strongly favourable to indifferent and even to negative feelings toward the brand. Position of [unaided] recall of a brand among total brands recalled is highly related to differences within the range of brand attitudes, and therefore to brand behaviour. Total [unaided] recall can be divided into three levels of consciousness, which successfully separate widely divergent attitudes towards brands. Brands that are recalled at the first level of consciousness (earliest) are more favourably viewed than those recalled in the second level of consciousness. The brands recalled in the second level of consciousness are more favourably viewed than those recalled in the third level of consciousness. Brands that produce favourable action (those regularly used and with a high switch-to potential) will be recalled almost exclusively in the first level of consciousness.

Axelrod (1968; 1986) demonstrates that top-of-mind-awareness (TOMA) of a brand is a sensitive and stable measure that can serve as an intermediate criterion for predicting brand-choice behaviour and brand-switching behaviour. Axelrod (1968) emphasised the need for developing valid and reliable intermediate survey indicators of whether or not marketing and advertising influence product and brand-choice behaviour because of the greater expense and time necessary for experiments to measure the impact of marketing and advertising actions on such behaviour. Based on the empirical findings, he suggested top-of-mind-awareness measures as one of two useful intermediate criteria to be associated strongly with product and brand-choice behaviour (the other measure found useful by Axelrod was the constant sum method). Other researchers demonstrate a strong link between (unaided) brand awareness and market share and offer the conclusion that managers can use awareness data for measuring potential market share (Gruber, 1969; Burke and Schoeffler, 1980).

Other measures of automatic-unconscious processing

MacLachlan (1977) and colleagues (e.g., Aaker et al., 1980) verify that response latency (defined by MacLachlan as the length of time taken by a respondent to make a paired-comparison choice) is a valid measure of strength of preference. Aaker et al. (1980) found that the combination of measuring response latency and paired comparisons is superior to constant sum measures, even though the best single indicator of brand preference is the constant sum. "Thus, in many situations, such as telephone interviewing, where the constant sum measure is unwieldy but the recording of response latency is not, the paired comparison/response latency approach might be preferable."

Hoyer and Brown (1990) demonstrate in a controlled experiment of peanut butter brand-choice that unaided brand awareness is a dominant choice heuristic among awareness-group subjects versus subjects with no brand awareness. Subjects with no brand awareness tended to sample more brands and selected the high-quality brand on the final choice trial significantly more often than those with brand awareness. Hoyer and Brown (1990) point out that the consumer in many purchase situations is, at best, a passive recipient of product information and one who tends to spend minimal time and cognitive effort in choosing among brands (also, cf. Hoyer, 1984); they refer to several streams of research beginning with the early work of Titchener (1912, p. 33): "What ... is the feeling [i.e., that experienced upon recognition]? In experiments upon recognition it is variously reported as a glow of warmth, a sense of ownership, a feeling of intimacy, a sense of being at home, a feeling of ease, a comfortable feeling. It is a feeling of pleasure in its affective quality, diffusively organic in its sensory character."

Research on retail store choice behaviour

In research on retail store choice behaviour, the limited value of using any intermediate criterion to indicate the impact of marketing actions on retail store choice has been implied strongly at least by Doyle (1977) and his colleagues (Doyle and Gidengil, 1977; Corstjens and Doyle, 1989). Corstjens and Doyle (1989) point out that "research into how consumers choose shops is usually dated from Martineau's (1958) concept of store image. Reviews of the stream of studies in this area have been presented by Wyckham, Lazer and Crissy (1971), May (1975), Ring (1979), Pessemier (1980), Peterson and Kerin (1983), and Downs and Haynes (1984). But despite the vast literature on store image and positioning the theoretical and practical implications are rather disappointing." As Rosenbloom (1983) concludes, direct evidence of a link between a store's image and its capacity to attract and maintain patronage is difficult to obtain. The evidence that is available is usually fragmentary and indirect and does not provide a sufficient basis for proving in a rigorous way the relationship of store image to consumer patronage.

While few would argue with Doyle (1977) and his colleagues that the most reliable means of measuring the impact of marketing actions on store choice behaviour is via field experimentation and direct sales measures, research on attitude-accessibility of retail store evaluations may indicate attitude-accessibility to be an important moderating variable affecting the value of image measures as intermediate criteria of store choice behaviour. Consequently, the additional benefit of using valid and reliable intermediate criteria measures of store choice might be added possibly to the benefits of low cost and high speed of store attitude research.

The term "intermediate criteria" is used here as intended by Axelrod (1968), that is, a variable between marketing actions (i.e., advertising, pricing, store layout, and others) and customer purchases. An intermediate criteria is an indicator of influence of marketing actions on customer purchases. One of the limitations of the study reported in this chapter is that the study does not include a marketing experiment involving manipulating marketing actions and examining the impact of such manipulations on both the intermediate criteria of attitude accessibility and customer purchases. Our aim is to confirm and extend the work of several scholars (cf. Cohen, 1966; Axelrod, 1968; Tigert, 1983; Kopp, Eng and Tigert, 1991) that customers' unaided top-of-mind retrieval of a brand or store name in response to a general category question or evaluative attribute question is associated positively and strongly with their primary purchase choice of brand or store.

Some indication of the substantial influence of attitude-accessibility as a moderating variable between store image and store choice is provided by the work of Tigert (1983). For three sets of studies of retail food, fast food, and do-it-yourself primary store choice, Tigert (1983) asked respondents, "Please tell me all things considered, the single most important reason you shop at the store where you shop most often." The respondents were also asked to name the second most important reason. Tigert (1983) used this open-ended, direct questioning method to learn the determinant attributes for store choice for each store among sets of competing stores; he used Alpert's (1971) definition of determinant attributes, "those attributes projected by the product's [store's] image which lead to the choice of the product [store] may be called determinant, since they determine preference and purchase."

For retail, food store-choice data collected in Toronto, Cleveland, and Tampa, Tigert (1983) performed a comparative analysis between the proportions of total mentions of attributes using the open-ended approach and logit coefficients estimated from forced-choice store ratings data for the same sets of competing stores. He reports that both approaches identified geographical convenience as the most determinant attribute. In all three cities, low prices was the second strongest attribute in the direct, questioning data, but in Tampa, friendly, courteous service ranked second in the logit analysis, followed by price. Tigert (1983) concludes that the high correlations ($r > .80$ for the data from two of the three cities) between direct-questioning and the rating data indicate "that the direct-questioning technique is a reasonably valid method of identifying determinant attributes [of store choice]."

Hypotheses

(H1) The most accessible attitudes that associate a given store with evaluative store attributes are highly predictive of primary store choice. Based on the discussion in the literature review, the primary objective of this study is to investigate the hypothesis (H1) that the most accessible attitudes that associate a given store with evaluative store attributes are highly predictive of primary store choice. Following the insights of Grunert (1988) and the research streams reviewed from psychology (e.g., Fazio et al., 1989) and marketing (e.g., Cohen, 1966), it is proposed that retail store customers are able automatically to access and retrieve from their long-term memories for associating first with evaluative attributes (e.g., lowest overall food prices, most convenient location, or largest selection of foods) and that such automatic associations accurately predict primary store choice, that is, the store where the customers shop for most of their product needs.

If the empirical study confirms the first hypothesis, a series of propositions related to the first hypothesis may be developed and tested as a set of additional hypotheses on attitude-accessibility and primary store choice. For example, for retail food stores, (H2) a store that dominates competing stores in being named most often by customers in a market area as their primary store will be the store named most often first (activated from memory) for one or both of the two most determinant attributes found by Tigert (1983): most convenient location and lowest prices. While accessibility to attitudes toward other attributes (e.g., quality, selection variety, speed of checkout) are likely to be associated with primary store choice, a given store identified most often by customers in a market area to be their primary store would also need to dominate its competitors in being named earlier when these customers are asked about store attributes found to be the most determinant of supermarket store choice.

However, not all competing stores are likely to be retrieved by their primary customers for specific evaluative attributes. For example, a store having noticeably higher overall food prices than its competitors' is unlikely to be retrieved by its primary store customers when asked which store first comes-to-mind as offering the lowest overall food prices.

The practical value of testing the automatic-unconscious processing among customers in linking store names to evaluative attributes is to learn the extent that such links are contributing or hurting the store in sustaining its primary store customer base. That is, which automatic links between the store and evaluative attributes are being made by customers that really do contribute to sustaining the store's share of primary store customers? It is demonstrated herein that (1) primary customers of different stores make automatic links to different evaluative attributes with their respective primary stores and that (2) such linkages provide accurate predictions of primary store choice.

(H3) Strong positive correlations exist between positive evaluative attributes and primary choice. The identification of a customer's primary store is associated positively with accessing the same store from his or her memory for positive evaluative attributes. Thus, (H3) strong positive correlations are predicted among the store being named for positive evaluative attributes and being named as the subject's primary shopping store.

(H4) A few and similar determinant attributes are useful in predicting a substantial share of the variance. Consequently, (H4) a few and similar determinant attributes are useful in predicting a substantial share of the variance of primary store choice for each store in a set of competing stores. These two hypotheses – H3 and H4, reflect the proposition that for store X to be identified by some customers as their primary store, then store X must be highest in accessibility for one or more positive determinant attributes even when only a few customers name store X as their primary store. Thus, customers identifying store X as their primary store will be likely to name store X first as having the lowest overall food prices, even when most other customers identify the same store as having the highest overall food prices.

Method

The hypotheses were tested using survey data collected from a telephone survey completed in 1989. A representative sample of 400 households was drawn from households with telephones from a small city (a population of 75,000) located in the southern region of the United States. Random-digit-dialing of the last four telephone numbers among banks of household telephone exchanges known to be in use was completed.

Adult female or male household members responsible for doing most of the shopping for groceries to be consumed at home completed the interviews. Four attempts during early evening hours and on Saturdays and Sundays were used to reach each household included in the sample. Adult members of 73 percent of the households reached agreed to complete the survey. A total of 301 useable interviews were completed.

Results

A total of 11 supermarkets were identified by one or more respondents as their primary store. However, as summarised in Table 2.1, one store, Super One, was identified by 47 percent of the 301 respondents as their primary store, and the three stores identified most often were the primary stores for 80 percent of the respondents. Table 2.1 summarises the details on store name and evaluative attribute accessibility for the three stores named by most of the respondents as their primary stores.

Table 2.1   Retail Food Store Top-of-Mind-Awareness Shares by Attribute for All Respondents and Primary Customers (decimals omitted)

	Super One		Brookshires		A&P	
	All	Primary	All	Primary	All	Primary
Lowest overall food prices	64	88	5	19	5	25
Best quality meat	31	49	20	54	16	52
Best quality produce	46	73	20	54	11	41
Largest selection of foods	69	87	7	21	7	32
Friendliest personnel	21	35	46	81	9	41
Fastest checkout	30	51	18	69	14	32
Most convenient location	24	43	22	65	30	41
Highest overall food prices	1	1	25	19	31	54
Poorest quality meat	10	11	8	13	14	84
Poorest quality produce	5	5	8	12	12	27
Smallest selection of foods	4	2	8	8	15	13
Most unfriendly personnel	11	6	3	2	11	14
Slowest checkout	18	17	7	6	11	9
Least convenient location	17	2	16	10	11	2
Sample Size	301	142	301	52	301	44

The results summarised in Table 2.1 are relevant for testing the second hypothesis: for food stores, if store X dominates by being named by most customers as the primary store in a shopping area, then a greater share of all shoppers should name store X versus other stores as first coming to mind as having the most convenient location and offering the lowest overall food prices. Partial support of this hypothesis is provided by the results in Table 2.1.

Each of the 11 supermarkets mentioned as being a primary store has only one location in the metropolitan area included in the study. Thus, none of the three stores mentioned most often as primary stores would be likely to dominate the others on the convenience of its location, unless a higher population concentration occurred near one of the stores. In reality, none of the three most-reported primary stores dominated the other in being mentioned as having the most convenient location. "Dominate" refers to a store being mentioned by a substantially greater share of customers as their primary store, or a greater share mentioning the store as first coming to mind for an evaluative attribute, compared to the shares mentioned for competing stores.

Note in Table 2.1 that nearly two-thirds of the total respondents identified Super One when asked to name the supermarket having the lowest overall food prices and the largest selection of foods. Thus, in partial support of the second hypothesis, the dominant primary store also dominates in one of the two determinant attributes reported by Tigert (1983), lowest overall food prices. In terms of being the supermarket that first comes-to-mind, Brookshires dominated the other most-reported primary stores on only one evaluative attribute (friendliest personnel) among the total respondents. The A&P store did not dominate the other two principal, primary stores as first coming to mind among the respondents on any of the positively worded evaluative attributes.

It is expected that compared to all respondents, a greater share of the respondents identifying a particular store as their primary store would access this store from their long-term memories for positive evaluative attributes but would be less likely to do so for negative evaluative attributes. Comparing the attitude-accessibility data for the total respondents versus primary store respondents confirms these expectations for each of the three stores (see Table 2.1). An additional finding that possibly would be surprising to the managers of Brookshires and A&P in this particular metropolitan area is that the majority of both groups of respondents identifying these stores as their primary stores identified Super One when asked the name of the supermarket with the lowest overall food prices and the largest selection of foods.

In support of the third hypothesis, the identification of a particular store as a customer's primary store was associated positively with accessing the same store from memory for positive determinant attributes. Thus, even though only 5 percent of the total respondents named Brookshires as offering the lowest overall food prices (LOFP), the correlation between naming Brookshires as offering the LOFP and being the respondents' primary store was .32 (p < .01)

The strengths of the relation between primary store and positive evaluative attributes do vary substantially within and between primary stores. For example, lowest overall food prices is associated more with Super One than Brookshires and A&P being the primary store (.48 versus .32 and .36, respectively, p < .05 for both of these comparisons). Also, the relationship is stronger between the evaluative attribute of best quality produce being associated with Super One and the store being named as the respondents' primary store compared with friendliest personnel and Super One being the primary store (.52 versus .32, p < .01).

Table 2.2 indicates that age is the only demographic variable found to be related with primary store choice. A significant negative relationship was found for age and Super One being the primary store choice, and a significant positive relationship was found for age and Brookshires being the primary store choice.

The findings support the fourth hypothesis. Some of the same attributes are useful in predicting a substantial share of the variance of primary store choice for each store in the set of competing stores. For predicting of the three stores as the primary store, for each store the stepwise multiple regressions indicated 3 to 5 of the 14 evaluative attributes to be determinant attributes in making unique contributions to explain the variance in primary store choice.

Table 2.2   Correlation Coefficients of Primary Store Choice with Store that "First Comes to Mind" For Each of 14 Attributes and Primary Store

	Super One	Brookshires	A&P
Lowest overall food prices	0.48 **	0.32 **	0.36 **
Best quality meat	0.37 **	0.38 **	0.40 **
Best quality produce	0.52 **	0.37 **	0.40 **
Largest selection of foods	0.36 **	0.27 **	0.39 **
Friendliest personnel	0.32 **	0.35 **	0.46 **
Fastest checkout	0.44 **	0.42 **	0.49 **
Most convenient location	0.42 **	0.49 **	0.49 **
Highest overall food prices	0.01	−0.06	−0.04
Poorest quality meat	0.03	0.09	0.00
Poorest quality produce	−0.02	0.07	0.02
Smallest selection of foods	−0.08	−0.04	−0.07
Most unfriendly personnel	−0.13	−0.03	0.00
Slowest checkout	−0.03	−0.03	−0.06
Least convenient location	−0.12 *	−0.08	−0.11 *
Age	−0.28 **	0.12 *	0.07

* $p < .05$; ** $p < .01$

The store evaluative attributes found to make unique contributions for predicting primary store choice match well with the predictions of Howard (1989) of store variables influencing store choice: convenience, price, and information.

For Super One, age made a significant contribution in explaining this store as being the respondents' primary store; the contribution of age was negative for Super One. Age was associated positively with Brookshires being the respondents' primary store, but including age in the logit or regression models did not add significantly to explaining Brookshires as a primary store choice; the size of the relationship of age and primary store choice was weaker for Brookshires compared to Super One (Table 2.2).

Age was not associated with A&P as the primary store choice. The logit and regression models for Super One and Brookshires are summarised in Tables 2.3 and 2.4, respectively. Regression model results for A&P are summarised in Table 2.10.

The results support H1: the most accessible attitudes that associate a given store with determinant store attributes were highly predictive of primary store choice. The ratios of primary store choices predicted correctly by the logit models shown for the three stores (Tables 2.3, 2.4, and 2.10) were .76, .85, and .88, for Super One, Brookshires, and A&P, respectively; degrees of accuracy similar to that reported in the study by Gensch and Recker (1979) and higher than the predictive accuracy reported by Hortman et al. (1990) for their unsegmented, overall model (a ratio of .75).

Table 2.3   Comparison of Logit Model and Multiple Regression Model of main Effects for Super One (SPR1) Supermarket as Primary Store

Independent Variable	Logit Design			Standard R^2
	Coefficient	Standard Error	Z Value	Design Beta[1]
Best Quality Produce	0.58	0.07	8.42	0.30
Lowest Overall Food Prices	0.49	0.06	7.43	0.30
Most Convenient Location	0.44	0.06	6.80	0.17
Fastest Checkout	0.45	0.06	7.01	0.14
Least Convenient Location	–0.04	0.06	–0.07	–0.12
Age	–0.27	0.06	–4.51	–0.10
Constant	0.08	0.06	1.29	

[1] Adjusted R^2 = 43.68; 6/285 d.f.; p < .000

The range of the predictive accuracies (R^2s) of the attitude-accessibility models for the three stores is from .37 for Brookshires to .45 for Super One when age is excluded as an independent variable. This range indicates levels of explained variance for one type of patronage behaviour (primary store choice) significantly above the levels usually found (15 to 20 percent) using store-image ratings to predict patronage behaviour (cf. Bellinger, Steinberg, and Stanton, 1976; Schiffman, Dash, and Dillon, 1977; Peterson and Kerin, 1983). The logit and regression models for each of the three stores included some of the same as well as unique evaluative attributes as having significant beta coefficients. (Age was not included in either the logit or the regression model as a significant influence on primary store choice for A&P, but age was included as a significant influence of primary store choice for Brookshires and Super One.) The relative sizes of both the logit and regression betas for Brookshires indicates the attitude-accessibility of Brookshires for location convenience is more important than the store's attitude accessibility for best quality meats (see Table 2.4).

Table 2.4   Comparison of Logit Model and Multiple Regression Model of Main Effects for Brookshires (BRK) Supermarket as Primary Store

Independent Variable	Logit Design			Standard R^2
	Coefficient	Standard Error	Z Value	Design Beta[1]
Best Quality Meat	0.72	0.07	0.97	0.27
Lowest Overall Food Prices	0.84	0.08	10.44	0.15
Most Convenient Location	0.83	0.08	10.37	0.39
Age	0.15	0.06	2.57	0.08
Constant	0.77	0.08	9.99	

[1] Adjusted R^2 = .35; F = 39.58; d.f. = 4,287; < .0001; all b coefficient significant (p < .03).

Given the robust ability of multiple regression in identifying significant independent variables and its usefulness for predictive purposes (R^2), multiple regression models may be useful to present side-by-side with logit models when the diagnostic information (betas) of the regression models is restricted to reporting significance and not relative impact.

Main effects of attitude-accessibility and age on Super One and Brookshires being the primary store

The correlations of the store attitude-accessibility of the determinant attributes and age associated with naming Super One as the primary store are summarised in Table 2.5. The variables in the models were examined for possible multicollinearity problems. For example, note in Table 2.5 that while the correlations between accessing the evaluative attributes for Super One are significant statistically (e.g., r's = .34 and .28 for SPR1LOFP-SPR1BQP and SPR1MCL-SPR1BQP, respectively), however, the correlations are low enough to indicate that each variable makes a unique contribution to explaining Super One being identified as the primary store. In Table 2.5 the top-of-mind accessibility of each of the positive evaluative attributes for Super One is associated more strongly with Super One being named as the primary store (r's > .40) compared to its association with the other evaluative attributes for Super One. Comparatively similar results were observed for the model results for the other stores.

Table 2.5 Correlation among Variables Used in Super One Models

Super One	BQP[2]	LOFP	MCL	XOUT	LCL	Age[3]
Primary Store[1]	0.52	0.48	0.42	0.44	–0.12	–0.28
Best Quality Produce		0.34	0.28	0.35	0.00	0.24
Lowest Overall Food Prices			0.23	0.33	0.12	–0.21
Most Convenient Location				0.36	–0.25	–0.17
Fastest Checkout					–0.06	–0.17
Least Convenient Location						–0.08

Note: > .16, p < .01.
[1] *"Super One"* was response to question, *"Which one supermarket do you shop most often?"*
[2] Abbreviations: Best Quality Produce (BQP); Lowest Overall Food Prices (LOFP); etc.
[3] Age: 0 is less than 40 years age; 1 represents 40 years age and greater

The cross-tabulations of the attitude-accessibilities and age for Super One are summarised in Table 2.6. Cross-tabulation results for Brookshires are summarised in Table 2.7; the cross-tabulation results for A&P are not included herein. All the cross-tabulations indicate highly significant relationships. The apparent strength of Super One versus Brookshires in being named by most respondents as the supermarket having the lowest overall food prices becomes clear from comparing these two tables and the results for the two stores in Table 2.1. Very few respondents (less than 5%) retrieved Brookshires from their long-term memories when asked the name of the supermarket offering the lowest overall food prices. Brookshires competes more effectively in gaining greater shares of top-of-mind mentions for having the most convenient location (17%) and the best quality meat (20%).

When a given store is identified as a shopper's primary store, what evaluative attributes are related first to that store? Answering this question helps identify a store's strength in building a customer equity. Several retail management implications may be suggested for Super One from examining the results of the possible combinations of responses to the determinant attributes. For example, the majority of the respondents named Super One as their primary store only when Super One is retrieved from their long-term memories as having the lowest overall food prices (SPRlLOFP) and either the most convenient location (SPRlXOUT) or the best quality produce (SPRlBQP).

Table 2.6   Main Effects of Attitude-Accessibility and Age Super One Named as Primary Store

Super One	% Naming Super One as Primary Store		X^2, 1 d.f.	$p <$
Best Quality Produce	*Yes*	75	81.24	0.0000
	No	23		
Lowest Overall Food Prices	*Yes*	65	70.00	0.0000
	No	16		
Most Convenient Location	*Yes*	80	57.15	0.0000
	No	33		
Fastest Checkout	*Yes*	85	53.53	0.0000
	No	35		
Least Convenient Location	*Yes*	34	4.18	0.0400
	No	50		
Age	<40	59	22.31	0.0000
	>=40	31		

Thus, Super One's strong top-of-mind association with lowest overall food prices is necessary but not sufficient for dominating its competitors in being identified most often as the primary store. Super One would likely need to continue its strong share of top-of-mind access to the other two determinant attributes to retain its majority primary store share. Because Super One has only one location and the majority of shoppers are likely to find at least one competing store more convenient, Super One's management might focus the store's marketing strategy on retaining its high share of food shoppers accessing Super One first as offering the LOFP and on gaining shoppers who first access Super One as offering the best quality produce (or some other positive evaluative attribute associated strongly with quality produce).

Table 2.7 Main Effects of Attitude-Accessibility on Brookshires Named as Primary Store

Brookshires		% Naming Brookshires as Primary Store	X², 1 d.f.	p <
Most Convenient Location	*Yes*	52	71.19	0.0000
	No	8		
Best Quality Meats	*Yes*	46	43.87	0.0000
	No	10		
Fastest Checkout	*Yes*	43	53.35	0.0000
	No	7		
Best Quality Produce	*Yes*	46	41.67	0.0000
	No	10		

Cross-validating of the regression models

The data from the 301 respondents were divided randomly into two nearly equal-sized subsamples. Stepwise regression models were run for predicting each store (Super One, Brookshires, and A&P) as the primary store choice using the data for each subsample. The predicted scores using the regression coefficients from the model estimated from the first subsample and the data for the independent variables of the second subsample were compared to the actual values for primary store choice for the second sample; the reverse procedure was also used to cross-validate the models.

Table 2.8 summarises the correlation coefficients between the predicted and actual primary store choices, the regression models for the two subsamples for Super One. The results for Brookshires and A&P appear in Tables 2.9 and 2.10.

The cross-validity coefficients are modest in size (ranging from .56 to .68 among the three stores), but they do demonstrate that modeling the store attitude/accessibility of determinant attributes is useful for predicting primary store choice. For the models from the subsamples for Super One, the beta coefficients for the determinant attributes are positive as would be hypothesised, and they are highly significant statistically for best quality produce, lowest overall food prices, and most convenient location. Similar levels of model performance are indicated in Table 2.9 for Brookshires and Table 2.10 for A&P.

Validation: comparing the models with open-ended responses

During the interviews, several questions after asking for the name of the respondents' primary store, the respondents were asked the following open-ended question, "What are your main reasons for shopping (name of primary store mentioned by the respondent early in the interview)?" The

Table 2.8 Cross-Validation Results: Regression Models for Super One as Primary Store

	Model for First Sample				
	b	SEb	β	t	p <
Best Quality Produce	0.24	0.07	0.24	3.52	0.00
Lowest Overall Food Prices	0.40	0.07	0.38	3.37	0.00
Most Convenient Location	0.25	0.009	0.21	2.82	0.00
Fastest Checkout	0.02	0.08	0.02	0.24	0.81
Least Convenient Location	−0.02	0.10	−0.01	−0.18	0.86
Age	−0.11	0.07	−0.11	1.58	0.12
Constant	−0.07	0.07		0.94	0.35

Adjusted R^2 = .42; 6/145 d.f.; F = 19.11; p < .0000

	Model for Second Sample				
	b	SEb	β	t	p <
Best Quality Produce	0.23	0.07	0.23	3.40	0.00
Lowest Overall Food Prices	0.34	0.07	0.33	3.88	0.00
Most Convenient Location	0.32	0.08	0.28	4.00	0.00
Fastest Checkout	0.09	0.08		0.24	0.81
Least Convenient Location	−0.22	0.09	−0.16	−2.52	0.03
Age	−0.14	0.07	−0.14	2.15	0.03
Constant	−0.13	0.07		1.78	0.08

Adjusted R^2 = .49; 6/130 d.f.; F = 22.62; p < .0000
Note: r = .68 on model 1 predictions and data second random sample; r = .64 for model 2 predictions and data from first random sample.

two principal responses to this question for Super One and Brookshires being selected as primary stores are summarised in Table 2.11.

Partial validation of the strengths of the associations between top-of-mind accessibility of store name with determinant attributes and primary store choice indicated from the logit and regression models may be examined by comparing the results from the models with open-ended responses: how well do the evaluative attributes that would most likely be determinant of store choice based on their accessibility and unique contributions to explaining store choice compare with the first and second, open-ended, main reasons reported by the respondents for shopping at the competing stores? Based on the results in Table 2.11 where Super One is shown to dominate all competing stores combined as first coming-to-mind for lowest overall food prices and largest selection of foods, these two evaluative attributes would be likely to be reported often as principal reasons for Super One being selected by some grocery shoppers as their primary store. The results in Table 2.11 support these expectations (by chi-square tests).

Table 2.9 Cross-Validation Results: Regression Models for Brookshires as Primary Store

	Model for First Sample				
	b	SEb	β	t	p <
Most Convenient Location	0.28	0.06	0.32	4.44	0.0000
Best Quality Meats	0.20	0.09	0.14	2.06	0.0411
Fastest Checkout	0.15	0.06	0.18	2.48	0.0142
Best Quality Produce	–0.27	0.07	0.28	4.07	0.0001
Constant	0.00	0.03		0.01	0.9900

Adjusted R^2 = .35; 4/152 d.f.; F = 22.35; p < .0000

	Model for Second Sample				
	b	SEb	β	t	p <
Most Convenient Location	0.25	0.07	0.29	3.74	0.0003
Best Quality Meats	0.13	0.06	0.15	2.04	0.0433
Fastest Checkout	0.20	0.06	0.25	3.27	0.0013
Best Quality Produce	0.27	0.09	0.22	3.00	0.0032
Constant	–0.01	0.03		0.43	0.6658

Adjusted R^2 =. 36; 4/139 d.f.; F = 20.70; p < .0000
Note: r = .58 on model 1 predictions and data second random sample; r = .56 for model 2 predictions and data from first random sample.

Given that nearly half (46 percent) of all the respondents retrieved Brookshires from their memories when asked to name the supermarket with the friendliest personnel and only 21 percent named Super One, this evaluative attribute would be more likely to be mentioned as a principal reason for Brookshires versus Super One being shoppers' primary store. This line-of-reasoning is supported by the results in Table 2.11; 37 percent of the respondents naming Brookshires versus 10 percent of the respondents naming Super One as their primary store gave friendly personnel as the first or second main reason for shopping at the respective stores.

While low prices, large selection, and convenient location were the three main reasons mentioned most often by the respondents for shopping at their named primary store, the accessibility responses for the store named for the evaluative attributes of lowest overall food prices and largest selection of foods were highly correlated (r = .40 for Super One with both loading highly [above .60] on the same rotated factor in a varimax factor analysis); thus, only one of these two variables made unique contributions to explaining the variation in primary store choice in the regression models.

In an open-ended question, each respondent was asked to name the supermarket "closest to your home (even though you may not shop

Table 2.10 Cross-Validation Results: Regression Models for A&P as Primary Store

	Model for Complete Sample (n = 301)				
	b	SEb	β	t	p <
Most Convenient Location	0.24	0.04	0.31	6.07	0.0000
Friendliest Personnel	0.21	0.07	0.16	2.81	0.0053
Best Quality Meats	0.19	0.05	0.20	3.95	0.0001
Fastest Checkout	0.21	0.06	0.20	3.43	0.0007
Constant	0.00	0.02		–0.06	0.9506

Adjusted R^2 = .41; 4/287 d.f.; F = 50.97; p < .0000

	Model for First Sample (n = 157)				
	b	*SEb*	β	*t*	*p <*
Most Convenient Location	0.39	0.09	0.29	4.160	0.0000
Friendliest Personnel	0.22	0.05	0.28	4.460	0.0053
Best Quality Meats	0.21	0.09	0.18	2.220	0.0001
Fastest Checkout	0.20	0.09	0.18	2.210	0.0007
Constant	0.01	0.02		–0.060	0.9506

Adjusted R^2 = .47; 4/152 d.f.; F = 36.02; p < .0000

	Model for Second Sample (n = 144)				
	b	SEb	β	t	p <
Most Convenient Location	0.23	0.10	0.20	2.180	0.0308
Friendliest Personnel	0.15	0.06	0.31	4.170	0.0001
Best Quality Meats	0.22	0.10	0.16	2.240	0.0263
Fastest Checkout	0.23	0.11	0.18	2.120	0.0356
Constant	0.02	0.03		–0.830	0.4060

Adjusted R^2 = .34; 4/139 d.f.; F = 19.87; p < .0000

there)?" Because Super One was named by 47 percent of all the respondents as their primary store but only 24 percent retrieved "Super One" when asked to identify the store having the most convenient location, it is reasonable to expect Super One to have the largest share identifying this store as their primary store among respondents naming a store other than their primary store as being closest to their homes. Of the three stores with the largest shares of respondents identifying stores as their primary stores, A&P was expected to have the largest share of their primary customers also naming A&P as being the closest store to their homes. These expectations were confirmed by an analysis of responses for primary store and store closest to the respondents' homes. Among the respondents, while only 27 percent of shoppers identifying Super One as their primary store also

Table 2.11   Open-Ended Responses for First and Second Mentioned Main Reasons for Shopping at Primary Store

| Open-ended Response | Primary Store | | | |
| | Super One | | Brookshires | |
	1st	2nd	1st	2nd
Low Prices	42	30	8	12
Large Selection	23	26	4	12
Convenient Location	11	8	44	10
Clean Store	6	6	6	10
Good Quality in General	3	6	2	10
Friendly Personnel	2	8	17	20
Fast Service	1	6	0	0
Number of Respondents	139	101	52	40

identified Super One as the supermarket closest to their homes, 56 percent of Brookshires' and 80 percent of A&P's primary store customers identified these respective stores as being closest to their homes.

Least favourite store analyses

The attitude-accessibility data for the 14 evaluative attributes were used to build logit and regression models for the three stores receiving 10 percent or more mentions of being the respondents least favourite store, "the store you don't like and rarely or never shop." Theoretical and empirical evidence exists that each customer is likely to identify one or more stores among competing stores that she or he rejects from purchase consideration at the initial stages of retail choice because of negative evaluation (cf. Narayana and Markin, 1975; Church, Laroche, and Rosenblatt, 1985; Spiggle and Sewall, 1987).

Is modeling the attitude-accessibility of stores associated with evaluative attributes useful for predicting the store primarily rejected? What evaluative attributes are included in such models? Both the logit and regression models gave nearly identical answers to these questions; the regression models are summarised in Table 2.12 for the three stores named most often as being the least preferred.

The A&P store in the study holds the dubious honor of being identified by the most respondents (16 percent) as the least preferred store. A&P's top-of-mind association with three negative and one positive evaluative attributes made unique contributions to explaining its selection of being the least favourite store. The selection of this A&P store as the least favourite store suffers from a triple whammy of the store's high accessibility with least convenient location, unfriendliest store personnel, and highest food prices. A&P's accessibility with offering the best quality

Table 2.12 Regression Models for Three Principal Least Favourite Stores ("Your Least Favourite Store, the Store You Don't Like and Rarely or Never Shop")

Variable	A&P Least Favorite Store				
	b	SEb	β	t	p <
Least Convenient Location	0.20	0.06	0.17	3.00	0.00
Unfriendly Personnel	0.16	0.06	0.14	2.50	0.01
Best Quality Produce	–0.14	0.07	–0.12	–2.12	0.03
High Food Prices	0.09	0.04	0.11	2.01	0.05
Constant	0.11	0.03		4.01	0.00

Adjusted R^2 = .07; 4/296 d.f.; F = 7.05; p < .0000

Variable	Country Market Least Favorite Store				
	b	SEb	β	t	p <
Unfriendly Personnel	0.27	0.07	0.23	3.98	0.00
Poor Quality Meat	0.14	0.05	0.15	2.61	0.01
Large Selection of Foods	–0.17	0.08	–0.12	–2.25	0.02
Constant	0.10	0.02		4.75	0.00

Adjusted R^2 = .09; 3/297 d.f.; F = 11.15; p < .0000

Variable	Brookshires Least Favorite Store				
	b	SEb	β	t	p <
High Food Prices	0.24	0.04	0.33	6.17	0.00
Fastes Checkout	–0.12	0.04	0.17	–3.19	0.00
Poorest Quality Produce	0.20	0.06	0.17	3.14	0.00
Constant	0.06	0.02		3.87	0.00

Adjusted R^2 = .17; 3/297 d.f.; F = 21.36; p < .0000

produce reduces its likelihood of being identified as the respondents' least favourite store. Details appear in Table 2.12.

While significant statistically, the amounts of explained variance of least favourite stores are much less than the variance explained for primary store choice. One explanation of the lower levels of explained variance for least favourite stores is that 22 percent of the respondents were unable to identify a least favourite store. Possibly, shoppers find retrieving and processing information from long-term memory on negative store choices to be more difficult and less useful.

Some support for the validity of the store attitude-accessibility for the evaluative attributes for least favourite store identified by the regression models is provided by the open-ended responses of reasons for least favourite store. These open-ended responses are summarised in Table 2.13.

Table 2.13 Open-Ended Responses for Reasons for Least Favourite Store

	Least Favorite Store		
	A&P	Country Market	Brookshires
High Prices	33%	5%	47%
Unfriendly Personnel	15	3	9
Location Too Far	23	33	25
Dirty Store	8	18	0
Poor Quality in General	4	5	3
Unpleasant Atmosphere	4	5	0
Other Reasons	13	31	16
Number of Respondents	48	38	32

The three negative evaluative attributes found to uniquely explain A&P as the least favourite store in the attitude-accessibility regression model were also mentioned most often as the reasons why A&P was the least favourite store. For Country Market, the store second most often identified as being the least favourite store, the reasons mentioned most often in the open-ended responses are not similar to the negative evaluative attributes for which Country Market was accessed and were predictive of Country Market as being the least favourite store. The most often mentioned reason for Brookshires being mentioned third most often as the least favourite store (11% of the respondents) was high prices; the partial regression coefficient for accessibility of Brookshires' with highest food prices was highly significant statistically for predicting Brookshires as the least favourite store (see Table 2.12). Thus, the results from an analysis of the data provides support that attitude-accessibility modeling of least favourite store is useful for understanding weaknesses in a store's image among some shoppers that decreases the store's likelihood of becoming these shoppers' primary store.

Discussion and conclusions

The results suggest that research on consumer automatic-unconscious processes in linking brand names with evaluative attributes would be useful for learning the principal associations a store or brand holds in the minds of customers. A few of these links are likely to be associated with a store or brand being identified as the customer's primary store. With this research method, advertising and marketing strategists also learn whether or not any customers retrieve their brand or store in association with important evaluative attributes.

For a given store or brand, marketing strategists may fall in the trap of advertising a link that their brand or store can not possibly "own," that is, be identified first as being the most, best, or lowest of a given evaluative attribute, because another brand dominates on this particular attribute. Or, such strategists may be advertising a feature or benefit that has little to do with their brand's or store's ability to gain primary customers. Unfortunately, too often strategists believe they know what their customers really are thinking without hard evidence of when their store or brand automatically comes to their customers' minds.

Customers can easily and quickly respond when asked to name a store or brand as first coming to mind for a given evaluative attribute. Their answers likely reflect an automatic-unconscious process that includes accessing an internal memory bank, retrieving a file of information, reviewing the file's contents, selecting and giving a response. A few such automatic associates are useful for predicting primary store choice or brand choice.

Research programs on customer automatic-unconscious processes will likely be useful for learning the "hot buttons" (Tigert, 1983) to use and to avoid for planning positioning strategies. Assuming that automatic associations of a store or brand with an evaluation are grounded in reality, then such research will likely be useful for improving product/service offerings to gain customers. For example, if substantial numbers of customers name store X for slowest checkout or highest prices, most likely checkout service needs to be improved and prices are indeed higher compared to competitors' prices.

The hypotheses developed and the results presented here are extensions of previous consumer behaviour research on automatic-unconscious processing (cf. Fazio and his colleagues, 1986; 1989; Herr et al., 1990; Cohen, 1966; Axelrod, 1968; Gruber, 1969; MacLachlan, 1977; Aaker et al., 1980; Hoyer, 1984; Hoyer and Brown, 1990). This cited related body of work examines theoretically and empirically the effect on choice of the earliest accessibility from long-term memory of attitude to a global concept, for example, a brand name (Fazio et al., 1989) or the accessibility from long-term memory of brand awareness (Cohen, 1966; Hoyer and Brown, 1990).

The theoretical propositions of level of consciousness (Cohen, 1966), top-of-mind-awareness (Axelrod, 1968), affect referral (Wright, 1975), attitude-accessibility (Fazio, 1986), and unaided brand awareness (Hoyer and Brown, 1990) are likely to be most applicable for routine problem solving (Howard, 1989) for buying frequently purchased consumer products (e.g., candy bars, brands of peanut butter).

Table 2.14 summarises the findings of 3 separate studies conducted by the author: 1) an experiment on brand recall among children, 2) a London bank study for PriceWaterhouseCoopers and 3) a PC study for Hewlett Packard. The first two studies are reported in further detail in later chapters.

These studies, varying by product category and involvement, when assimilated help develop a general rule on the size of the TOMA set (i.e., the number of different brands recalled in a unaided brand recall question). It

Table 2.14 Towards a General Rule on the size of the Retrieval Set Retrieval Set Size Varying by Brand TOMA Position

Recall Position	Children & Adolescents								Price Waterhouse Banks	Hewlett Packard PC's	Set Size Overall Mean
	Drinks	Makeup	Fast Food	Spt Gds	Cars	Cigs	Banks	Mags	Banks	PC's	Mean
1	8	17	6	6	12	10	10	12	10	21	11
2	14	17	5	8	18	12	12	13	12	21	13
3	15	14	7	12	17	11	10	17	19	22	14
4	16	10	12	15	21	5	12	18	18	21	15
5	15	10	10	13	15	3	7	17	31	22	14
6	17	9	6	11	17	2	6	14	28	22	13
7	15	4	4	8	15		5	10	24	17	11
8	9	4	1	5	11		1	9	21	16	9
9	5			4	6			6		15	7
10	3				6			3		12	6
11	3				3					11	6
12	3				3					9	5
13					3					9	6
14					2					7	5
15										5	
Mean	10	11	6	9	11	7	8	12 #	20	15	
Sample N	34	34	34	34	34	34	34	34	129	672	

can be seen in the table that the TOMA set size varies as a function of the position of brand recall.

What is of specific use and interest however is the fact that the nature of the TOMA set size function is curvilinear – irrespective of product category and/or level of involvement. The first set (brands recalled 1st) is usually rather small – about the size of the mean across all recall positions. Brands recalled in the 1st set apparently act as the initial node in a neural nexus of all possible brands. Once this node is activated, it triggers off the network. Thereafter the set size increases generally (a chain reaction) up until about the 4th recall position. After this, when subjects begin to exhaust their memory search the set sizes gradually diminish as the strength of the links in network weaken. See Figure 2.1.

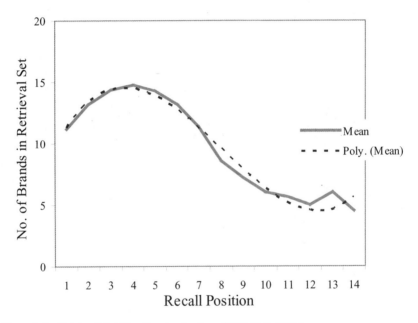

Figure 2.1   Retrieval Set Size Varying by Brand TOMA Position

The first position of unaided recall is almost always dominated by a few very strong brands; thereafter (positions 2–5) the sets become increasingly crowded with major and (mostly) minor brands. Beginning in about the 5th recall position, as the set sizes diminish they generally become dominated by minor and/or obscure brands.

An important additional benefit exists (besides the most obvious) of a brand being recalled in the 1st position vs. the 2nd, 3rd, 4th and 5th positions. Because the set size in the 1st position is generally smaller than the 2nd–5th position set sizes, if a brand makes it into that set, its probability of being recalled is increased substantially. For example, a brand recalled in the 1st position can increase its probability of recall to about 1 in 6–10 from 1 in 15–20 in 4th and 5th positions. So, the general rule for the TOMA set size looks something like this:

Set size = 7.97 + (0.0297 * recall position3) – (0.7153 * recall position2) + (.017 * recall position1), the R^2 for this empirical model is 0.97.

Perhaps it is not the position of the recall that affects the favourability of the brand but the set size. Brands in limited set sizes produce more favourable attitudes because they are more likely to serve as the primary nodes in the brand neural nexus – firing initially in a chain reaction through a network of all possible brands in memory.

Thus, the theoretical underpinnings and empirical research presented here are related but distinct from the work of Cohen (1966), Axelrod (1968), MacLachlan (1977), Fazio et al. (1989), and Hoyer and Brown (1990). It is proposed that the attitude-accessibility of competing stores or brands as indicated by primacy of responses to evaluative attributes is useful for accurately predicting primary choice. Data on attitude-accessibility linking stores with evaluative beliefs are useful for building paramorphic models of consumer cognitive processes, especially cognitive processes involving bottom-up agendas. Both multinomial logit and multiple regression models may be useful for building such models.

The empirical models described in the results section fits well with Howard's (1989) proposal of three key dimensions of store image affecting store choice for limited problem-solving situations. Supermarket store choice versus convenience store choice is assumed to represent more of the characteristics of limited problem-solving situations versus routine problem-solving, given that food stores represent one of the most complex elements of consumers' environments; food and beverage shopping are important activities representing 16 percent of the average U.S. household budget (Ambry, 1990), with expenditures likely to average more than $100 per visit to the shopper's primary supermarket.

Little loss in predictive accuracy is likely to be experienced from building primary store choice models from store attitude-accessibility data using the same evaluative attributes for competing stores. For example, largest selection of foods may be substituted for best quality meats in some cases, without little reduction occurring in explained variance. However, to some extent, unique store-image dimensions are likely to be found for each competing store in a given metropolitan area that do affect the store's selection as a primary store. This speculation matches with another: not all food stores can claim effectively to be the one with the lowest overall food prices.

If a store is not believed by buyers to offer the lowest overall food prices and can not hope to change this evaluation, then the store's management may want to encourage shoppers to use hierarchical agendas that favor those store aspects that the store can dominate competing stores (cf. Hauser, 1986). Longitudinal research is recommended to assess the impact of such strategies, research that includes assessments of the images of competing stores using the described attitude-accessibility modeling approach. A cross-sectional field study limited to one group of stores in one retail industry, supermarkets, in one metropolitan area has been reported in the present article. Before attempting to generalise the empirical results, research on store attitude-accessibility toward evaluative attributes held by customers needs to be extended to other retail store types, metropolitan areas, as well as through time.

While Corstjens and Doyle (1989) are correct in asserting that the most reliable means currently available of evaluating alternative store-image strategies is via experimentation and direct sales measures, field applications of such research methods are expensive and lengthy. Nevertheless, assessing store attitude-accessibility of evaluative attributes does appear to meet the requirements proposed by Axelrod (1986) for intermediate criteria that predict choice or purchase: sensitivity (discriminations between stores using small samples), stability (the same answers results from repeat testing), and predictive power (high explained variance). Schwartz (1989) correctly states that food retailers need to know what their customers think. However, it is essential to add that much of retail customers' thinking is represented by automatic-unconscious processes. Attitude-accessibility, programmatic research on a monthly, quarterly, or annual basis to assess changes in store images is recommended as a useful method for auditing such consumer thinking.

Appendix: survey instrument, procedure, and analysis

Based on prior research on the determinant attributes of customer food store decisions (Lindquist, 1975; May, 1975; Gensch and Recker, 1979; Pessemier, 1980; Tigert, 1983), a total of seven possible determinant attributes were used in the study: food prices, quality of meat, quality of produce, selection of foods, personnel, checkout speed, and location convenience. The seven store attributes include what Howard (1989) identifies as the three key dimensions of a retail store image: convenience of the store's location, the price of its products, and the information it provides about its products. Responses were collected for both positive and negative statements of these possible determinant attributes. For example, each respondent was asked to name "the food store that first comes to mind when I say, 'lowest overall food prices'," and "the food store that first comes to mind when I say, 'poorest quality meats'." Thus, in presenting the list of possible determinant attributes to the subjects both the attribute and the direction of the evaluation (positive to negative, or negative to positive) were changed. To control for order bias both the order of presentation of the 14 questions as well as the starting point were varied among the respondents.

This procedure was used for several reasons. First, this procedure would likely cause the respondent to retrieve the names of more than one food store because the same food store would be unlikely to be recalled as offering both the highest and lowest overall food prices or having the most and least convenient location. Thus, the procedure used would be likely momentarily to clear the respondent's focus in her or his working memory on the store named in answering the previous question. The chances of giving a rote answer of naming the same food store in response to each positively-worded attribute would be reduced. Also, accessible negative associations may be found to be associated negatively with the identification of a store as the respondent's primary store; while not hypothesised, this possibility is examined in the results section of this study.

After asking initial screening questions to reach the adult household member responsible for most grocery purchases for consumption in the home, the questioning began with asking the respondent to name all the supermarkets she or he was familiar with. Initially the words "food stores" were used in the telephone interviews. However, the word "supermarkets" was used in the final version of the survey form because the majority of 10 subjects in a pretest of the survey form asked the enumerator if "food stores" meant "supermarkets." In the main study, all the subjects were able to answer the questions with ease when the questions referred to "supermarkets." The respondents were prompted to name all the supermarkets that might come to her or his mind.

Thus, customers' attitude-accessibilities of stores related to evaluative attributes was measured by collecting data on the top-of-mind store name associated with positive and negative evaluative attributes. Such a measure is unique and represents an extension of previous research on brand awareness accessibility (e.g., Cohen, 1966; Axelrod, 1968; Hoyer and Brown, 1990) and global attitude-accessibility toward a brand (Fazio, 1989; Herr, Farquhar, and Fazio, 1990). It is proposed here that assessing the automatic-unconscious processing of a customer in retrieving the first store name (or brand) from her or his long-term memory to associate with evaluative attributes is useful for predicting the customer's primary store (or brand) choice.

The respondents were then asked to identify their primary food store, "Which one supermarket do you shop most often (your main store)?" The respondents were also requested to identify their least favourite supermarket, "Which supermarket is your least favourite store, the store you don't like and rarely or never shop?" Open-ended questions were asked to learn the main reasons for shopping at the customers' primary stores and the reasons for the store identified as their least favourite store. The open-ended questions were used as one step to examine the validity of the attitude-accessibility approach for predicting primary store choice. Data were also collected on total weekly expenditures at all grocery stores, how many persons including the respondent live in their households, age, race, gender, employment of the female head of the households, zip code, and total annual family income.

For choice modeling of primary store, both multinomial-logit and multiple-regression approaches were used. Rationale: for multiple-regression analysis, the partial regression coefficients represent the estimated increase in likelihood of primary store choice if the store is associated first with the evaluative attribute; however, several violations in classical statistical assumptions occur with using MRA on dichotomous dependent and independent data.

In a comparison of using the two approaches to model store choice, Gensch and Recker (1979) emphasised the limitations of the multiple regression, "unfortunately, the beta coefficients (diagnostic information) really should not be interpreted because the dichotomous dependent variable forces the error term to violate two of the assumptions underlying the linear model." As Goldberger (1964) points out, it is inherent in the model using a dichotomous dependent variable that the classical assumption of homoscedasticity is violated. More important, Thiel (1969) illustrates that in order for the error term to have an expected value of zero it would have to take on specific values with probabilities greater than one or less than zero. Thus, though one may use the foregoing model for predictive purposes (R^2), an interpretation of the beta coefficients is not advisable because they were generated in a manner that violates assumptions underlying the linear model (also, cf. Malhotra, 1986). Empirically, Gensch and Recker (1979) demonstrate the multinomial-logit model to result in better fit than the regression approach.

In practice, the evaluative attribute found to be most significantly related to primary store choice using logit modeling has also been reported to have the largest, absolute beta coefficient using a multiple-regression approach, and most of the same independent variables are found to have significant coefficients using the two approaches (cf. Gensch and Recker, 1979). Also, Tigert (1983) reports high correlations between the proportions of respondents who mention each store attribute as first or second most important in choosing their primary store and logit coefficients estimated from store ratings data.

A logit is defined as the log of the odds of the occurrence of a certain event; logits provide a convenient way to meaningfully apply the linear model to a dependent variable that is dichotomous. In the present study the dependent variable was primary store choice. For store X, primary store choice is assigned a 1 when the respondent identifies store X as her or his primary store and 0 when store X is not identified as her or his primary store. The independent variables consisted of the 14 evaluative attributes with respect to store X with each variable being assigned a 1 when store X is mentioned and 0 if another store is mentioned.

Main-effects logit and stepwise-regression models were tested for each of the stores that were identified by more than 10 percent of the respondents as their primary store. The models were tested both with and without the use of additional dummy variables for gender, race, household size (less than three versus three or more persons), age (a median split of equal or less than 40 versus above 40 years old), and income (a median split of less than $30,000 versus $30,000+). Such model building and testing was intended to improve the predictive accuracy of customers' primary store choices. The resulting models do not reflect necessarily how customers actually make their primary store choice decisions. However, the open-ended answers from additional questioning of the respondents of the study do indicate some correspondence between the store attributes found to be determinant from the logit and regression analysis and the evaluative attributes reported to be used by the respondents for selecting their primary stores. Comparisons of the open-ended responses and the logit and regression model results are presented in the results section.

References

Aaker, D. A., Bagozzi, R. P., Carman, J. M. and MacLachlan, J. M. "On Using Response Latency to Measure Preference," *Journal of Marketing Research*, 17, 2 (1980): 237–44.

Alpert, M. "Identification of Determinant Attributes: A Comparison of Methods," *Journal of Marketing Research*, 8, 2 (1971): 184–91.

Ambry, M. "The Age of Spending," *American Demographics*, November 1990.

Axelrod, J. N. "Attitude Measures That Predict Purchase," *Journal of Advertising Research*, 8, 1 (1968): 3–17.

Axelrod, J. N. "Minnie, Minnie Tickled the Parson," *Journal of Advertising Research*, 26, 1 (1986): 89–96.

Bellinger, D. N., Steinberg, E. and Stanton, W. "The Congruence of Store Image and Self Image as It Relates to Store Loyalty," *Journal of Retailing*, 52, 1 (1976): 617–32.

Burke, W. L. and Schoeffler, S. *Brand Awareness as a Tool for Profitability*. Boston: Cahners Publishing Company, 1980.

Church, N. J., Laroche, M. and Rosenblatt, J. A. "Consumer Brand Categorization for Durables with Limited Problem Solving: An Empirical Test and Proposed Extension of the Brisoux-Laroche Model," *Journal of Economic Psychology*, 6, 4 (1985): 231–53.

Cohen, L. "The Level of Consciousness: A Dynamic Approach to the Recall Technique," *Journal of Marketing Research*, 3, 2 (1966): 142–48.

Corstjens, M. and Doyle, P. "Evaluating Alternative Retail Repositioning Strategies," *Marketing Science*, 8, 2 (1989): 170–80.

Downs, P. and Haynes, J. B. "Examining a Retail Image Before and After a Repositioning Strategy," *Journal of the Academy of Marketing Science*, 12, 4 (1984): 1–24.

Doyle, P. "Experimental Methods in Retailing," In *Consumer and Industrial Buying Behaviour*, Arch G. Woodside, Jagdish N. Sheth, and Peter D. Bennett (eds) New York: North-Holland, 1977.

Doyle, P. and Gidengil, B. Z. "A Review of In-Store Experiments," *Journal of Retailing*, 53, 2 (1977): 47–62.

Fazio, R. H. "How Do Attitudes Guide Behaviour?" In *The Handbook of Motivation and Cognition: Foundation of Social Behaviour*, Richard M. Sorentino and E. Tory Higgins (eds) New York: Guilford Press, 1986.

Fazio, R. H., Powell, M. C. and Williams, C. J. "The Role of Attitude Accessibility in the Attitude-to-Behaviour Process," *Journal of Consumer Research*, 16, 4 (1989): 280–88.

Fazio, R. H., Powell, M. C. and Herr, P. M. "Toward a Process Model of the Attitude-Behaviour Relation: Accessing One's Attitude Upon Mere Observation of the Attitude Object," *Journal of Personality and Social Psychology*, 44, 6 (1983): 723–35.

Gensch, D. and Recker, W. W. "The Multinomial, Multi-attribute Logit Choice Model," *Journal of Marketing Research*, 16, 1 (1979): 124–32.

Goldberger, A. S. *Econometric Theory*. New York: Wiley, 1964.

Gruber, A. "Top-of-Mind Awareness and Share of Families: An Observation," *Journal of Marketing Research* 6, 2 (1969): 227–31.

Grunert, K. "Research in Consumer Behaviour: Beyond Attitudes and Decision-Making," European Research: *The Journal of the European Society for Opinion and Marketing Research*, 16, 5 (1988): 172–83.

Grunert, K. "Automatic and Strategic Processes in the Perception of Advertising," Paper presented at the *22nd International Congress of Applied Psychology*, Kyoto, Japan, July 22–27, 1990.

Haley, R. I. and Case, P. B. "Testing Thirteen Attitude Scales for Agreement and Brand Discrimination," *Journal of Marketing*, 43, 4 (1979): 20–32.

Hauser, J. R. Agendas and Consumer Choice. *Journal of Marketing Research*, 23 (August 1986): 199–212.

Herr, P., Farquhar, P. H. and Fazio, R. H. "Extending Brand Equity to New Categories," *Working paper*, Graduate School of Business, Indiana University, 1990.

Howard, J. A. *Consumer Behaviour in Marketing Strategy*. Englewood Cliffs, NJ: Prentice-Hall, 1989.

Hoyer, W. D. "An Examination of Consumer Decision Making for a Common Repeat Product," *Journal of Consumer Research*, 11, 4 (1984): 822–29.

Hoyer, W. D. and Brown, S. P. "Effects of Brand Awareness on Choice for a Common, Repeat-Purchase Product," *Journal of Consumer Research*, 17, 3 (1990): 41–48.

Kassarjian, H. H. "Low Involvement: A Second Look," In *Advances in Consumer Research*, 8, Kent B. Monroe (ed.) Ann Arbor, Michigan: Association for Consumer Research, 1981.

Kopp, R. J., Eng, R. J. and Tigert, D. "Competitive Structure and Segmentation Analysis of the Fashion Retailing Marketing: A Replication," Paper presented at the *1991 Patronage Behaviour and Retail Symposium: Cutting Edge II*, Baton Rouge, LA: Louisiana State University, 1991.

Lindquist, J. D. "Meaning of Image," *Journal of Retailing*, 50, 4 (1975): 29–38.

MacLachlan, J. *Response Latency: New Measure of Advertising*. New York: Advertising Research Foundation, 1977.

MacLachlan, J. and LaBarbera, P. "Response Latency in Telephone Interviews," *Journal of Advertising Research*, 19, 3 (1979): 49–56.

MacLachlan, J., Czepiel, J. and LaBarbera, P. "Implementation of Response Latency Measures," *Journal of Marketing Research*, 16 (1979): 573–77.

Malhotra, N. K. "Modelling Store Choice Based on Censored Preference Data," *Journal of Retailing*, 62, 2 (1986): 128–44.

Martineau, P. "The Personality of the Retail Store," *Harvard Business Review*, 36, 1 (1958): 47–55.

May, E. G. "Practical Applications of Recent Retail Image Studies," *Journal of Retailing*, 50, 4 (1975): 15–20.

Narayana, C. L. and Markin, R. "Consumer Behaviour and Product Performance: An Alternative Conceptualization," *Journal of Marketing*, 39, 4 (1975): 1–6.

Pessemier, E. A. *Retail Patronage Behaviour.* Report Number 80–112. Cambridge, MA: Marketing Science Institute, 1980.

Peterson, R. A. and Kerin, R. A. "Store Image Measurement in Patronage Research: Fact and Artifact," In *Patronage Behaviour and Retail Management*, William R. Darken and Robert F. Lusch (eds) New York: North-Holland, 1983.

Ring, L. L. "Retail Positioning: A Multiple Discriminant Analysis Approach," *Journal of Retailing*, 55, 1 (1979): 25–35.

Rosenbloom, B. "Store Image Development and the Question of Congruency." In *Patronage Behaviour and Retail Management*, William R. Darken and Robert F. Lusch (eds) New York: North-Holland, 1983.

Schiffman, L. G., Dash, J. F. and Dillon, W. R. "The Contribution of Store-Image Characteristics to Store-Type Choice," *Journal of Retailing*, 53, 2 (1977): 3–14 ff.

Schwartz, J. "Why They Buy." *American Demographics*, March 1989.

Shiffrin, R. M. and Dumais, S. T. "The Development of Automatism," In *Cognitive Skills and Their Acquisition*, John R. Anderson (ed.) Hillsdale, NJ: Lawrence Erlbaum, 1981.

Spiggle, S. and Sewall, M. A. "A Choice Sets Model of Retail Selection," *Journal of Marketing*, 51, 2 (1987): 97–111.

Thiel, H. "A Multinominal Extension of the Linear Logit Model," *International Economic Review*, 10, 4 (1969): 251–59.

Tigert, D. J. "Pushing the Hot Buttons for a Successful Retailing Strategy," In *Patronage Behaviour and Retail Management*, William R. Darken and Robert F. Lusch (eds) New York: North-Holland, 1983.

Titchener, E. B. *A Textbook of Psychology.* New York: Macmillan, 1912.

Wright, P. "Consumer Choice Strategies: Simplifying Vs. Optimizing," *Journal of Marketing Research*, 12, 1 (1975): 60–67.

Wyckham, R. G., Lazer, W. and Crissy, W. J. E. *Image and Marketing: A Selected and Annotated Bibliography*, Chicago: American Marketing Association, 1971.

3
Customer Portfolio Analysis among Competing Retail Store Brands

Introduction: how and why customers buy and do not buy

Customer portfolio analysis (CPA) may be useful for improving retailers' attempts to successfully position their stores in the minds of consumers. A customer portfolio for a store includes new-primary, loyal-primary, and defector (formerly primary) customers, as well as occasional customers who shop primarily at competing stores. Customers' attitude-accessibility with respect to first-linking a given store with evaluative attributes may offer useful information about the reasons for the shopping behaviour of customers in a store's customer portfolio.

Several hypotheses related to customer portfolio analysis and store attitude-accessibility are offered in this chapter. The principal hypothesis (H1) examined is that the attitude-accessibility of the major supermarkets competing in the same metropolitan area will differ substantially among loyal, new, competitors' customers, and defector customer segments for each supermarket. More specifically, for a given store, greater shares of loyal and new customers will exhibit positive, store attitude-accessibility profiles compared to non-customers and defectors (H2). A greater share of customer defectors will exhibit a negative attitude-accessibility profile compared to each of the loyal and new shopper segments (H3).

The results of a cross-sectional telephone survey of 317 supermarket shoppers are described, and the findings support these hypotheses. The chapter concludes with recommendations for planning changes in retailing positioning strategies and for monitoring success of implementing these strategies.

Customer portfolio analysis

CPA includes segmenting customers by their contributions to sales and profits, as well as segmenting customers by the length and type of their relationships with a marketing organisation. New, loyal, defector, and non-customers are examples of buyers segmented by their relation with a marketing organisation.

Several research reports demonstrate the value of performing customer portfolio analysis for developing a deeper understanding of both how and why customers buy and do not buy (Sevin, 1965; Wells, 1968; Beik and Buzby, 1973; Hartley, 1976; Fulgoni and Eskin, 1983; Campbell and Cunningham, 1983; Dubinsky and Ingram, 1984; Dubinsky, 1986; Dwyer, 1989; Jackson, 1989a, 1989b; Rost and Salle, 1989; Woodside and Soni, 1991). Most of these research reports of work related to customer portfolio analysis are based on industrial versus retail customer databases [(for two exceptions, see Fulgoni and Eskin (1983) and Woodside and Soni (1991)].

This chapter deals specifically with customer portfolio research – segmenting retail store shoppers into loyal, new, defector, and non-customers. The principal aim of the research is to learn what these customers think about each of the major stores competing for the shoppers' expenditures – the primary cognitive associations (relevant to store choice) in these shoppers' long-term memories with respect to each store. The study is grounded in the theoretical work on attitude accessibility (Fazio, 1989; Fazio, Powell and Williams, 1989) and automatic-unconscious processing (Grunert, 1988, 1990). The empirical results reported here provide strong evidence that store attitude-accessibility differs substantially between food shoppers who have been segmented into loyal, new non-customers, and defectors in relation to a given store (Winn-Dixie, for example). The detailed information on the attitude-accessibility of a store's portfolio of customers leads to strategy implications for attracting new customers, retaining existing customers, and reducing the flow of defectors to competing stores.

First, previous research on automatic-unconscious processing and attitude-accessibility is described. Second, how this research may be applied to retail customer portfolios is examined. Third, the method and results of an empirical study of customer portfolios of competing retail stores that incorporates automatic-unconscious processing are illustrated. Finally, the chapter concludes with examples of strategic implications for retaining and gaining customers and reducing the flow of defectors to other stores based on the empirical study.

Automatic-unconscious processing and attitude accessibility

Grunert (1988) emphasises that the vast majority of consumer decisions is in fact not based on a large degree of conscious thinking, what he identifies as" strategic cognitive processing." A lot of information processing is unconscious.

> To name just a few examples : the recognition of outside stimuli and the decision to select them for conscious attention or not are unconscious

processes. The integration of new information with information already stored in memory is an unconscious process. Retrieval of information from long-term memory into working memory is unconscious as well. The basic pattern is clear: unconscious information processing sets the limits within which the conscious information processing can occur. (Grunert, 1988, pp. 177–178).

Such unconscious cognitive processes are also referred to as automatic-unconscious processing. These processes include mental associations made between two or more beliefs, feelings, and/or emotions within working memory and between working memory, external stimuli, and/or long-term memory that occur without trying. Consequently, memory associations are made automatically and below the threshold of conscious processing.

Research on top-of-mind-awareness (TOMA) is an example of applying automatic-unconscious processing. TOMA measures have been applied to both unaided brand, and store retrieval from long-term memory into working memory. For example: What brand first comes to mind in the soft drink product category? What fast food chain first come to mind? These questions are TOMA operational statements. TOMA measures of brand advertising are used in a monthly, national study in the US by Gallup and *Advertising Age* to report the shares of respondents who first retrieve advertising of competing brands from their long-term memories – advertising the respondents" have seen, read, or heard in the past 30 days. "

TOMA advertising shares for several competing brands and stores and across several product and store categories are reported in one weekly issue each month in *Advertising Age*. Independent empirical support of the positive linkages among TOMA-advertising, TOMA-brand measures of competing brands and stores with preferences and behaviour in support of the Gallup/*Advertising Age* studies have been reported (cf. Woodside and Wilson, 1985).

Asking TOMA-store or TOMA-brand questions is the first step in measuring awareness-accessibility of a store or brand – that is, the location of a store or brand in a customer's long-term memory. To measure the awareness-accessibility more completely, the names of the stores that came second, third, fourth and fifth to mind for a respondent is useful. Strong empirical relationships have been reported that support several hypotheses related to awareness-accessibility. For example, (1) the higher the awareness-accessibility location of a brand (i.e., being mentioned first or second versus fourth or fifth), the more likely the brand is the regular brand used by the customer; (2) in unaided recall, customers strongly tend to name in second place the brand to which they would switch if they were to leave their present regular brand (Cohen, 1966).

The basic hypothesis related to such measures of automatic-unconscious processes is that TOMA-advertising is positively related to TOMA-brand and

TOMA-store; second, increasing TOMA-brand or TOMA-store increases the ability of customers to recognise, prefer, and buy the brand or shop the store. The most well-known support of the hypothesised positive link between unaided, order of brand awareness and attitude towards the brand may be Axelrod's 1968 study of attitudes that predict purchase (Axelrod, 1968, 1986) and the testing of 13 attitude scales for agreement and brand discrimination by Haley and Case (1979).

However, prior to Axelrod (1968) and Haley and Case (1979), a theory of automatic-unconscious processing was introduced in the marketing literature by Cohen (1966). The following theoretical rationale was developed for what Cohen called" the level of consciousness concept":

1. Total [unaided] recall of brand relates to brand attitudes, which range from strongly favourable to indifferent and even to negative feelings toward the brand.
2. Position of [unaided] recall of a brand among total brands recalled is highly related to the differences within a range of brand attitudes, and therefore to brand behaviour. The earlier the [unaided] recall; the more favourable the attitude towards the brand; the later the [unaided] recall, the less favourable the attitude.
3. Total [unaided] recall can be divided into three levels of consciousness, which successfully separate divergent attitudes, and therefore to brands. Brands that are recalled in the first level of consciousness (earliest) are more favourably viewed than those recalled in the third level of consciousness. Brands that produce favourable action (those regularly used and with high switch-to potential) will be recalled almost exclusively in the first level of consciousness. (Cohen, 1966, p. 142).

This theoretical rationale for the levels of consciousness concept is very similar to the automatic-unconscious processing model of attitude-accessibility proposed by Fazio (1986, 1989; Fazio et al., 1989). According to Fazio's model, the accessibility of the attitude from memory is postulated to act as a critical determinant of whether the attitude-to-behaviour process is initiated. Fazio and his colleagues have reported the use of three measures of attitude-accessibility including TOMA measures and latency measures – the number of milliseconds taken by a subject to respond with" like" or" dislike" when shown the names of brands presented on a computer screen.

Whereas Fazio's (1989) hypothesis of attitude-accessibility is based on automatic-unconscious processing and is similar and related theoretically to Cohen's (1966) level of consciousness theory, the two propositions are unique. Cohen's work is focused on the relationship between order (or latency) of brand awareness (retrieval) with brand attitude and brand choice, whereas Fazio's work is focused on the relationship between order (or latency) of global brand (object) attitude with brand (object) attitude with brand (object) attitude and choice.

Thus Cohen's work is parallel to Fazio's work. Cohen suggests that customers have a built-in retrieval bias to think first of one object and (say a brand or store) they like the most (and prefer to but) from among a set of competing objects held in their long-term memories. Cohen addresses the linkages of awareness-accessibility with behaviour, and he recognises that this relationship is likely to be mediated by attitude.

Cognitive processing and store choice

In retaining store image research, Tigert (1983) has successfully applied what might be identified as top – down, automatic-unconscious processing to learn customers' determinant attributes for primary store choice. Determinant store attributes are store characteristics that lead to choice of particular store to shop (cf., Alpert, 1971; Tigert, 1983).

Tigert (1983) asked retail store shoppers to mention the reasons first and second most important in choosing the store (e.g., supermarket) where they shopped most often. He found that shares of mentions for the determinant attributes using this direct questioning technique were directly correlated highly with logit coefficients in modelling primary store choice. The approach taken by Tigert (1983) is top-down, because he began his questioning with attitude-object, by asking for the name of the primary store, and then asking the respondent for the first and second store attribute that the respondent associated with his/her primary store.

However, the argument may be valid that Tigert's open-ended questioning procedure caused strategic cognitive processing by the respondents, because the respondents were asked to report the first and second store attributes most important to themselves that came to their minds in choosing the store where they shop most often. Such a question requires two steps in answering: first, a network of several store attributes related to the respondent's primary store would be created from long-term memory and entered into working memory; second, the respondent would need to evaluate which of the associations between these store attributes and his/her primary store was determinant of his/her primary store decision. Thus, elements of both automatic and strategic cognitive processing are present in answering the question posed to shoppers by Tigert.

In contrast with Tigert's (1983) approach, Trappey and Woodside (1991) used a bottom-up questioning procedure to measure automatic-unconscious processing of the linkage of store attributes and store names. Using a telephone survey, respondents were asked to name the store that" first comes-to-mind" when hearing each of 14 possible store evaluative attributes, for example," lowest overall food prices,"" most convenient location," and" best quality produce." Both logit and multiple regression models were tested of respondents' primary store choices based on their TOMA responses of store names linked with each of these 14 attributes. These results supported an attribute-accessibility hypothesis of the association of primary store choice based on evaluative attributes and TOMA of store name, and what Hauser (1986) defines as bottom-up consumer agenda of selecting among choice alternatives (cf., Trappey and Woodside, 1991).

Both top-down and bottom-up research approaches to measure attitude-accessibility used by Tigert (1983) and Trappey and Woodside (1991), respectively, indicate direct relationships between store image and the store's ability to attract and maintain patronage exist. Prior research on store image using rating scales (e.g., 5-point or 7-point, strongly disagree to strongly agree scales) has been criticised severely for its inability to account for only small proportions of the variance in store patronage (cf., Doyle, 1977; Doyle and Gidengil, 1977; Corstjens and Doyle, 1989).

The attitude-accessibility approaches are likely to provide moderate to high levels of explained variance in store patronage (more than 40 percent) and are quicker and less expensive to implement than employing in-store experiments and direct sales measures to learn the affects of retailing strategy on customer behaviour [(as advocated by Doyle and his colleagues, see especially Corstjens and Doyle (1989, p. 171)]. Thus, although the higher validity of the results from properly executed, true experiments is not questioned here, a few" intermediate criteria" [measures of customers' awareness and affective states to learn if an association is occurring between marketing action and customer behaviour, see Axelrod (1968, 1986)] do indicate that store image is linked strongly with store patronage.

The principal hypothesis (H1) examined here is that the attitude-accessibility of the major supermarkets competing in the same metropolitan area will differ substantially among their loyal, new, competitors' customers, and defector customer segments for each supermarket. More specifically, for a given store, greater shares of loyal or new customers will exhibit positive, store attitude-accessibility profiles compared to non-customers and defectors (H2). A greater share of customer defectors will exhibit a negative attitude-accessibility profile compared to each of the loyal and new shopper segments (H3). In reference to what store first comes to mind with respect to specific store attributes, shoppers who identify competing stores as their primary store (i.e., competitors' customers) will least likely think first of the store identified by loyal, new, and defectors as their primary store (H4). Among loyal and new customers, the profiles of the store attributes most accessible with respect to each of the major supermarkets will differ substantially across stores (H5). For example, the loyal and new customers of major supermarkets will not identify their primary stores first equally as often as having the lowest overall food prices, the largest selection of food, and the most convenient location. Loyal customers of different stores are likely to associate the store principally with the store attributes that differ between the stores. In part, it is suggested here that not all major supermarkets will be perceived as offering the lowest overall food prices (LOFP) by their primary store customers; this lack of perception of being the stone with the LOFP does not mean that a store is necessarily unable to compete effectively.

For a given store: loyal, new, competitors', and defector customer groups will differ by demographic and food expenditure profiles (H6). The loyal customers across competing stores will differ in their average total grocery expenditures – that is, not all loyal customers are equally valuable in terms of their amount of total purchases (H7).

Attitude-accessibility in associating a store with store attributes explains a substantial share of primary store choice behaviour (PSC) beyond the level explained by previous primary store choice (PPSC) behaviour (H8). This hypothesis is analogous to Jacobson and Aaker's (1985) predictions and findings about the influence of market share on return on investment (ROI): market share positively influences ROI but does not contribute much to the explained variance of ROI beyond that explained by lagged ROI. Lagged ROI acts as a surrogate for firm specific factors occurring in previous periods that tend to be constant on a year-to-year basis.

The inclusion of lagged dependent variables as explanatory factors in regression or logit models helps to capture some of the impact of past factors (such as the influence of precedence and habit of shopping most of the time at the same store) even such factors as luck, and a host of other factors. Previous primary store choice (PPSC) may be associated with both primary store choice (PSC) and the shoppers' attitude-accessibilities associating a store with specific store attributes. The question raised here is whether or not including attitude-accessibility variables explains some unique variance in primary store choice (PSC) that is not spurious (the results of a common association with some other factors).

Thus, the study examines models of PSC including and excluding a measure for PPSC:

$$PSC = a + b1 \, (PPSC) \tag{1}$$
$$PSC = a + b1 \, (A1) + b2 \, (A2) + b3 \, (A3) + e \tag{2}$$
$$PSC = a + b1 \, (A1) + b2 \, (A2) + b3 \, (A3) + b4 \, (PPSC) + e \tag{3}$$

With A_i representing a given store's attitude-accessibility with respect to attribute i. More or less than three store attributes may be included in the model, but three are included in models 2 and 3 based on Howard's (1989, p. 170) proposition that about three store attributes represent the key dimensions of retail store image in limited problem solving, buying situations.

The specific store attributes (thus, store images) in attitude-accessibility models differ substantially across competing stores (H9). For example, given that one store might be more often perceived as having the most convenient location (MCL), then this store would be accessed more often from shopper's long-term memories as having the MCL, and the store's link with MCL should be associated strongly with the store being identified as the primary store choice.

Method

A two-page survey form was used to collect both store awareness-accessibility data. Telephone interviews were conducted in two areas of New Orleans (Metairie and the uptown area). Store awareness-accessibility data were collected by asking respondents," Name all the supermarkets in the New Orleans area that you are familiar with [note order of mention in space provided]." Store attitude accessibility data were collected by asking the respondent," What supermarket first comes to mind when I say," for 10 positively and 10 negatively worded store attributes: lowest (highest) overall food prices, best (worst) quality meat, best (worst) quality produce, largest (smallest) selection of foods, friendliest (most unfriendly) personnel, fastest (slowest) checkout, best (worst) quality bakery, best (worst) quality deli, fresh (unfresh) seafood, and most (least) convenient location.

Results

A total of 317 interviews was completed. Most (76%) of the respondents' primary store choices involved three supermarket chain stores: Winn-Dixie (36%) of the respondents' primary store), Schwegmann's (22%), and Superstore (18%). Winn-Dixie has 26 stores in the greater New Orleans metropolitan area, Schwegmann's has 11 stores, and Superstore has two stores. The findings reported here are for these three major supermarkets; no other supermarket was reported by more than 7 percent of the respondents to be their primary store.

The store positioning strategies for each of these three stores includes advertising the respective stores as offering the lowest overall food prices, a feat impossible for all three stores to achieve. Winn-Dixie's strategy also includes promoting the store to be" the beef people."

H1 and H2: do store attitude-accessibilities differ among loyal, new, competitors', and defector customers?

The results of the data analyses support H1 and H2. For most of the 20 store attributes, the store attitude-accessibilities for Winn-Dixie, Superstore, and Schwegmann's do differ among each of the store's four customer portfolio segments; these results are summarised in Tables 3.1, 3.2 and 3.3, respectively.

The fact that Winn-Dixie has more stores in the two areas included in the study than the other two competing supermarket chains combined provides a way to examine one aspect of the validity of the responses. Because the greater number of store locations, among all the respondents Winn-Dixie was expected to be identified most often as first coming to mind for having the most convenient location. This expectation was confirmed: 46 percent of the total respondents identified Winn-Dixie as first coming to mind as offering the most convenient location; only 4 percent identified Superstore and 16 percent identified Schwegmann's as having the most convenient location.

Note that Winn-Dixie is not associated with LOFP, but the store chain is associated by half all the respondents, and even half of the store chain's loyal customers, as offering the highest overall food prices (HOFP). Less than 1 percent of the total respondents identified Superstore, and 4 percent identified Schwegmann's as offering the HOFP.

H3: defector versus loyal and new customers

The results support H3 for each of the three stores. Greater shares of defector customers identify the respective stores first most negatively worded store attributes in comparison with the loyal and new customer segments. Particularly noteworthy are the shares of the defectors who identify Winn-Dixie first as having the HOPF (79%), the slowest checkout (46%), and the smallest selection of foods (43%) – shares substantially higher than loyal and/or new customers for this store chain.

For Superstore in the following Table 3.2, particularly noteworthy are the lower shares in positive store attributes among defectors first identifying Superstore as having these attributes compared to shares of loyal and new customers: LOFP, the largest selection of foods, best quality bakery, and the best quality deli. If Superstore did a better job at maintaining its image among its customers for these store attributes, the store could probably reduce some of its losses of primary store customers.

In Table 3.3, Schwegmann's has noteworthy lower shares of defectors versus loyal and new customer segments first identifying the store as offering the LOFP, best quality meat, fastest checkout, and especially best quality produce. Also, note that none of the defectors first identified Schwegmann's as having the best quality produce, but 25 percent did identify Schwegmann's as having the poorest quality produce. None of the Schwegmann's defectors identified the store as having the poorest quality bakery, and 25 percent did identify the store as having the best quality bakery. Thus, Schwegmann's perceived produce quality appears to be increasing defection, but its bakery quality is not stemming defection among the store's primary customers. These observations are based on survey data only. A limitation of the research method is that only

Table 3.1 Attitude Accessibility of Winn-Dixie for Evaluative Attributes by Winn-Dixie Customer and Non Customer Segments

Winn-Dixie Evaluative Attributes	Winn-Dixie Customer Portfolio Segment					F; p < 3/313 d.f.
	Total	Loyal	New	Defectors	Competitors'	
Lowest overall food prices	3	7[a]	7	0	0	4.98; 0.00
Best Quality Meat	28	53	52	32	11	23.87; 0.00
Best quality Produce	20	37	33	18	10	11.34; 0.00
Large selection foods	5	10	11	7	2	3.60; 0.01
Friendliest personnel	18	33	37	18	7	12.94; 0.00
Fastest checkout	17	32	26	4	10	8.63; 0.00
Best quality bakery	13	20	30	14	6	6.84; 0.00
Best quality deli	19	35	30	14	9	10.39; 0.00
Freshest seafood	14	25	22	14	6	6.78; 0.00
Most convenient location	46	89	81	57	17	79.81; 0.00
Highest overall food prices	50	50	40	79	48	3.54; 0.01
Poorest quality meat	15	11	11	21	16	0.77; 0.51
Poorest quality produce	23	24	22	21	23	0.03; 0.99
Smallest selection of food	38	38	15	43	40	2.29; 0.08
Most unfriendly personnel	15	20	15	11	13	0.95; 0.42
Slowest checkout	25	30	22	46	20	3.43; 0.02
Poorest quality bakery	19	23	11	29	16	1.52; 0.21
Poorest quality deli	19	20	19	18	18	0.06; 0.98
Most unfresh seafood	14	8	7	25	17	2.49; 0.06
Least convenient location	6	0	0	0	11	5.77; 0.00
Sample Size	317	88	27	28	174	

[a] Note: Read that 7% of customers loyal to Winn-Dixie identified Winn-Dixie when asked the name of the store having the lowest overall food prices.

Table 3.2 Attitude-Accessibility of Superstore for Evaluative Attributes by Superstore Customer and Noncustomer Segments

Superstore Evaluative Attributes	Superstore Customer Portfolio Sement					F; p< 3/313 d.f.
	Total	Loyal	New	Defectors	Competitors'	
Lowest overall food prices	53	92[a]	81	67	44	14.33; 0.00
Best quality meat	11	43	24	6	5	19.97; 0.00
Best quality produce	31	73	67	50	20	25.02; 0.00
Largest selection fo foods	56	95	86	72	46	15.37; 0.01
Friendliest personnel	17	41	43	11	12	10.40; 0.00
Fastest checkout	26	51	71	22	18	16.22; 0.00
Best quality bakery	37	70	62	39	29	10.84; 0.00
Best quality deli	32	81	67	50	20	31.25; 0.00
Freshest seafood	21	65	38	11	13	22.72; 0.00
Most convenient location	4	27	5	0	1	20.19; 0.00
Highest overall food prices	0	0	0	0	0	0.01; 0.96
Poorest quality meat	10	8	14	6	10	0.33; 0.80
Poorest quality produce	7	5	10	6	7	0.13; 0.94
Smallest selection of foods	3	3	10	11	2	2.08; 0.10
Most unfriendly personnel	8	11	10	17	7	0.98; 0.40
Slowest checkout	11	16	50	11	10	0.65; 0.58
Poorest quality bakery	4	3	10	11	3	1.46; 0.23
Poorest quality deli	5	8	5	6	5	0.21; 0.89
Most unfresh seafood	7	8	5	11	6	0.29; 0.83
Least convenient location	54	51	62	72	53	1.06; 0.36
Sample size	317	37	21	18	241	

[a]*Note:* Read that 7% of customers loyal to Superstore identified Superstore when asked the name of the store having the lowest overall food prices.

association, not cause-and-effect relationships, may be uncovered. Thus, the strategic implications suggested are based on useful but not conclusive evidence.

Schwegmann's is less often seen to be distinct among its own primary customers compared to how competing stores are perceived by primary customers of these stores.

Given that a substantial share (36%) of the total respondents identified Winn-Dixie to be their primary store, Winn-Dixie is able to compete effectively at gaining primary customers even through only a handful access Winn-Dixie as offering the lowest overall food prices, and nearly half of the store's primary customers access Winn-Dixie as having the highest overall food prices. Most likely, these attitude-accessibilities for Winn-Dixie, along with its primary store customers' perception that the store has the most convenient location, are grounded in reality.

H4: customers of competing stores thoughts about store X

The results support the fourth hypothesis. In general, competitor's customers think first of Winn-Dixie across the store attributes less often than loyal, new, and defector customers of Winn-Dixie. Substantial shares of competitor's customers think first of Winn-Dixie only for the highest overall food prices (48%) and smallest selection of foods (40%). Only a few of the competitor's customers identify Winn-Dixie first when thinking about most convenient location (17%).

The results for Superstore and Schwegmann's also support H4. Details appear in Tables 3.2 and 3.3. At least one, and many instances all three of the loyal, new, and defector customer groups, think first of these respective stores compared to competitors' customers across the 20 store attributes. Thus, gaining high versus low attitude-accessibility is associated with primary store customer behaviour versus not being a customer of a store. Not being thought about first is highly associated with not being a customer.

H5: profiles of attitude-accessibilities across competing stores.

The results Tables 3.1, 3.2 and 3.3 support H5: substantially different proportions of the different loyal and new customers of competing stores think first of their respective primary stores for the same evaluative attribute. For example, consider the store attitude-accessibilities among the loyal and new customers for each of the three stores for most convenient location (see Figure 3.1).

We next consider the store attitude-accessibilities among these same customer groups for each of the three stores for lowest overall food prices. These results support the view that most current and new

Table 3.3 Attitude-Accessibility of Schwegmann's for Evaluative Attributes by Schwegmann's Customer and Noncustomer Segments

Schwegmann's Evaluative Attributes	Schwegmann's Customer Portfolio Segment					F; p < 3/313 d.f.
	Total	Loyal	New	Defectors	Competitors'	
Lowest overall food prices	33	79a	67	33	20	36.29; 0.00
Best quality meat	11	34	33	25	4	20.48; 0.00
Best quality produce	12	38	33	0	5	22.86; 0.00
Largest selection fo foods	27	64	50	42	16	23.45; 0.00
Friendliest personnel	11	36	17	17	4	20.42; 0.00
Fastest checkout	14	38	33	25	6	17.85; 0.00
Best quality bakery	7	17	17	25	3	7.39; 0.00
Best quality deli	15	52	42	25	4	41.08; 0.00
Freshest seafood	17	45	25	42	8	18.42; 0.00
Most convenient location	16	50	50	50	4	44.13; 0.00
Highest overall food prices	4	5	0	8	4	0.36; 0.70
Poorest quality meat	11	16	8	8	10	0.58; 0.63
Poorest quality produce	12	22	17	25	19	3.70; 0.01
Smallest selection of foods	5	3	8	0	5	0.41; 0.79
Most unfriendly personnel	16	24	17	8	15	1.16; 0.32
Slowest checkout	17	24	17	25	15	1.24; 0.29
Poorest quality bakery	7	15	0	0	6	2.82; 0.04
Poorest quality deli	25	22	29	0	27	0.46; 0.71
Most unfresh seafood	16	9	0	0	7	0.69; 0.56
Least convenient location	16	14	17	17	17	0.09; 0.96
Sample size	317	58	12	12	235	

[a]Note: Read that 7% of customers loyal to Schwegmann's identified Schwegmann's when asked the name of the store having the lowest overall food prices.

Store	New	Loyal
Winn-Dixie	89%	81%
Superstore	27%	5%
Schwegmann's	50%	50%

Figure 3.1   Most Convenient Location

Winn-Dixie primary store customers recognise the same distinct advantage of Winn-Dixie versus its competitors (Winn-Dixie's most convenient locations) and what is not a distinct advantage (its prices); and that most current and new Superstore primary customers recognise the same distinct advantage of Superstore (its prices), and what is not (its locations).

Schwegmann's is often caught in the middle between the other two competitors in the proportions of its loyal and new customers identifying Schwegmann's as first coming to mind for the 20 evaluative attributes. Thus,

Store	New	Loyal
Winn-Dixie	7%	7%
Superstore	92%	81%
Schwegmann's	79%	67%

Figure 3.2   Lowest Overall Food Prices

If so, then Winn-Dixie's principal advertising message may be counterproductive – trying to increase shoppers' attitude-accessibility that Winn-Dixie offers the LOFP when the LOFP position is "owned" by Superstore and Schwegmann's in most shoppers' long-term memories (88%). Winn-Dixie is asking food shoppers to focus their attention on an evaluative attribute that these customers perceive the store's competitors to excel in compared to Winn-Dixie.

Is the principal positioning message used by Winn-Dixie counterproductive? Does focusing on Winn-Dixie's advertising on LOFP drive away loyal customers? Some circumstantial evidence supports an affirmative answer: 79 percent of Winn-Dixie defectors access Winn-Dixie as offering the highest overall food prices, a percent substantially higher ($p < .01$) than loyal, new, and primary customers of competing stores. Such an analysis is one of the benefits of considering customer portfolio analysis.

H6 and H7: demographic and food expenditure profiles do differ within a store's customer portfolio; loyal customers are not equally valuable

Tables 3.4 and 3.5 summarise the results for examining H6. The average ages estimated for each store differ for the four customer segments. For example, the average age (45) of Schwegmann's loyal customers is substantially higher compared to the average age (35) of competitors' loyal customers; the opposite findings occurs for Superstore.

Average household sizes varies substantially among the four customer groups for Winn-Dixie and Schwegmann's, but not for Superstore. The average household is larger for Schwegmann's loyal customers (3.1) versus loyal customers of competing stores (2.3); the opposite finding is observed in Table 3.4 for Winn-Dixie.

Table 3.4 Age and Household Size Profiles of Customer Portfolios for Three Supermarket Chains in New Orleans

Supermarket	Customer Portfolio Segment					Sig. F;
	Total	Loyal	New	Defectors	Competitors'	p <
Age:						
Winn-Dixie	37	37	31	30	40	5.13; 0.00
Sample Size	287	73	26	27	161	df - 3/283
Superstore	37	32	27	32	40	6.74; 0.00
Sample Size	287	33	20	16	218	df - 3/283
Schwegmann's	37	45	39	39	35	5.04; 0.00
Sample Size	287	53	12	12	210	df - 3/283
Household Size:						
Winn-Dixie	2.5	2	2.3	2.1	2.8	5.95; 0.00
Sample Size	317	88	27	28	174	df - 3/313
Superstore	2.5	2.6	2.2	1.9	2.5	0.97; 0.41
Sample Size	317	37	21	18	241	df – 3/313
Schwegmann's	2.5	3.1	3.1	2.8	2.3	4.63; 0.00
Sample Size	317	58	12	12	235	df - 3/313

The analysis for total annual household income does not indicate significant differences among the four customer groups for each of the three stores. This lack of significance may be due, in part, to a nonresponse error for the income question; 25 percent of the respondents refused to answer the income question.

The average weekly expenditures for groceries did vary substantially across the four customer groups for each store. In Table 3.5, the average weekly grocery expenditures for Winn-Dixie's loyal customers (both loyal and new customers combined) are less compared to loyal customers of competitors' stores. The opposite finding is observed for Superstore and Schwegmann's.

Table 3.5 Weekly Expenditures at All Supermarkets and Grocery Stores and Total Annual House-hold Income by Customer Portfolios for Three Supermarket Chains

Supermarket	Total	Customer Portfolio Segment				Sig. F; $p <$
		Loyal	New	Defectors	Competitors'	
Weekly expenditures for food:						
Winn-Dixie	$85	$75	$72	$72	$93	4.54; 0.00
Sample Size	309	84	25	27	173	df – 3/305
Superstore	$85	$107	$81	$84	$82	3.30; 0.01
Sample Size	309	37	21	18	233	df – 3/305
Schwegmann's	$85	$95	$120	$89	$80	3.83; 0.01
Sample Size	309	57	11	11	230	df – 3/305
Total annual household income (000's)						
Winn-Dixie	$51	$38	$35	$44	$59	0.84; 0.47
Sample Size	238	61	19	19	139	df – 3/234
Superstore	$51	$45	$39	$36	$54	0.29; 0.83
Sample Size	238	35	16	16	171	df – 3/234
Schwegmann's	$51	$45	$54	$35	$52	0.14; 0.94
Sample Size	238	43	10	8	177	df – 3/234

The demographic food expenditure results supports the following conclusions. Winn-Dixie's compared to Superstore's primary customers are younger, smaller in household size, and they spend less money on groceries. These findings are intuitively appealing, given the finding that a distinct advantage associated with Superstore LOFP. Shoppers living in households with several persons (3 or more) that have higher food expenditure requirements will seek out the store with the LOFP, compared to shoppers from smaller household sizes and having lower average food bills.

Thus, the results support H7. The average sales expenditures for Winn-Dixie loyal customers are lower than Superstore and Schwegmann's loyal customers. It takes about 14 loyal customers at Winn-Dixie to equal the expenditures of 10 loyal customers at Superstore. The analyses for other demographic data did not indicate significant associations with customers segmented into the four portfolio groups.

H8: modelling primary store choice by previous store choice and attitude-accessibility

Dichotomous attitude-accessibility variables were created for each store with a value of 1 assigned if the store was named by the respondent as first coming to mind for a given evaluative attribute, for example, lowest overall food prices. A value of 0 was assigned to the store when the store was not accessed for each of the 10 evaluative attributes and the additional attitude-accessibility variable of the store perceived closest to the respondent's home. Similarly, dichotomous variables (1, 0) were created for primary store choice and previous primary store choice for each store. Both logit and stepwise regression models were run to examine the affects of attitude-accessibilities of evaluative attributes (Ai) and previous primary store choice (PPSC) on primary store choice (PSC). For ease of interpretation and because the same variables were found to provide very similar significant, unique contributions to the explained variance of PSC for the logit and OLS regression models results, this chapter reports only the OLS regression models. However, several violations of important theoretical assumptions have been noted when using regression to model dichotomous dependent variables (cf. Goldberger, 1964, p. 249). Also, Gensch and Recker (1979) have demonstrated that the multinomial logit model results in better fit than the regression approach.

The regression results models for Winn-Dixie, Superstore and Schwegmann's are summarised in Tables 3.6, 3.7 and 3.8, respectively. For model 1, the adjusted variances of primary store choice (PSC) for Winn-Dixie, Superstore and Schwegmann's explained by PPSC alone were 0.37, 0.32, and .059, respectively. For model 2, the predictive accuracies (R^2's) for primary store choice using the unique contributions of attitude-accessibility variables were 0.46, 0.35, and 0.48, for Winn-Dixie, Superstore and Schwegmann's, respectively.

Thus, the comparisons of the regression models that include only atti-tude-accessibility variables versus the more parsimonious PPSC only models do not indicate a consistent finding that the predictive accuracy is higher with one approach versus the other.

However, the results for model 3 support H8: the use of both PPSC and attitude-accessibility variables adds substantial increases in the ex-plained variances of PSC for each store. The predictive accuracies for the three stores are 0.54, 0.46, and 0.69 for Winn-Dixie, Superstore and Schwegmann's, respectively. Also, insights into likely causes of PSC behav-iour with respect to each store are provided by examining the evaluative attributes contributing to increasing the predictive accuracies.

Both the logit and regression model results indicated that Winn-Dixie being thought of first as offering the most convenient location was the important attitude-accessibility in influencing shoppers' selection of Winn-Dixie as their primary store. As shown in Table 3.6, being perceived first as offering the best quality meat and fastest checkout are the two other variables contributing to the predictive accuracy of primary store choice of Winn-Dixie.

In first glancing at Table 3.7, it may be surprising not to see LOFP as contributing to the explained variance of Superstore as the primary store

Table 3.6　Attitude-Accessibility Regression Models for Winn-Dixie

Winn-Dixie	Regression Model				
	b	SEb	β	t	p
Evaluative Attributes Only Model:					
Most convenient location	0.51	0.04	0.52	12.09	0.00
Best quality meat	0.19	0.05	0.18	3.86	0.00
Fastest checkout	0.17	0.05	0.14	3.19	0.00
Best quality produce	0.14	0.05	0.12	2.62	0.00
Constant	0.02	0.03		0.60	0.55

Adjusted R2 = 0.46; F= 69.63; 4/312 df; p < .00

Evaluative Attributes Plus Previous Behaviour Model:					
Winn-Dixie six months ago	0.36	0.05	0.36	7.78	0.00
Most convenient location	0.35	0.04	0.36	7.97	0.00
Best quality meat	0.16	0.04	0.15	3.72	0.00
Fastest checkout	0.16	0.05	0.13	3.26	0.00
Constant	0.00	0.02		–0.17	0.86

Adjusted R2 = 0.54; F = 94.50; 4/312 df; p < .00

Table 3.7　Attitude-Accessibility Regression Models for Superstore

Superstore	Regression Model				
	b	SEb	β	t	p
Evaluative Attributes Only Model:					
Best quality deli	0.22	0.04	0.26	5.12	0.00
Best quality produce	0.19	0.04	0.23	4.69	0.00
Fastest checkout	0.19	0.04	0.22	4.62	0.00
Most convenient location	0.38	0.09	0.20	4.23	0.00
Constant	–0.01	0.02		–0.48	0.63

Adjusted R2 = 0.35; F = 43.33; 4/312 df; p < .00

Evaluative Attributes Plus Previous Behaviour Model:					
Superstore six months ago	0.43	0.05	0.42	9.12	0.00
Fastest checkout	0.18	0.04	0.21	4.80	0.00
Best quality deli	0.15	0.04	0.18	3.71	0.00
Best quality produce	0.13	0.00	0.16	3.40	0.00
Constant	–0.02	0.02		–1.21	0.23

Adjusted R2 = 0.46; F = 67.30; 4/312 df; p < .00

Table 3.8   Attitude-Accessibility Regression Models for Schwegmann's

Schwegmann's	Regression Model				
	b	SEb	β	t	p
Evaluative Attributes Only Model:					
Best quality deli	0.24	0.06	0.21	4.25	0.00
Most convenient location	0.35	0.05	0.31	6.92	0.00
Lowest overall food prices	0.23	0.04	0.26	5.78	0.00
Best quality produce	0.28	0.04	0.22	4.69	0.00
Constant	0.02	0.02		0.91	0.36

Adjusted R2 = 0.48; F = 73.01; 4/312 df; p < .00

Schwegmann's					
Evaluative Attributes Plus **Previous Behaviour Model:**					
Schwegmann's six months ago	0.58	0.04	0.58	15.03	0.00
Lowest overall food prices	0.13	0.03	0.15	4.19	0.00
Closest to my home	0.23	0.04	0.19	5.33	0.00
Best quality produce	0.23	0.04	0.18	5.21	0.00
Constant	–0.01	0.02		–0.43	0.67

Adjusted R2 = 0.69: F = 174.88; 4/312 df; p < .00

choice. The attitude-accessibility of Superstore for LOFP does not significantly add to the explained variance of Superstore as shoppers' primary store, but Superstore-LOFP as an accessibility variable is associated also with some of the independent variables that do not enter the final model shown in Table 3.7, and consequently, the attitude accessibility variable of Superstore-LOFP does not enter the final regression model.

Note that in Tables 3.7 and 3.8 the standardised regression coefficients are about the same size for the attitude-accessibility variables, that is, the influence of each of these variables on primary store choice for Superstore and Schwegmann's is about the same. However, in Table 3.1 the attitude-accessibility of Winn-Dixie for most convenient location dominates the other two attitude-accessibility variables in the models. The regression models and results in Table 3.1 provide specific evidence of how much primary store choice of Winn-Dixie is influenced by the store's top-of-mind position as having the most convenient location for grocery shoppers. These findings may also suggest that Winn-Dixie is more vulnerable to competitive attacks if either Superstore and Schwegmann's could gain higher shares of attitude-accessibility for most convenient location.

For the models in Tables 3.6, 3.7 and 3.8 that included previous primary store choice (PPSC), the number of attitude-accessibility variables included in the models were restricted to three. This limitation was used to help compare the relative increase in explained variance in predicting primary store choice (PSC) between the proposed theoretical models (models 2 and 3) by eliminating the effect of increasing the number of variables in the models. For all three stores for the models that include PPSC, one or two additional attitude-accessibility variables did not contribute significantly to explaining PSC beyond the three attitude-accessibility variables that entered first, second, and third in the models. However, the increase in the explained variance provided by these additional models was less than 2 percent for all three stores.

Cross validation

The total sample of respondents was split randomly into nearly two equal subsamples. Regression models were developed for each subsample for each of the three stores. The predictions of the first models from the first sub-sample were compared with the actual PSC values in the second subsample, and vice versa. The cross-validation adjusted explained variances ranged from 0.34 to 0.49 for the six models.

When the cross-validation model predictions were restricted so that the low values through 0.5000 equals 0 and 0.5001 through the high values equals 1.0, the proportion of correct model predictions for the cross-validation models ranges from 0.75 to 0.87.

Conclusion and strategic implications

A store's attitude accessibility toward evaluative store attributes is likely to vary within a store's portfolio of customers. The attitude-accessibility of any given store, say Store X, toward evaluative attributes is likely to vary considerably among new, loyal, and defector Store X customer groups, as well as customers of competitors' stores. Information of the differences in store attitude and accessibility among these customer groups is likely to be very helpful in identifying competitive opportunities and vulnerabilities for a given store.

For example, a strong positive trend is found among several negative evaluative attributes being associated first with Winn-Dixie as some customers move from new to loyal to defector locations in Winn-Dixie's portfolio. Specifically, in Table 3.1 the proportions of these three respective customer groups increases from 0.15 to 0.38 to 0.43 for the smallest selection of food, from 0.22 to 0.30 to 0.46 for the slowest checkout, and from 0.40 to 0.50 to 0.79 for the highest overall food prices. The presence of such data trends for Winn-Dixie and their absence for Superstore and Schwegmann's indicates potentially serious problems for Winn-Dixie and opportunities for retailers of these two other stores.

The application of customer portfolio analysis to retail customers and store attitude-accessibility joins together two research literatures and extends the work of Tigert (1983) and Trappey and Woodside (1991). The moderately high levels of variance in primary store choice explained by the attitude-accessibility models indicates that additional research on attitude-accessibility and store choice is warranted.

The survey results presented here are based on one cross-sectional study. Tigert (1983) demonstrates convincingly that store evaluative attributes do vary over time in the same market for the same retailer. For that reason, the use of longitudinal designs in future studies of store attitude-accessibilities and the use of such measures as intermediate criteria to estimate the likely ultimate revenue and profit impact of retailer strategies to improve their stores' positions in the minds of the consumers is advocated.

Retailers do need to recognise that their customer portfolios are changing constantly. In fact, based on BehaviourScan, single-source data, Fulgoni and Eskin (1983) indicate that it might be more useful to conceptualise retail supermarket patronage in terms of store switching rather than store loyalty. The evidence from supermarket scanner-data linked to household information is that almost no household is 100 percent loyal to one store and about one-fifth of supermarket shoppers but 70 percent of their groceries from one store over a 24-week period. Most customers switch their primary store choice among three or four stores within a two-year period (cf., Fulgoni and Eskin, 1983, pp. 270–271). Thus, understanding the amount and reasons for flows within a store's portfolio of customers and competitors' customers is important. Identifying key customer portfolio segments and these customers' attitude-accessibilities appears useful for developing such an understanding. The point has been made by others (Shepard, 1990; Chakraborty, et al., 1991) that the forward stepwise regression method used in the present study" is notorious for finding subsets of variables that do not 'hang' together." That is, the selected variables are difficult to justify because they appear not to be related in any logical order or reasonable way to the dependent variable (Shepard, 1990 p. 205). Model building requires both analytic skills and theoretical foundation on the part of the researchers (Chakraborty et al., 1991).

Consequently, when using attitude-accessibility theory to model primary store choice it is that recommended modeling begin with testing the hypotheses presented in this article. That is, customer portfolio analyses of major competing stores (resulting in tables similar to 3.6, 3.7 and 3.8) are likely to indicate a logical set of likely independent variables affecting primary store choice. A few subsets of different independent variables are likely to include different variables that influence primary store choice significantly. Some variables may be excluded from entering forward stepwise regression models that have a profound influence on primary store choice, for example, the attitude-accessibility influencing primary store choice.

Appendix: details of the field study method

Store attitude-accessibility information may be useful for modelling customers' least favourite stores (i.e.," the store you don't like or rarely shop"). Such models indicate the evaluative attributes associated most with deciding actively not to shop at a particular store. From the data in the present study for example, the attitude-accessibility of Winn-Dixie first coming to mind for HOFP influences Winn-Dixie being selected as the respondents least favourite store. For detailed examples of modelling least favourite store choice using attitude-accessibility data from supermarket customers of store in Monroe, Louisiana, see Trappey and Woodside (1991). Customer portfolio analysis should include such research on what stores customers refuse to shop and why they refuse, as well as research for understanding and predicting primary store choice.

To reduce the continuing yea- or nay-saying responses, these attributes were rotated from one respondent to the next; a positively worded attribute was followed by a negatively worded attribute for a different word dimension, and vice-versa. Thus, asking for the name of the store offering the lowest overall food prices was never followed by asking for the name of the store offering the highest overall food prices.

The 10 store attributes were selected for the study based both on a literature search of store attributes and found to be important determinant attributes of store choice (cf., Lindquist, 1975; Gensch and Recker, 1979; Tigert, 1983; Howard, 1989) and on previous research on testing logit and regression attitude-accessibility models of store choice in a small southern city, Monroe, Louisiana (cf. Trappey and Woodside, 1991). The questions on fresh seafood and deli store features were asked because some of the stores involved in the New Orleans market areas studies offer these services and some do not; thus, it was necessary to learn if such features would affect primary store choice differently among the competing stores.

Information on the supermarket closest to the respondent's home was requested. Also, the following question was asked to learn the respondent's primary store," Which one supermarket do you shop most often? (Your main store)." To measure whether or not the respondent was loyal to his/her primary store, the following question was asked," Six months ago, at which supermarket did you shop most?" Responses to this question were used to estimate each respondent's previous primary store[1] choice.

For any store, say Store X, a respondent was classified as a loyal customer to the store if his/her primary store choice (say Store X) was reported to be the same at the time of the interview and six months ago (same response to

---

[1] The fact that the longitudinal data collection procedure was not used to collect primary store choice data among the same sampled respondents at two points in time is a limitation of the study.

the two questions just described). A respondent was classified as a defector from a given store if her/his current primary store choice (say, Store Z) at the time of the interview was different from her/his reported primary store choice six months ago (Store X). A respondent was classified as a new customer if her/his current primary store choice (Store X) was different from her/his primary store choice six months ago (Store Y). Competitors' customers, that is, non-customers, were respondents who neither a primary store customer of Store X six months ago nor at the time of the survey data were collected.

The data for the study were collected in the autumn, 1990. Only households with telephone numbers in the telephone books of the respective areas were included in the study. Thus, the exclusion of households with unlisted telephone numbers is a limitation of the study.

Pages were selected randomly from the telephone book, and all numbers with exchanges listed in the areas included in the study were called. A total of five attempts was made to reach each household selected for the study with eight telephone rings per call; one or more members of 84 percent of the households was reached by telephone. A total of 87 percent of the households contracted participated in answering all the questions in the survey.

Demographic data were also collected: age, household size, race, employment outside home, gender, years of education completed, zip code area, annual household income, marital status, and number and ages of children. Information on the respondent's estimated total expenditures per week for groceries was also collected.

References

Alpert, M. "Identification of Determinant Attributes: A Comparison of Methods," *Journal of Marketing Research*, 8 (May 1971): 184–191.

Axelrod, J. N. "Attitude Measures that Predict Purchase," *Journal of Advertising Research*, 8 (February/March 1968): 3–17.

Axelrod, J. N. "Minnie, Minnie Tickled the Parson," *Journal of Advertising Research*, 26 (February/March 1968): 89–96.

Beik, L. L. and Buzby, S. L. "Profitability Analysis by Market Segments," *Journal of Marketing*, 37 (July 1973): 48–53.

Campbell, N. C. G. and Cunningham, M. T. "Customer Analysis for Strategy Development in Industrial Marketing," *Strategic Management Journal*, 4 (December 1983): 369–380.

Chakraborty, G., Woodworth, G., Gaeth, G. J. and Ettenson, R. "Screening for Interactions between Design Factors and Demographics in Choice-based Conjoint Analysis," *Journal of Business Research*, 23 (1991).

Cohen, L. "The Level of Consciousness: A Dynamic Approach to the Recall Technique," *Journal of Marketing Research*, 3 (May 1966): 142–148.

Corstjens, M. and Doyle, P. "Evaluating Alternative Retail Repositioning Strategies," *Marketing Science*, 8 (Spring 1989): 170–180.

Doyle, P. *Experimental Methods in Retailing, in Consumer and Industrial Buying Behaviour*, Arch G. Woodside, Jagdish N. Sheth, and Peter D. Bennett (eds), North-Holland, New York. 1977.

Doyle, P. and Gidengil, B. Z. "A Review of In-Store Experiments," *Journal of Retailing*, 53 (Spring 1977): 47–62.

Dubinsky, A. J. and Ingram, T. N. "A Portfolio Approach to Account Profitability," *Industrial Marketing Management*, 13 (February 1984): 57–62.

Dubinsky, A. J. "Customer Portfolio Analysis," in *Advances in Business Marketing 1*, Arch G. Woodside (ed.) Greenwich, CT: JAI Press, 1986, pp. 113–141.

Dwyer, R. F. "Customer Lifetime Valuation to Support Marketing Decision-Making," *Journal of Direct Marketing*, 3 (Autumn 1989): 8–15.

Fazio, R. H. "How Do Attitudes Guide Behaviour?" In *The Handbook of Motivation and Cognition: Foundation of Social Behaviour*, Richard M. Sorentino and E. Tory Higgins (eds) New York: Guilford Press, 1986.

Fazio, R. H. "On the Power of Functionality of Attitudes: The Role of Attitude Accessibility," in *Attitude Structure and Function* Anthony R. Pratkanis et al., NJ: Lawrence Erlbaum Associates, 1989, pp. 153–179.

Fazio, R. H., Powell, M. C. and William, C. "The Role of Attitude Accessibility in the Attitude-to-Behaviour Process," *Journal of Consumer Research*, 16 (December 1989): 280–288.

Fulgoni, G. and Eskin, G. J. "The BehaviourScan Research Facility for Studying Retail Shopping Patterns," in *Patronage Behaviour and Retail Management*, William R. Darden and Robert F. Lusch (eds), New York: Elsevier, North-Holland, 1983, pp. 261–274.

Gensch, D. and Recker, W. W. "The Multinomial, Multiattribute Logit Choice Model," *Journal of Marketing Research*, 16 (February 1979): 124–132.

Goldberger, A. S. *Economic Theory*. New York: Wiley, 1964.

Grunert, K. "Research in Consumer Behaviour: Beyond Attitude and Decision-Making," *Journal of European Society for Opinion and Marketing Research*, 16 (1988): 172–183.

Grunert, K. "Automatic and Strategic Processes in the Perception of Advertising," Paper presented at the *22nd International Congress of Applied Psychology*, Kyoto, Japan (July 22–27, 1990).

Haley, R. and Case, P. B. "Testing 13 Attitudes Scales for Agreement and Brand Discrimination," *Journal of Marketing*, 43 (Fall 1979): 20–32.

Hartley, R. F. "Use of Customer Analysis for Better Marketing Penetration," *Industrial Marketing Management*, 3 (February 1976): 57–62.

Hauser, J. R. "Agendas and Consumer Choice," *Journal of Marketing Research*, 23 (August 1986): 199–212.

Howard, J. A. *Consumer Behaviour and Marketing Strategy*, NJ: Prentice-Hall Englewood Cliffs, 1989.

Jackson, D. "Determining a Customer's Lifetime Value, Part One," *Direct Marketing*, 52 (March 1989a): 60–62.

Jackson, D. "Determining Customer's Lifetime Value, Part Two," *Direct Marketing*, 52 (May 1989b): 24–32.

Jacobson, R. and Aaker, D. A. "Is Market Share all That It's Cracked Up to Be?" *Journal of Marketing*, 49 (Fall 1985): 11–22.

Lindquist, J. D. "Measuring of Image," *Journal of Retailing*, 50 (Winter 1975): 29–38.

Rost, C. and Salle, R. "Customer Portfolio Analysis as an Opportunity to Improve Marketing Strategy: A Case Study," *Working Paper, Lyon Graduate School of Business*, Ecully Cedex, France. 1989.

Sevin, C. H. *Marketing Profitability Analysis*. New York: McGraw-Hill, 1965.

Shepard, D. *The New Direct Marketing*, Homewood, IL: Business One Irwin.1990.

Tigert, D. J. "Pushing the Hot Buttons for a Successful Retailing Strategy," in *Patronage Behaviour and Retail Management*, William R. Darden and Robert F. Lusch (eds), New York: Elsevier North-Holland, 1983, pp. 89–113.

Trappey III, R. J., and Woodside, A. G. "Attitude-Accessibility and Primary Store Choice," *Working Paper, Freeman School of Business*, Tulane University, New Orleans, LA. 1991.

Wells, W. D. "Backward Segmentation," in *Insights into Consumer Behaviour*, Johan Arndt (ed.). Boston, MA: Allyn and Bacon, 1968, pp. 85–100.

Woodside, A. G. and Wilson, E. J. "Effects of Consumer Awareness of Brand Advertising Preference," *Journal of Advertising Research*, 4 (August/September 1985): 41–48.

Woodside, A. G. and Soni, P. K. "Customer Portfolio Analysis for Strategy Development in Direct Marketing," *Journal of Direct Marketing*, 4 (1991).

4

Automatic Thinking and Store Choices by Near and Distant Customers

Background: finding what causes customers to think about your brand

Holden and Lutz (1992) propose that the reason consumers evoke different brands from long term memory into working memory is that different associates (e.g., benefits, attributes) have stronger links to some brands than others.

This chapter examines this proposition for associate-to-store evocations for supermarket shopping, in a market environment where several competing supermarkets are readily accessible for shopping. This chapter expands on Holden and Lutz (1992) central proposition by offering additional related hypotheses: (H_1) each competing store has a unique constellation of a few (3 to 7) associates that evoke the store's name among its primary customers; (H_2) in associate-to-store retrievals, substantial differences occur in the proportions of a store's primary consumers evoking the store's name for a benefit among those consumers living closest to their primary store versus consumers living closest to competing stores; (H_3) consumers are able to retrieve one or more competing stores (versus their primary store) for being "worst" on one or more benefits, for example, when asked to name the supermarket having the highest overall food prices.

The results (described in detail in the following sections) from telephone survey data previously used in Chapter 3 are utilsed here again to provide substantial support for hypotheses for the stores included in the study. Applying theory to store choice research provides retailing strategists an understanding of the causes for the gains and losses between competing stores. A positive retrieval bias was found: while two to five stores were retrieved as being best for each of ten benefits, almost all consumers reported "no store" came-to-mind readily as being the worst for these ten benefits. However, all consumers were able to retrieve the name of a store as being worst on one or more associates (e.g., highest overall food prices and least convenient location).

Brand retrieval theory and research

An initial burst of theoretical interest and research on what cues evoke what brands in what order-of-retrieval occurred in the 1960s and 1970s (see Cohen, 1966; Axelrod, 1968; Haley and Case, 1979). Cohen's (1966, p. 143) work is profound: "position of [unaided] recall of a brand among total brands recalled is highly related to differences within the range of brand attitudes, and therefore to brand behaviour. The earlier that [unaided] recall, the more favourable the attitude toward the brand; the later the [unaided] recall, the less favourable the attitude."

Without referring to Cohen (1966), the empirical studies by Axelrod (1968), Haley and Case (1979), and Nedungadi and Hutchinson (1985) strongly support the proposals made by Cohen including the central proposition that top-of-mind-awareness (TOMA) of a brand's retrieval from long-term memory is associated strongly with brand choice. Empirically, Haley and Case (1979) and Hauser (1978) find that the TOMA retrieval position is more important than attitude; using an information theoretic approach; Hauser (1978) reported that the probability of inclusion of the brand in the evoked set accounts for more variation in brand choice than does brand attitude.

Holden and Lutz (1992) and Woodside and Trappey (1992) extended the view that TOMA brand accessibility is associated strongly with brand choice because brand choice is a function of brands retrieved for specific benefits sought by the consumer. "It is suggested that research aimed at identifying the situational goals that act as cues in the evocation process will provide more insight into the cues that guide consumer evocation. In particular, one element that represents an important cue and which has not been included in the associative model of brand memory [and retrieval] is the consumer's underlying motives; that is his/her needs and wants" (Holden and Lutz, 1992, p. 104). In a study of shoppers' benefits-to-store retrievals, a limited number of such retrievals were found to be associated highly with primary store choice (Woodside and Trappey, 1992).

Separately, Tigert (1983) and his associates (Arnold, Handelman, Tigert, 1996; Arnold, Oum, and Tigert, 1983; Tigert, Arnold, Powell, and Seiders, 1991) reason that a potential customer of competing stores first thinks about a limited number of goal-derived categories of store attributes and benefits and shops at the store that is "best", even if only marginally (but noticeably) better, on one or more of these attributes/benefits.

Consequently, asking a customer to retrieve (access from memory) the name of the store or brand that is "best," for each of a limited number of benefits or attributes is likely to be useful for understanding the stores or brands the customer shops/buys. While unlikely to be observed for all, customers who report most often buying a given brand or shopping at a given store, will retrieve this brand/store first for the same, or a very similar, constellation of benefits (e.g., see Tigert, 1983).

Theoretical grounding for the prediction of a strong association between associate-to-brand/store retrieval and choice is found in the attitude-accessibility work of Fazio (1986, 1989) and his colleagues and the automatic-unconscious processing work by Grunert (1988, 1989). According to Fazio's model, the accessibility of an attitude from memory is postulated to act as a critical determinant of whether or not the attitude-to-behaviour process is initiated. Grunert (1988) views most information processing to be unconscious, automatic and not based on a large degree of conscious thinking.

Holden (1993) emphasises the role of situation and motives in influencing brand evocation. He points out that research from the categorisation literature (e.g., Roth and Shoben, 1983) describe how contextual factors can change the graded structure of a category. As for motives, different brands may be evoked depending on the goal-derived categories presented to a consumer, such as "things to take on a camping trip" (see Barsalou, 1985). Consequently, different stores may be associated (linked) in long-term memory as being the best solutions for achieving specific goals. Which store is evoked by a consumer depends on the salience of a given motive. Because consumers are more likely to focus on achieving salient goals rather than only to avoid poor outcomes, evoking the "best" store for a given motive is easier than evoking the "worst" store for the same motive. However, for the most salient motives in a given situation, avoiding the worst outcomes associated with these motives may increase the ease of retrieving store names linked with such outcomes.

While some variance is likely to occur, the same (and limited number of) benefits (about 2 to 5) are likely to evoke the name of a given store among the store's primary customers. Illustrations of such associations include the following statements. "I always come to Albertson's because it has the biggest assortment and the lowest prices." "I shop at Winn-Dixie because it is most convenient to my home and it has the best quality meats."

Because some benefits are less salient (e.g., only come-to-mind for situations that occur infrequently), only a partially graded structure has been formed by the consumer, that is, she or he is able to automatically evoke the "best" for the benefit category but not the "worst." For example, a store may easily be evoked for "best quality bakery" but not for "worst quality bakery," for the consumer not automatically associating "bakery" when thinking about making a trip to the supermarket.

A consumer who has frequently experienced a negative event when using a given brand, or shopping at a given store, may be likely to automatically evoke the brand or store for this event. For example, "slowest checkout" may be associated automatically with a given store after long waits in queues; and, such an association may be linked with this store not being evoked as the consumer's primary store. Therefore, for a few associates consumers may be trained by their experiences to automatically evoke a store name as "worst" on a given attribute or benefit.

The hypotheses and example applications comply with "a standard assumption in the memory literature that relations can be asymmetrical in strength and that the direction processed more frequently develops stronger relations (Barsalou and Sewell (1985, p. 650). Consequently, most consumers likely are able to evoke one or more store-names automatically for all benefits but most of these same consumers are unable to name stores automatically for several of the same associates when worded negatively.

Near and distant customers evocations

Research findings based on scanner data include the following store-choice information: most shoppers spend the majority of their food dollars (70%) at one store over a 1-week period, but only about 1 in 5 shoppers spend 70 percent of their dollars at the same supermarket over a six-month period. Thus, most shoppers exhibit some amount of food store loyalty in the very short term, but many shoppers change their primary store-choice once or more each year. "Primary store" is defined as the store named by a consumer when asked, "Please name the supermarket where you shop most often for groceries."

Given the importance in the retailing literature of location as a store-choice attribute (Linquist, 1975; Gensch and Recker, 1979; Howard, 1989), it is particularly important to understand how benefits-to-store evocations occur among primary customers for the store named for most and/or least convenient location. What are the benefits that evoke a given store name when the consumer names a different store for "most convenient location"?

Given that retailing strategists focus on pulling customers away from competing stores which are more conveniently located for some customers, what pulls distant customers, and what associates are linked with what stores for nearby customers gained or lost, are valuable bits of information. "Distant" customers for a given store (say, X) are defined as primary store customers evoking the name of another store (e.g., Y or Z) when asked to "please name the supermarket closest to your home." "Nearby" customers for a given store are consumers who evoke their primary store's name when asked to "please name the supermarket closest-to-your home."

Several studies have been devoted to profiling and comparing in-shoppers versus out-shoppers (for reviews, see Lumpkin, Hawes, and Darden, 1986; LaFief and Hensel, 1991). Out-shoppers are those consumers purchasing goods and services outside of local retail trading area; in-shoppers are those consumers buying from local retail stores. Buying from distant supermarket may be viewed as a form of micro-out-shopping behaviour. Based on the findings from the literature on out-shopping behaviour (see Lumpkin et al., 1986) the associations of more distant stores with better selections and/or lower prices than nearby stores are motivators for such behaviour. Consequently, the relative frequencies of these two benefit-to-store evocations and others for consumers selecting distant stores as their primary stores are examined herein.

Usually, but not always, the supermarket closest to a consumer's home likely is evoked also for "most convenient location." The supermarket evoked both for closest-to-home and most convenient location may be viewed as starting with a location advantage for gaining a large share-of-business of this customer's grocery needs. What other associates evoke the same store for such consumers located nearby this store? What associates evoke other store names for these same consumers who select and do not select their nearby store as their primary store?

Results

A total of 317 interviews were completed. Most (76%) of the respondent's primary store choices involved three supermarket chain stores: Winn-Dixie (the primary supermarket chain for 36 percent of the respondents), Schwegmann's (22%) and Superstore (18%). At the time of data collection, Winn-Dixie had 26 stores in the greater metropolitan area, Schwegmann's had 11 stores, and Superstore had 2 stores. The average total sales-floor space per store was largest for the two Superstore locations and smallest for the 26 Winn-Dixie stores. The findings reported here are for these three major supermarket chains; no other supermarket was reported by more than 7 percent of the respondents to be their primary store.

Supermarket Chain	Number of Stores	Share Primary Customers Nearby
Winn-Dixie	26	79%
Schwegmann's	11	44
Superstore	2	16

The retailing strategies within each of the three supermarket chains are designed to be the same across all stores in the respective chains. However, some individual store differences might be perceived among consumers identifying individual stores in the respective chains as their primary stores. The findings reported in this section refer only to associate-to-store retrievals by store name at the chain level, not to individual stores within a chain. Thus, this data collection method represents a limitation of the study in that perceptions may differ among stores within a given supermarket chain.

Table 4.1 is a summary of the proportions of consumers living nearby and distant to their primary store for each of the three supermarket chains for the ten positively and ten negatively worded attributes.

Table 4.1   Nearby and Distant Customers' Perceptions of their Primary Store

Store Attributes	Superstore		Winn-Dixie		Schwegmann's	
	Nearby	Distant	Nearby	Distant	Nearby	Distant
Lowest Overall Food Prices	1.00	0.86	0.07	0.08	0.71	0.82
Best Quality Meat	0.55	0.33	0.48	0.71	0.32	0.36
Best Quality Produce	0.89	0.67	0.33	0.50	0.26	0.46
Largest Selection of Foods	1.00	0.90	0.08	0.21	0.55	0.67
Friendliest Personnel	0.67	0.37	0.29	0.54	0.32	0.33
Fastest Checkout	0.78	0.55	0.26	0.46	0.39	0.36
Best Quality Bakery	0.89	0.63	0.19	0.38	0.13	0.21
Best Quality Deli	1.00	0.71	0.35	0.29	0.48	0.51
Freshest Seafood	0.67	0.53	0.21	0.38	0.45	0.38
Most Convenient Location	1.00	0.04	0.92	0.67	0.81	0.26
Highest Overall Food Prices	0.00	0.00	0.44	0.62	0.08	0.00
Poorest Quality Meat	0.00	0.12	0.14	0.00	0.19	0.10
Poorest Quality Produce	0.00	0.08	0.27	0.08	0.26	0.18
Smallest Selection of Foods	0.11	0.04	0.40	0.04	0.06	0.03
Most Unfriendly Personnel	0.00	0.12	0.23	0.04	0.13	0.31
Slowest Checkout	0.00	0.14	0.32	0.12	0.19	0.26
Poorest Quality Bakery	0.11	0.04	0.23	0.08	0.03	0.21
Poorest Quality Deli	0.00	0.08	0.23	0.08	0.06	0.05
Most Unfresh Seafood	0.00	0.08	0.10	0.00	0.06	0.08
Least Convenient Location	0.00	0.65	0.00	0.00	0.03	0.23
Loyal Six Months Ago	1.00	0.57	0.84	0.46	0.81	0.85
Sample Size (n =)	9	49	91	24	31	39

Note: Read that 86 percent (86%) of customer loyal to Superstore who report a competing store closest to their homes identified Superstore as having the lowest overall food prices. Significant comparisons between the two groups of primary store customers are highlighted in **bold** font.

Note in Table 4.1 that the majority of customers who reported a Winn-Dixie store to be their primary store also reported a Winn-Dixie store to be closest to their homes (91/115 = 79%). However, only 44 percent of Schwegmann's primary customers reported a Schwegmann's store to be located closest to their homes. Only 16 percent of Superstore's primary customers reported a Superstore to be located closest to their homes. Thus, the shares of the three stores' primary customers living closest to these stores are associated substantially with the number of stores located in the greater metropolitan area.

Note in Table 4.1 substantial majorities of nearby primary customers evoke the names of their primary store for "most convenient location (MCL)," while the shares evoking the same store were substantially lower for distant primary store customers. For example, 100 percent of the 9 primary store customers for Superstore evoked Superstore for MCL, only 4 percent of the distant primary customers of Superstore evoked the store for MCL. Such findings provide strong evidence for the nomological validity of the study. Higher location convenience should be reported for the store chain having the greatest number of stores and high shares of MCL-to-store evocations should be found for the nearby store; both findings were observed.

A summary of primary store loyalties and shifts in store loyalties is provided in Figure 4.1. Based on the survey results, Winn-Dixie was found to have the largest share of primary store customers (37% of all respondents) and 28 percent of all customers reported that Winn-Dixie was both their current primary store and their primary store six months previously.

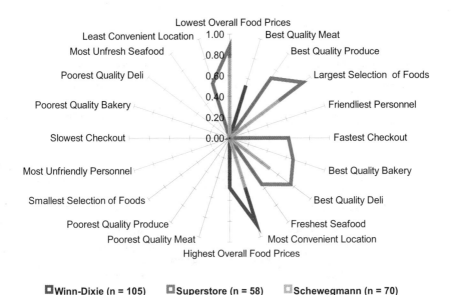

☐ Winn-Dixie (n = 105)   ☐ Superstore (n = 58)   ☐ Schewegmann (n = 70)

Figure 4.1 Principal Thoughts Evoked by Primary Customers for Each of Three Competing Supermarkets

Note that the shares of total primary customers for the three supermarket chains follow the same rank order of the number of stores each chain has located in the greater metropolitan area. Winn-Dixie has the largest share of respondents identifying this chain as their primary store (37%) and Superstore has the smallest share of respondents identifying this chain as their primary store (19%). However, given that Superstore had only two stores operating at the time of the study, 19 percent of the total respondents identifying Superstore as their primary store is very impressive.

Note in Table 4.1 that 65 percent of Superstore's distant primary customers evoke the store's name for least convenient location. None of the nearby and distant primary Winn-Dixie customers evoked Winn-Dixie's name for least convenient location. Such results provide further evidence in support of the nomological validity of the study.

H1: unique constellation of associate-to-store evocations

The results include strong support for H1. Each store has a unique constellation of a few associate-to-store evocations. The three associates evoking Winn-Dixie among the largest shares of this store's primary customers are summarised in Figure 4.2.

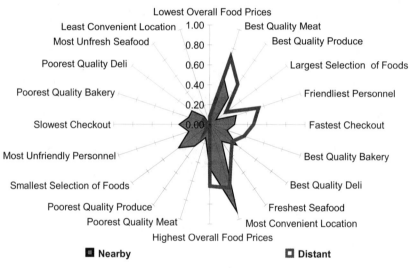

Figure 4.2 Winn-Dixie's Near and Distant Customer Perceptions

Note in Figure 4.2 that two benefits evoke Winn-Dixie for the majority of the chain's primary customers: best quality meats and most convenient location. A substantial share (48%) of the store's primary customers also evoked the store's name for "highest overall food prices." Even though all three major supermarket chains advertise weekly to have the lowest food prices, Winn-Dixie's price message is likely to be believed by fewer shoppers. In fact, Winn-Dixie was named most often by primary store customers for each store chain for highest overall food prices (results not shown).

Figure 4.1 summarises the unique constellations of associates-to-store evocations for all primary customers for Superstore and Schwegmann's.

Note in Figure 4.1 that Superstore is evoked by the majority of its primary customers for "least convenient location" but such a finding is not observed among Schwegmann's primary store customers. Thus, the conclusion appears supportable that Superstore has a location problem for most of the chain's primary customers but the many other associate-to-store evocations help the store gain its primary customers and overcome the store being evoked for least convenient location.

Note the shares for Schwegmann's primary customers for lowest overall food prices, largest selection of foods, and best quality of deli are all substantially lower ($p < .05$ by t-tests) compared to Superstore's primary customers evoking Superstore's name for these benefits. When comparing the shares of total primary customers evoking their store's names, Schwegmann's shares of evocations among its primary customers for different benefits fall between Superstore's and Winn-Dixie's with Winn-Dixie dominating on one benefit: most convenient location (87%). Superstore dominates on most other benefits; exceptions include "best quality meats" and "friendliest personnel."

Such analyses provide information on the achieved positioning of competitors in the minds of customers. Achieved positioning is defined here as the top-of-mind associate-to-store (or brand) retrievals for an individual consumer or segments of consumers (e.g., primary customers). The achieved positioning is a form of automatic thinking, or "unconscious information processing" (Grunert, 1988).

The achieved positioning for a given store (or brand) is likely to include clues useful for understanding customer behaviour, such as her or his selection of a primary store and rejecting a particular competing store. For example, the subset of supermarket shoppers automatically retrieving Schwegmann's in response to all four associates in Figure 4.3 are likely to retrieve the same store when asked to name their primary store.

Measuring achieved positioning among primary customers may provide information on shortcomings linked by most customers to "their" store, for example, "least convenient location" for Superstore and "highest overall food prices" for Winn-Dixie. Also, such measurement may provide information about benefits a store may be striving, yet failing, to have customers link to its name, a possible example being "friendliest personnel" for Superstore.

H2: substantial differences in benefit-to-store retrievals among nearby and distant primary customers

The results include partial support of H2. For two of the stores examined, one or more benefit-to-store retrievals are different for the store among its nearby and distant primary customers.

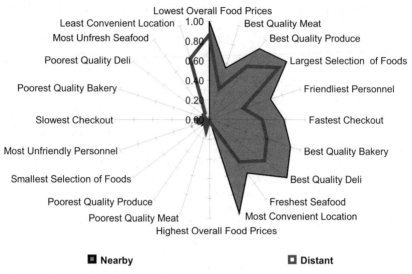

Figure 4.3 Superstore's Near and Distant Customer Perceptions

With the benefit-to-store retrievals in Figure 4.1 including "highest overall food prices" and only one benefit beyond "most convenient location," how can a supermarket chain like Winn-Dixie possibly attract distant primary customers? Separating primary customers into nearby and distant shoppers as shown in Figures 4.2 provides the answer. For most (67%) distant, primary Winn-Dixie customers, Winn-Dixie is still retrieved for "most convenient location," even though the share is substantially lower compared to nearby primary customers (92%). Also, Winn-Dixie is retrieved for "friendliest personnel" by 54 percent of the store's distant primary customers.

Note in Figure 4.2 that the retrieval of Winn-Dixie for "highest overall food prices" is more secure among the store's distant versus nearby primary customers (62% versus 44%, respectively). Possibly for these distant primary customers, a Winn-Dixie store not closest-to-home is very convenient to shop at, and one or more store employees have been particularly friendly, even though the store is associated with high prices. These customers may be willing to trade-off the benefit of getting lower prices elsewhere for one or all three benefits shown in the right-side of Figure 4.2.

The findings in Figure 4.2 emphasise the strategic importance of location convenience as an associate-to-store retrieval for Winn-Dixie. Whether planned or unplanned by store executives, being retrieved for "most convenient location" serves to retrieve Winn-Dixie for most nearby and distant primary customers. Unfortunately this competitive advantage is somewhat thwarted: findings related to H3 include data that Winn-Dixie is associated first with "slowest checkout" among a high share of its primary customers (reported in the next findings section).

In Figure 4.3, at first sight the benefit-to-store, retrieval profiles for Superstore, nearby and distant, primary customers look the same, except for most convenient location. Note, however, that all the benefit-to-store shares are lower for distant versus nearby primary customers in Figure 4.3, even though the shares for largest selection of foods and lowest overall food prices remain very high (90% and 86%, respectively). Possibly the greater effort in travelling to the less convenient Superstore affects the associative network for distant versus nearby primary customers. In particular, the drop in share for "friendliest personnel" retrieving Superstore is startling among the store's nearby versus distant primary customers (67% to 37%).

The findings in Figure 4.4 do not provide much support for H2. Beyond most convenient location, the three principal benefit-to-store retrievals for Schwegmann's remain the same for nearby and distant primary customers. Note also in Figure 4.4 that Schwegmann's has similar shares of nearby and distant primary customers (n's of 31 and 39, respectively). In contrast, most Winn-Dixie primary customers live nearby and most Superstore primary customers live distantly from these stores.

Figure 4.4   Schwegmann's Near and Distant Customer Perceptions

H3: store retrieval for being worst

The findings provide strong support for H3. All respondents did retrieve one or more store names for at least one negatively worded associate for stores competing with their primary stores. However, less than 10 percent of the total respondents retrieved store names for all ten negative associates.

Figure 4.5 is a summary of the associate-to-Winn-Dixie retrievals for distant primary customers of Superstore and Schwegmann's. Along with high shares of retrieval for "highest overall food prices," nearly half of these customers retrieved Winn-Dixie for "smallest selection of foods available." Also, the majority of distant, Superstore primary customers retrieve Winn-Dixie for most convenient location. Such findings provide clues for the strategic changes that may be necessary for Winn-Dixie to implement to gain additional nearby customers.

Distant Primary Customers of Superstore and Schwegmann's

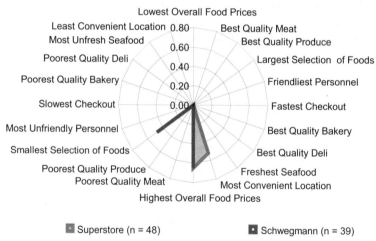

Superstore (n = 48)   Schwegmann (n = 39)

Figure 4.5   Principal Thoughts Evoking Winn-Dixie

Principal associate-to-store retrievals for Superstore among distant primary customers of Winn-Dixie and Schwegmann's include mostly benefits, not shortcomings, in the case of Winn-Dixie customers, and nothing at all in the case of Schwegmann's customers. These results are summarised in Figure 4.6.

Results for Schwegmann's being retrieved among distant primary customers of competing stores are not shown because few (< 25%) such customers

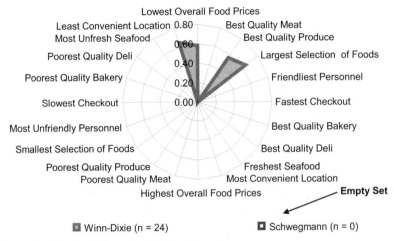

Distant Primary Customers of Winn-Dixie and Schwegmann's

Figure 4.6 Principal Thoughts Evoking Superstore

retrieved Schwegmann's name for benefits or shortcomings. This finding and additional findings (see Figure 4.8) indicate that fewer customers not shopping at Schwegmann's retrieve the store first for any associates compared to the shares of customers not shopping at competing stores retrieving these stores' names. "Thus, among distant primary customers of competing stores, Schwegmann's is likely to belong to the inert set" (Spiggle and Sewall, 1987) of stores. The inert set is defined here to be the retail stores the consumer is aware, but which are not retrieved readily (e.g., first) for any positively or negatively worded associate.

Principal associate-to-store retrievals among defector customers

Clues for the retailing strategist for the reasons for lost customers may be found by examining the store retrievals among customers who report a different primary store now versus six months previously. For former Winn-Dixie primary customers, most reported Superstore to be their current primary store. The principal store retrievals for these Winn-Dixie defectors are summarised in Figure 4.7.

Note in Figure 4.7 that the majority of Winn-Dixie defectors retrieve Winn-Dixie for most convenient location and Superstore for least convenient location. What is particularly striking is that the majority of these consumers retrieve Winn-Dixie for slowest checkout, possibly a linkage contributing to the loss of these customers.

Winn-Dixie Primary Customers Who Defected

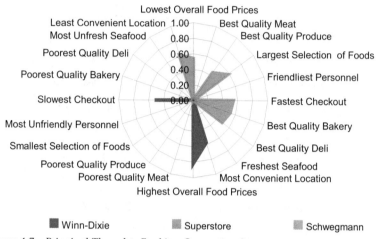

Figure 4.7   Principal Thoughts Evoking Competing Stores

Figure 4.8 summarises the principal retrievals for Superstore defectors. Comparing the results in Figure 4.8 with Figure 4.3 points to large declines in the shares of defector customers retrieving Superstore first for each of the benefits, and half of the defectors retrieving the store for least convenient location. Possibly, an effective strategy for Superstore would include reminding primary customers of the multiple principal benefits of shopping at Superstore.

Conclusions and implications

The findings presented in this chapter support the conclusion that supermarket shoppers can retrieve specific store names as "best" representing specific associative cues. A subset of such benefit-to-store retrievals is linked to the consumer's primary store choice. Some negatively worded associates may be associated with retrieval of a consumer's primary store choice, such as high overall food prices linked with Winn-Dixie among many of this chain's primary customers.

The associate-to-store retrievals among distant primary customers for a store are valuable especially for providing clues of why some consumers will shop primarily at less convenient stores. A few subtle, but strategically insightful, associate-to-store retrievals differences are likely to be observed by comparing nearby versus distant primary store customers.

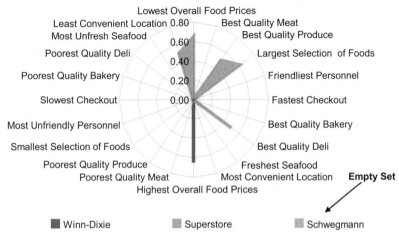

Figure 4.8   Principal Thoughts Evoking Competing Stores

The findings provide circumstantial evidence in support of the associate-to-cue proposition and choice sequence proposed by Holden (1993, p. 387): "By placing cues known to facilitate retrieval in the choice situation, the probability of brand evocation is increased, and thereby increases the probability of choice of the brand – without evocation, the probability of choice is zero."

Additional empirical evidence using experimental designs (Banks, 1965) with test and control groups is needed for confirming this proposition and the core proposition that the probability of brand choice is likely to increase as a function of the increase in the probability of evocation (Nedungadi, 1990).

Based on the findings reported here, a corollary proposition is likely to be supported: certain associate-to-store retrievals serve to decrease the likelihood of brand or store choice. Possibly, retailing strategists for Winn-Dixie may be causing more harm than good by communicating the message, "lowest overall food prices," given that the store chain is retrieved by a large share of this chain's primary customers as well as primary customers of competitors' stores.

Focusing on "lowest overall food prices" may result in a double-whammy. First, the lowest-price message is associated strongly with retrievals of "Superstore" and "Schwegmann's" among Winn-Dixie primary customers; consequently, more attention may be devoted to these competing stores resulting in their choice.

Second, by communicating an associate-to-store message, that is, not held by target consumers, relatively less attention may be attended to a retrieval that is held which is helpful for building primary store choice. For example, Winn-Dixie might benefit more by focusing the store's strategy on positive associates known to result in high shares of retrievals for the store: most convenient location, best quality meats, and friendliest Personnel compared to trying to cause customers to reverse an associate known to be linked negatively for store retrieval.

Finally, nearly all the respondents interviewed in the study reported here reported, "None come-to-mind," for one or more negatively worded associates. Such a finding, compared to the same respondents being able to retrieved stores easily for positively worded associates, serves to support "the notion that evoked sets are better described as goal-derived categories and vary by context" (Holden and Lutz, 1992, p. 102) versus thinking of evoked sets as being relatively static. An initial evoked set of brands or stores (which may be modified before choice) is generated automatically most likely because each alternative in the set is "best" for one or more salient goals – a view concerning store choice that Tigert (1981, 1983) expresses several times.

References

Arnold, S. J., Handelman, J. and Tigert D. J. "Organizational legitimacy and retail store patronage," in *Journal of Business Research*, 35, 3 (March 1996): 229–239, Cutting Edge Research in Retailing.

Arnold, S. J., Oum, T. H. and Tigert, D. J. "Determinant Attributes in Retail Patronage: Seasonal, Temporal, Regional, and International Comparison," *Journal of Marketing Research*, 20 (May 1983): 149–157.

Axelrod, J. N. "Attitude Measures that Predict Purchase," *Journal of Advertising Research*, 8 (February/March 1968): 3–17.

Banks, S. *Experimentation in Marketing*, New York: McGraw-Hill, 1965.

Barsalou, L.W. "Ideals, central tendency and frequency of instatiation as determinants of graded structures in categories," *Journal of Experimental Psychology*, 11 (1985): 629–654.

Barsalou, L. W. and Sewell, D. R. "Contrasting the Representation of Scripts and Categories," *Journal of Memory and Language*, 24, 6 (1985): 646–665.

Cohen, L. "The Level of Consciousness: A Dynamic Approach to the Recall Technique," *Journal of Marketing*, 3 (May 1966): 142–148.

Fazio, R. H. "How Do Attitudes Guide Behaviour?" in *Handbook of Motivation and Cognition: Foundations of Social Behaviour* (eds) R. M. Sorrentino and E. T. Higgins, New York: Guilford Press, 1986, pp. 204–243.

Fazio, R. "On the Power and Functionality of Attitudes: The Role of Attitude Accessibility," in *Attitude Structure and Function* (eds) Anthony R. Pratkanis et al., Hillsdale, NJ: Lawrence Erlbaum Associates, 1989. 153–179.

Gensch, D. and Recker, W. W. "The Multinomial, Multiattribute Logit Choice Model." *Journal of Marketing Research*, 16 (February 1979), 124–132.

Grunert, K. "Research in Consumer Behaviour: Beyond Attitude and Decision Making." *Journal of the European Society for Opinion and Marketing Research*, 16, 5 (1988).

Grunert, K. "Consumer Behaviour: Beyond Attitudes and Decision-making", European Research: *The Journal of the European Society for Opinion and Marketing Research*, 16 (1989): 16–25.

Haley, R. I. and Case, P. B. "Testing Thirteen Attitude Scales for Agreement and Brand Discrimination," *Journal of Marketing*, 43 (Fall 1979): 20–32.

Hauser, J. R. "Testing, Accuracy, Usefulness and Significance of Probabilistic Models: An Information Theoretic Approach," *Operations Research*, 26 (May–June 1978): 406–421.

Holden, S. J. S. and Lutz, R. J. "Ask Not What the Brand Can Evoke: Ask What Can Evoke the Brand?" *Advances in Consumer Research*, Vol. 19 (eds) J. F. Sherry, Jr. and B. Sternthal, Provo, UT: Association for Consumer Research, 1992: 101–107.

Holden, S. J. S. "Understanding Brand Awareness: Let Me Give You a C(I)ue!" in *Advances in Consumer Research*, 20, Provo, UT: Association for Consumer Research (1993): 383–388.

Howard, J. A. *Consumer Behaviour in Marketing Strategy*, Englewood Cliffs, NJ: Prentice-Hall, 1989.

Linquist, J. D. "Measuring Image," Journal of Retailing, 50 (Winter 1975): 29–38.

LaFief, W. C. and Hensel, P. H. "Outshopping and Hedonic Consumption," *American Marketing Association Summer Educator's Conference Proceedings*, Chicago: American Marketing Association (1991): 106–116.

Lumpkin, J. R., Hawes, J. M. and Darden, W. R. "Shopping Patterns of the Rural Consumer: Exploring the Relationship between Shopping Orientations and Outshopping," *Journal of Business Research*, 14, 1 (1986): 63–81.

Nedungadi, P. and Hutchinson, J. W. "The Prototypicality of Brands: Relationships with Brand Awareness, Preference and Usage," in *Advances in Consumer Research*, Vol. 12 (eds) Elizabeth C. Hirschman and Morris B. Holbrook, Provo, UT: Association for Consumer Research (1985): 498–503.

Nedungadi, P. "Recall and Consideration Sets: Influencing Choice Without Altering Brand Evaluations," *Journal of Consumer Research*, 17 (December 1990): 263–276.

Roth, E. M. and Shoben, E. J. "The Effect of Context on the Structure of Categories," *Cognitive Psychology*, 15, 4 (1983): 346–378.

Spiggle, S. and Sewall, M. A. "A Choice Sets Model of Retail Selection," *Journal of Marketing*, 51, 2 (1987): 86–96.

Tigert, D. J. "Comparative Analysis of Determinants of Patronage," in *Retail Patronage Theory 1981 Workshop Proceedings* (ed.) Robert F. Lusch, Norman, OK: Centre for Economic and Management Research, School of Business Administration, The University of Oklahoma (1981): 118–124.

Tigert, D. J. "Pushing the Hot Buttons for a Successful Retailing Strategy," in *Patronage Behaviour and Retail Management* (eds) William R. Darden and Robert F. Lusch, New York, NY: North-Holland, 1983: 89–113.

Tigert, D. J., Arnold, S. J., Powell, L. and Seiders, M. K. "Service, Service and Service: Why Nordstrom is So Successful," in *The Cutting Edge, Proceedings of the 1991 Symposium on Patronage Behaviour and Retail Strategy* (eds) William R. Darden, Robert F. Lusch, and J. Barry Mason, Baton Rouge, LA: Louisiana State University, 1991: 181–194.

Woodside, A. G. and Trappey III, R. J. "Incorporating Competition in Attitude-Accessibility Models of Customers' Primary Store Choices," in *The Cutting Edge, Proceedings of the 1991 Symposium on Patronage Behaviour and Retail Strategy* (eds), William R. Darden, Robert F. Lusch, and J. Barry Mason, Baton Rouge, LA: Louisiana State University, 1992: 295–310.

5
Modelling Bank Loyalty

Introduction: gaining and retaining customer commitment

Financial service institutions today recognise that customer commitment is a notion that can no longer be treated casually in today's banking environment. More than ever, customer retention is regarded as a critical component of long-term profitability and survival in the financial services sector. Competition within the banking sector has caused financial services institutions to introduce permanent measures aimed both at maintaining and retaining profitable customer relationships. Yet keeping customers appears to be more and more difficult as the industry continues to change at an increasing rate. Much of the revolution is technology driven, and Internet banking will continue to play a key role in a plethora of new products, services and brands aimed simultaneously at wooing new customers and retaining existing ones. Consequently, insight into brand switching behaviour amongst financial services customers is central to understanding how retention can be affected in the new economy.

Prior research (Mittal & Lee, 1989; Goldsmith et al., 1991) reports a positive relationship between customer involvement and commitment. The research suggests that commitment is a part of brand loyalty. Hence, a positive relationship exists between the two. However, in the past there has been little systematic and empirical work aimed at evaluating the role of customer involvement and commitment in the choice of a financial services institution. More interestingly, little work exists that explores the relationship between a customer's involvement and/or commitment with the financial services institution and the propensity to switch between institutions. Moreover, an examination of the role Internet banking may play in brand switching behaviour is absent. Online account ownership, Internet usage for retail purchases, and attitudes towards this technology may likely interact and play a part in the behaviour – both from a retention standpoint as well as switching.

Colgate and Stewart (1998) demonstrate significant variations pertaining to how remotely the customer wishes to deal with his or her bank.

Nevertheless, little effort has been directed towards investigating whether or not the individual customer's perception of switching costs (both monetary and non-monetary) has an impact on the type of relationship he or she has with the financial services institution. Research reported herein takes this issue a step further and examines several questions amongst which two are paramount: (1) To what extent do perceived switching costs affect a customer's propensity to switch financial services institutions, and (2) will Internet banking change all that?

Prospect theory (Kahneman and Tversky, 1979) is a descriptive model of decision-making under risk. This theory builds from the observation that individual decision-making often violates the postulates of expected utility theory. The core concept of prospect theory is that an individual evaluates the outcomes of any decision with respect to the perceived deviation from a reference point rather than with respect to net asset levels. It is possible to examine this proposition for brand switching behaviour amongst financial services customers and in particular amongst holders of Internet accessible bank accounts.

Rotter (1966) defines "action control" as a personality characteristic – one which differentiates individuals to the extent they believe they can control their lives. The action control paradigm is used as an intervening variable between customer loyalty and customer retention. Mindful of this theory, research reported herein evaluates how it may be linked to customer switching behaviour amongst financial institutions.

Insight from Keller (1993) demonstrates in the structure of brand top-of-mind-awareness research that raising awareness of the brand increases the probability the brand will be a member of a set of brands that receive serious purchase consideration. Cohen (1966) in much earlier research introduced the brand level of consciousness concept and in doing so put forth the argument that the earlier the [unaided] brand recall, the more favourable the attitude towards the brand. Brands that are regularly used will be recalled almost entirely in the highest levels of consciousness. So too is this the case with brands with high switch-to potential. This case is examined in specific regards to bank switching behaviour. Woodside and Trappey (1996) illustrate a brand's attribute-to-brand evocations will vary amongst the brand's portfolio of customers – ranging from new, loyal, defector and competitor. To what extent these evocations differ between various levels of brand consciousness is studied in detail along with how they may interact with switching behaviour, loyalty, commitment and perceptions of risk.

Electronic commerce is changing the face of marketing in the new economy. Changing customer expectations will require marketers to interact differently and in most cases in an anticipatory manner. Because financial institutions will seek to offer increased convenience to bank customers by encouraging them to engage in virtual interactions, branding and customer loyalty issues will become particularly important in testing the validity and extending the theory of the previously mentioned constructs. Will the concomitant higher levels of satisfaction and control connected with the virtual bank account increase customer loyalty? On the other hand, will the perception and reality of lower switching costs associated with Internet accessible online bank accounts result in lessening the perceived risk linked with change and increase the propensity of customers to switch financial institutions? To date, very little research has addresses this issue (Hermanns & Sauter, 1999).

What follows is an analysis of the current competitive environment in retail banking. The review places emphasis on illustrating how e-commerce is shaping the banking industry today. In particular we examine how and in what ways e-commerce will challenge financial services institutions to attract and maintain customers who have become accustomed to competitive offers.

Why retail banking is changing

The market for financial services worldwide is experiencing a fundamental change that will reshape the way in which banking services are provided. Financial services cover a wide range of products. The products vary from commodity level, that is, sold on price, to providing of consulting advice. Advice may be the product or a part thereof (Morgan Stanley, June 1990). Globalisation of capital markets has diminished the traditional role of banks as intermediaries. Concurrently, deregulation has allowed non-bank competitors to enter into the market for financial services (http://www. kpmg.net/library 'Banking on the Future', July 1999). Today, mergers and reorganisation signify survival of the biggest. Not only are small and medium-sized banks struggling in a fiercely competitive marketplace, but also they are progressively more exposed to acquisition and take-overs.

Financial services and products are by their very nature intangible. Because of this, inventive ideas can be quickly copied. Consequently the number of products and services in development, available and on offer is growing at an ever-faster pace (Spectrum, 1996). Markets have become increasingly more dynamic, spurring changes in customer expectations, technology and competition. In this environment retail banks have had to realign thinking and strategic decision making to survive the new economic realities of the 21st century.

Information technology

Information technology has changed financial services forever. Today, digits – ones and zeroes, represent money and transactions occur at electronic speeds. Not only has the technology had a major impact on consumer attitudes, but business as well. Iconoclastic non-bank institutions have been enabled by information technology to enter markets with products and services that would have been unthinkable a decade ago. Though the technological change in the way financial services conduct business began effectively in the 1950s and 1960s, the real digital revolution came about as the result of wholesale e-flows from electronic funds transfers (Solomon, 1997). Contributing also to the transformation and adding to the competitive environment has been the rapid development of outsourcing as a feasible option for in-house IT departments. In the European Private Banking Survey conducted by PriceWaterhouseCoopers in 1996–97 (p. 28), 58 percent of the respondents stated outsourcing had increased flexibility within the organisation and improved efficiency. Outsourcing of investment research, custody, information technology and banking back-office had been initiated by 35 percent of the subjects.

Just as in the U.S., expenditures on outsourcing in the European banking sector are expected to continue to rise rapidly even after reaching the summit of $21.7 billion in 1999. Though information technology usually competes after people as the second greatest contributor to costs for financial institutions, it nevertheless accounts for twelve-percent (PriceWaterhouseCoopers, 1996–97). Outlays on information technology by U.K. banks alone will increase significantly as they seek both to bring information systems up to U.S. standards and meet rising customer expectations. The case for the rest of Europe remains yet to be seen. Expenditures for transaction processing and improvements in channels of distribution are expected to be considerable. These two enhancements will account for the largest share of financial services institutions information technology disbursements (Morgan Stanley, June 1999).

Table 5.1 How Financial Services Customers in North America Utilise the Channels Available

	% Within	Total %
Electronic Only		18%
Multiple Channels		
ATM	46%	
Branch	28%	
Telephone	20%	
Mail	3%	
PC	3%	
	100%	61%
Branch Only		21%
		100%

Source: Morgan Stanley, June 1999.

Though much of the spending by financial services institutions on information technology can be accounted for as improvements to infrastructure, much of it has to do with how customers now expect to interact with banks across a number of channels (Holmson, Palter, Simon, and Weberg, 1998). Table 5.1 indicates in summary form how financial services customers in North America typically utilise the channels available. Multiple channel usage can be seen to account for 61 percent of the total. Electronic delivery – namely ATM's, PC's and telephone account for more than two-thirds (69%) of the total usage within multiple channels. Electronic channels alone comprise 18 percent of all the usage and the rival branch only usage of 21 percent.

While most people use a variety of channels to purchase financial products and services, only a few are used regularly (Holmson, Palter, Simon and Weberg, 1988). Bank customers will typically shop at all the channels and select the one that best suits their needs at the time. Requirements may vary across a wide range – from the complexity of the product to the convenience of the service. Bearing this lesson in mind, bank marketers today have learned the importance of tracking the details of channel usage by customer and product-service categories. Channel preferences are checked against profitability in an endeavour to restructure the delivery mix so as to enhance convenience to the customer while at the same time minimising the overall expense.

At the current rates of growth it is expected that Internet banking will soon become the most important channel of distribution for North American and European banks. Consumers in Finland and Sweden are already the most advanced users of Internet technology in Europe. Finland and Sweden consider the Internet as part of an integrated strategy for the payments system. Finland became the first country in the world to abolish personal check and the clearing system. By 1996, 77 percent of all retail customer transactions were completely automated. The data processing system covers all banks in Finland. Usage rates for ATM's and giro ATM's in Finland are the highest in the world. In the United Kingdom, Barclays established an Internet banking service that duplicates the same range of retail financial services provided through its telephone banking service. By reproducing payments, credit cards, and savings services already in place, Barclays has been able to leverage the current operating infrastructure of the telephone through which Internet banking is linked (Morgan Stanley, 1999).

European and American banks disagree very little on what bank channel will become the most important by the year 2006. Table 5.2 demonstrates Internet banking to be unsurprisingly the number one channel in terms of importance within the next five to six years. In the United States, PC and telephone banking follow in second and third position. Telephone banking and the traditional bank branch occupy these ranks in Europe. No doubt

Table 5.2   Bank Channel Importance by Year 2006

Europe	Importance Rank	USA
Internet	1	Internet
Telephone	2	PC Banking
Traditional Bank Branch	3	Telephone
PC Banking	4	Smart Cards
Smart Cards	5	Interactive TV
Interactive TV	6	Traditional Bank Branch

Source: Booz, Allen & Hamilton 1997.

this is due to the fact that Europe lags what has already occurred in U.S. banking infrastructure and product development. Significantly, U.S. banks expect the traditional bank branch to be the least important of all distribution channels.

Customers' expectations

Just as financial institutions are experiencing new complications and uncertainties in the markets, so too are their customers. Numerous factors are contributing to the changes in consumer markets, but seven are noteworthy and worth reporting (The Economist Intelligence Unit Limited; Coopers & Lybrand, 1996):

1. *An aging population*: Forecasts show that by the year 2005, seventeen percent of the European Union population will be comprised of people aged 65 years and older. This is in stark contrast to figures in 1991 that show the same population comprised only fifteen percent. Affected most will be the demand for pensions and healthcare – both of which will see significant increases.
2. *Family Structure:* Because marriage rates will continue to decline in most countries, there will be more single parents. Divorce rates will continue to increase. Double income marriages will continue to be a trend as more and more couples find the need for the additional earnings.
3. *Disappearing Safety Nets*: By the year 2005, fewer people will rely upon the government for retirement income and insurance. Because a greater proportion of the population will be essentially independent from state support, state pension provisions will decline. This trend is already clearly recognisable in the United States and growing in the United Kingdom.
4. *Workforce Changes*: The notion of employment for life has passed. Job switching has become more and more attractive to larger segments of the workforce as employees become willing to trade-off security for

rising rates of income. Part-time work, shared jobs and temporary employment contracts have been successful in North America and Europe at increasing the flexibility of the labour markets. Signs of change in this direction have recently appeared in Asia along with expectations they will continue.

5. *Technology Know-how*: Consumers today are technology savvy and will be even more so in five years. In the year 2005 nearly all consumers will have grown up with computers as a part of their lives. Systems interaction and interfaces will be more user-friendly. At the same time, consumers will be more accustomed to and secure with the technology and use of the Internet. Consequently, they will be more willing to adopt innovative electronic and digital systems for delivery of products and services.

6. *Wealth Accumulation*: Consumers between the ages of 35 and 55 years comprise the single largest segment of the population in most developed countries. These are the primary earning years for most people. Persons fifty-five years old and senior who will have accumulated equity in their home and pension will have considerable spending power. Diminished support from the state for income in the retirement years will continue to push this group to become prime customers for investments and savings products.

7. *Income and Knowledge:* As the global economy continues to become ever more information, technology and knowledge driven, society and the nature of work will change persistently. While commercial markets become increasingly global in reach, local, regional, and national economies will become indistinguishable. Just as the Internet will change the distinction between regional economies, so too will it transform the value of labour. Information, capital, and knowledge will supplant the roles of skilled, unskilled labour, and production in the new economy. Although consumers are wealthier today than in years gone by, the unskilled- and elderly-poor continue to grow. The distribution of wealth will continue to be uneven, with knowledge-workers becoming even more affluent as the information economy transforms. This irregular distribution may be a transitory effect of the fundamental changes taking place in the economy.

As a consequence of the fundamental changes occurring in the new economy, retail banks and financial institutions will come under increased pressure to anticipate and meet the needs of customers. In the future, banks will need to become more innovative in delivering services. A thorough review of the current mix of products and services will be essential. Improvements in information technology and the Internet in particular will give consumers access to a wealth of competing products and services information. Virtually free right of entry to information will confer unprecedented power to consumers of financial services. Consumers will have the capability via the Internet to shop around for value-for-money like never before. Twenty-first century financial services customers will as a result be able to choose from a wide variety of products and services on offer from a large number of providers globally and cream-off the best (Holmsen, Palter, Simon and Weberg, 1998). Meeting the changing values and lifestyle needs of the new customer will be a trial for financial services seeking to instil and gain brand loyalty from consumers who will have the ability to change institutions with the click of a mouse button. A study titled "Consumer Electronic Access Project" conducted by PriceWaterhouseCoopers in October of 1998 demonstrated a link between propensity to switch and satisfaction with the services on offer. Ten percent of the customers in the study indicated a willingness to switch banks eventually if not offered online access to bank services.

Financial institutions' expectations

Financial institutions have great hopes the new electronic commerce economy and the Internet in particular will payoff handsomely with increased customer loyalty (PriceWaterhouseCoopers). Senior executives from financial services institutions were questioned in a PriceWaterhouse-Coopers conference board; 75 percent of the respondents stated the success of any e-business project would best be measured by its ability to build customer loyalty (Electronic Business Outlook, PriceWaterhouseCoopers, 1999).

Institutions further expect that since Internet accessible accounts will allow customers to conduct virtually all normal banking transactions online, loss of customers due to relocation will be reduced. Both scenarios are tentative and yet to be demonstrated. Indeed, an argument to the contrary (i.e., reduced switching costs associated with Internet accounts will *encourage* bank brand switching) looks just as likely and is tested herein. However, it is a near certainty that the costs for processing transactions and number of branches required to facilitate comparable numbers of customers will be substantially reduced by Internet banking (Engelhardt and Freiling, 1995; Meyer and Oevermann, 1995).

Table 5.3 presents some results from the "Technology in Banking" survey conducted by Ernst & Young in 1998. Financial services institutions in both Europe and the United States clearly expect customer retention to be the main benefit derived from Internet banking. Nearly fifty-percent of the American institutions and one-third of the Europeans in the survey agree on this point. From the financial performance standpoint though, American financial services institutions expect the main benefit of Internet banking to be increased revenues (35%) while European anticipate decreased costs (26%).

Table 5.3   Findings from "Technology in Banking" Study

Expected Payoff	Europe	USA
Improve speed of delivery	7	6
Sell more products	3	4
Gain new customers	16	6
Open new markets	12	12
Increase revenues	10	35
Decrease costs	26	18
Customer retention	32	47

Source: Ernst & Young 1998.

Customer segmentation

Changes in information technology will continue to have a significant impact on the way banks market products and services to their customers. Financial services customers more so today than in the past require the institutions with whom they bank to provide them with individualised products and services that are customised to fit their needs at the time (Hermanns and Sauter, 1999). Internet technology will allow banks to integrate the customer into the value-chain process with real-time personalised offerings (Piller, 1997). Internet and information technology enhancements will assure that in the delivery of financial services each customer interaction will be treated as a unique relationship.

Viewed from the lens of a customer-relationship-management (CRM) approach to marketing, in the information intensive world of financial services, enhancements in information technology give rise to improved communication with the customers and a greater understanding of the specific needs of both individuals and groups. Because the resultant higher rates of customer acquisition and retention generally improve profits (Abela and Sacconaghi, 1996), banks and financial services institutions will become progressively more reliant upon information-based CRM. Concurrently, as the technology disseminates and improves, consumers will become more comfortable with the benefits. A substantial American bank saw a three hundred percent increase in the number of products it sold per household in a two-year period by utilising needs-based customer segmentation and profiling (Adolf, Grant-Thompson, Harrington and Singer, 1997).

As financial services institutions offer more individually made-to-order products and services, they will be required to not only segment customers according to transaction habits, needs, lifestyle, demographics and the like, but also according to profitability (Kotler 1995). Financial services customers can be generally separated into three primary categories. These categories are the highly profitable, marginally profitable and unprofitable customers. Highly profitable customers typically have income levels in the upper ten- to twenty-percent of the population. They by and large maintain high bank balances and frequently utilise automatic teller machines and automated transaction devices. Marginally profitable customers are routinely referred to as the "middle 40 percent." They make little or no use of electronic banking, write lots of cheques, and maintain lower balances than highly profitable customers. Though these customers are required to provide the volume needed to maintain the institution's fixed costs, they characteristically engage in switching behaviour, are difficult to retain and costly to acquire. Unprofitable customers write lots of cheques, maintain low balances and never or rarely use the bank's electronic transaction facilities (Coopers and Lybrand, 1996).

Brand advantage

Marketers rely upon brands to communicate essential information to the market to affect purchase decisions and behaviour (Alpert and Kamins, 1995). Irrespective of the industry, not only do brands offer a key means for product and service differentiation, but they play a very important role when 1) consumers lack information to make informed product choices, and 2) when differences between competitors' versions of the product are small and/or non-existent (Keller, 1993).

The product differentiation and informational roles brands play can be seen to be of particular noteworthiness in the financial services market. Today, a surfeit of financial services product offerings from a multitude of providers guarantees a wide variety of choice available to consumers. At the same time, because so few differences exist between many of the products and services on offer, consumers find themselves overwhelmed and virtually unable to distinguish both between the providers and the products. The matter has become further complicated by the growing use of new and remote channels like telephone and Internet banking. Convenience is no longer a differentiating factor (Morgan Stanley, June 1999). In all of these regards and more, financial services brands meet the acid test for brand importance. Not only must financial services differentiate products and services, but they must also communicate key information, trustworthiness and value to consumers. This heralds the continued role for the brand as an even more decisive competitive force in a financial services marketplace that is becoming all the time more competitive.

Financial services brands are not only important in communicating essential information and value to consumers but to financial markets and shareholders as well. Booz, Allen & Hamilton recently conducted an analysis of a banking and brokerage client's brand equity. Brand equity was calculated using the principle of attributable brand-related revenues and expenses (see: http://www.bah.com/viewpoint/insights/bank_branding.html).

Equity for the brand comprised the equivalent of approximately $4 billion in market capitalisation. While the debate carries on in the accounting profession about how to account for this value in the balance sheet of the firm, investors and institutions continue to rely upon it as a critical measure of the firm's competitive position in the market and the consequent likely future cash flows.

The value of the brand in financial services has not gone unnoticed by players outside the conventional banking world. Credit card companies like American Express and Visa as well as investment brokerage houses akin to Merrill Lynch and Charles Schwab are aggressively pursuing strategies to build brand recognition and equity amongst consumers. Household brands like Coca Cola and Sears were recalled and recognisable by 94 percent of consumers in a up- to-date study conducted by Booz Allen Hamilton. This figure stands in stark contrast to only 29 percent for financial services firms. Brand recall, recognition and awareness are key elements of customer loyalty (Aaker, 1991).

This finding is important for many reasons, not least of which pertains to the environment of today's global marketplace. Global brands like Coca Cola have clear competitive advantages – most important of which is the ability to leverage the power of the brand across markets and product categories (Worcester, 1997; Edgett & Parkinson, 1994; Gray & Smeltzer, 1985). Given the relatively low levels of brand recall and recognition (29%) for financial brands demonstrated in the Booz Allen Hamilton study, it is apparent there is both an opportunity and a need for financial services institutions to establish dominant brands if they are to compete effectively in the emerging global market for consumer financial services.

Customer retention in the banking sector

The move from transactions with customers to enduring interactive relationships with customers has become the standard model for business in the 21st century (Gummesson, 1987; Webster, 1992; Gronroos, 1997). For financial services institutions generally and banks in particular, the move towards establishing interactive relationships with customers is now the norm. Though marketers today who seek greater profits through customer orientation regard relationship marketing favourably, in actual fact it has been always in some form a part of financial services. This is because the genuine character of banking and financial services has through the centuries entailed long-term relationships. Trust-based bonds are implicit and are as important today as in years long gone by.

Customer environment

Customers and the competitive and regulatory environment in which banks and financial institutions operate continue to change. Just as customers have become more sophisticated and attuned to competitive offers from institutions, institutions have responded by creating new products and services to meet the changing demand. An October 1996 study by Georgia Tech's Graphics, Visualisation and Usability Centre demonstrates that worldwide web users are predominantly male (69%), have a college and/or advance degree (56%) and a mean income of $60,800 (Source: Morgan Stanley, 1997). Thus, the common perception of Internet users as young, poverty-stricken nerds looks unfounded. In the past it was a routinely held notion that customer inertia would inhibit the exit behaviour of a financial institution's clientele. Yet more and more today customers tend to maintain multiple accounts and look more prepared to leave one institution for better offers from another.

Not only will the number of account relationships customers' maintain continue to change but so too will the permanence. Predatory practices like those of Alliance and Leicester whereby customers are offered £20 to move their current account only adds to the impetus. Complicating matters further is a new service operated by the bank central clearinghouse BACS. A system put in place in October 1999 enabled all customer payment instructions such as direct debits for utility bills and the like to be transferred from one bank to another automatically upon a customer's request. Though the system is currently paper-based, plans are that it will be entirely electronically automated by 2001 (*Financial Times*, August 9, 1999).

The last decade of the 20th century saw a considerable expansion in consumerism. However, even as banks and financial institutions have in the past interacted with consumers to play a positive role in the recurrent growth in the consumption of goods necessary for a sound economy, there has nevertheless developed amongst many consumers today a trendy contempt for banks (Jones, 1996; Ennew et al., 1993). This contempt has many marketers questioning what types of relationships banks and financial services customers currently have and want to have in the future. One question of particular interest is whether or not financial services customers want to have a relationship at all with the institution with whom they deal. Still a case can be made that all bank customers have an affiliation whether they choose to or not once they buy an institution's services or products. Then again, the structure of that relationship and its meaning to an individual will differ from customer to customer. Previous studies have demonstrated that a significant amount of this variation can be accounted for by understanding how remotely the customer wishes to deal with the bank (Colgate & Stewart, 1998).

Historically banks and financial institutions have relied upon personal contact and in-the-flesh dealings as the primary means of establishing and maintaining customer relationships. All the same, the personal nature of banking has been forever changed in the past two decades – and information technology has been the main engine. Customer convenience has become the marketer's mantra. However, as more and more consumers engage in electronic commerce and banks and financial institutions offer

Internet services and products, customers will perceive all institutions as equally convenient. Banks and financial institutions could soon come to realise that though convenience may well have been a major factor in understanding and predicting customer switching behaviour in the 20th century, it is no longer in the 21st.

Determinants of customer loyalty and choice

Johnson (1998) states, customer loyalty is *"...a psychological predisposition toward repurchase."* In general however, the term tends to envelop all loyal behaviour an individual may exhibit. The behaviour may take on numerous forms – for example loyalty towards a company, brand, technology, location, dealer, country of origin and the like (cf. Herrmann, 1998). Much attention in the marketing realm has centred upon ascertaining how consumer loyalty is formed. Research into the occurrence demonstrates that customer loyalty is initially and principally a consequence of the customer's satisfaction with the brand and/or the service (cf. Dichtl, Schneider, 1994). Therefore loyalty stands for a volitional factor in the selection of a brand and/or service (Homburg, Rudolph, 1995) by means of which consumers may convey their liking (Bloemer, Kasper, Lemmink, 1990).

Customer satisfaction

Considerable thought has been devoted towards evaluation of customer satisfaction and retention a means of assessing the creation and configuration of customer loyalty. With respect to customer satisfaction, two denotations have been acknowledged by Johnson, Anderson and Fornell (1995). The first is a transaction-specific point of view whereby customer satisfaction is portrayed as *"... a customer's evaluation of a particular product experience or service encounter."* The second denotation takes on a snowballing viewpoint whereby customer satisfaction emanates from *"...an overall evaluation of a customer's purchase and consumption experience to date."* Because overall satisfaction ratings by bank and financial services customers are utilised in the research reported herein rather than episodic transactions and contact points, the latter perspective is more appropriate for understanding and predicting behaviour.

Nevertheless, it should be noted both denotations of customer satisfaction are multi-attributive in nature. That being the case, discrete levels of an evaluation object (bank or financial services institution) can be both the source of satisfaction and/or dissatisfaction (Yi, 1991; Lingenfelder, Schneider, 1990; Churchill, Suprenant, 1982). Supporting the research are further studies that point to the multi-dimensional facet of the general satisfaction rating. Thus it is possible to model pre-purchase, purchase-dealer, product, and after-sales levels of customer satisfaction as a function of the relevant purchase and/or consumption phase in which the consumer is engaged (Danaher, Matsson, 1994; Korte, 1995). To illustrate further, for bank and financial services customers, overall satisfaction with the bank's conveyance is comparable to product satisfaction. Purchase-dealer satisfaction can be compared to consumer levels of satisfaction with the institution's sales representatives, bank clerks and officers. Performance of the institution's administration can be juxtaposed to overall performance.

Product quality

Customer satisfaction is not the only factor relevant in loyal behaviour. Economic, social and psychological barriers to change may also play a role in the reasons why a consumer would choose to repeat purchase the same brand, product, or service and shop the same store again and again. Product-related attributes however are equally important in loyal behaviour. Product quality is of particular interest. Research findings reported by Henning-Thurau and Klee (1997) stress the importance of comparative quality as a determinant attribute of customer loyalty. The "relative quality" paradigm is the product of a consumer's comparison of the quality of the product selected with the qualities offered by alternative and competing products and brands. From this standpoint, a consumer's appraisal of the quality of the product or brand selected matches up with his or her cumulative satisfaction rating (Henning-Thurau, Klee, 1997).

Regret theory (Bell, 1982; Loomes, Sudgen, 1982) explains in part the underlying reason why the perceived quality of competing brands and products is thought to be an influencing variable when a consumer forms a judgement on satisfaction. The theory put forward by Bell, Loomes and Sudgen states plainly that satisfaction with a brand, product or service is influenced too by the expected suitability of the alternative(s) that has been rejected (cf. Herrmann, 1998). The interaction between the suitability of the rejected alternative(s) and the product or brand selected is explained in the following quote from Loomes (1998, p. 463):

> "...the psychological intuition behind regret theory is that if an individual chooses A (and therefore rejects B) and state j occurs, the overall level of satisfaction he experiences will depend not simply upon x_{Aj} but also upon how x_{Aj} compares with x_{Bj}. If what he gets is worse than what he might have had, it is suggested that the satisfaction associated with x_{Aj} will be reduced by a decrement of utility due to regret."

Customer loyalty is therefore a function not only of a customer's satisfaction with the brand, product or service but also the perceived quality the alternatives offered by competitors (Peter, 1997). Accordingly, as the cost-benefit ratio of a competitor brand or product escalates, the likelihood the customer will be persuaded to take up the offer increases.

Brand choice involvement

Though customer satisfaction looks as if it is an essential precursor of brand loyalty, closer inspection demonstrates the correlation is imperfect. All brand loyal customers are not necessarily satisfied customers. At the same time, all non-loyal customers are not automatically dissatisfied. Studies that report similar findings in support of this proposition have been authored by La Barbera and Mazursky (1983), Bearden and Teel (1983), Woodside, Frey and Daly (1989) and Oliver and Swan (1989). More recent research (Fornell, 1992; Anderson et al., 1994) demonstrates that for some services like insurance, mail and telecommunications the correlation between customer loyalty and customer satisfaction may be in fact very low.

The apparent discrepancy between customer satisfaction and brand loyalty may be explained and mitigated by another factor however. That factor is brand choice involvement and it is considered to be another important antecedent of brand loyalty. Mittal and Lee (1989) explain the factor as "...*the interest in or the concern with the brand choice.*" Engel, Blackwell and Miniard offered further explanation (1990) when they put forth the following proposition: "*Brand loyalty, then, can reflect a motivated and difficult to change habit because it is rooted in high involvement.*" Schiffman and Kanuk (1994) and Solomon (1994) presented supplementary support for the theory that high involvement and brand loyalty are related. Three principal justifications that support the findings from this stream of research emerge:

1. High involvement leads to extensive information search and ultimately to brand loyalty, whereas low involvement leads to exposure and brand awareness and then possibly to brand habits (Schiffman and Kanuk, 1994).
2. High involvement leads to emotional bonds with a product and therefore to brand loyalty (Solomon, 1994).
3. Consumers are more likely to notice differences in the attributes offered by various products/brands, and a common outcome is greater brand loyalty (Engelhardt et al., 1995).

In a separate but related stream of research (Mittal and Lee, 1989; Goldsmith et al., 1991), there is a reported positive correlation between brand choice involvement and commitment to the brand. Inasmuch as commitment is considered to be a component of brand loyalty, a positive relationship between involvement and loyalty would confirm a direct positive effect of the former upon the latter. As a result, it is likely brand choice involvement is both an independent variable that influences the direction and a moderating factor that influences the intensity of the association between the variables concerned in the consumer's decision-making process.

Cognition

Cognitive information processing (Foxall, 1986; Olshavsky and Garrbois, 1979) is an accepted theory for consumer research. The theory proposes that intrapersonal mental actions within a consumer come before any discernible behaviour. Furthermore, the theory maintains such mental actions can explain the behaviour (Foxall, 1986; Shimp, 1997). As a result, archetypes grounded in this principle tend to represent the consumer as a processor of information who first seeks out and appraises the accessible alternatives before final selection (Foxall, 1986; Shimp, 1997).

Bank and financial services sector research increasingly seeks to establish the means by which customers develop an alternative set of branches to frequent and transact business. Additional and related research focuses on developing a better understanding of the attributes that influence bank choice behaviour (Mulhern, 1997). Accordingly, two competing theories have evolved with respect to how individuals select a bank and/or financial services brand.

One model of cognitive information processing for bank choice behaviour is grounded in economic theory. The theory postulates that an individual evaluates each alternative and then chooses the option that offers the maximum utility or gain (Fotheringham, 1988). This implies each consumer has at hand at any given time, vast information processing potential. In contrast, research has demonstrated that an individual decision maker's capability to process information may be restricted by a number of factors (Peter and Olson, 1996; Sheth and Parvatiyar, 1995). Energy, time, cognitive capacity and so forth are few of the factors that may impede and constrain the individual's ability to process information.

To offset this problem, a second model has been proposed (Peter and Olson, 1996; Sheth and Parvatiyar, 1995). This prototype proposes individual consumers want to achieve efficient information processing. Accordingly, the number of choice options is reduced by the consumer's cognitive information processing to an abbreviated set. From this limited set, a choice is made. Because the decision process involved in this model begins with a narrowing of the existing alternatives and ends with a choice from a limited set, it is thought to be sequential and require a reduced amount of processing capacity.

Brand image

The image of a brand has long been recognised as one of the most important components in the successful marketing of a product or service. Its importance cannot be underestimated. No doubt its magnitude is revealed in part by the amount of money spent each year by marketers and advertisers in efforts to better and bolster their brands. Further evidence of its significance can be garnered from a cursory review of the annual and cumulative amount of academic and scholarly research specifically devoted to understanding it. Yet for all the money spent and research effort devoted to it, brand image remains still a hotly debated and elusive topic for academicians and practitioners alike.

Notwithstanding this, in the course of years of industry practice and research a consensus of sorts has evolved. Brand image can be thought of as a perception reflected by the associations a brand holds in the memory of a consumer. These associations are the supplementary and complementary informational intersections connected in a neural nexus together with the brand node in a consumer's memory. Brand associations hold the essence and comprise the fundamental nature of the brand for the consumer. Specific associations like brand strength, inimitability and favourability are measures that have been shown to differentiate brand knowledge. These associations play a significant role in shaping the degree of difference in customer response that makes up brand equity. Customer-based brand equity relates to how familiar consumers are with the brand and in what way they hold favourable, strong, and unique brand associations in memory (Keller, 1993).This is especially the case in high-involvement brands and decision settings (Keller, 1993).

Brand image is not the only component of brand knowledge, however. Brand awareness, as defined by Aaker (1991) can be deemed as *"...the ability of a potential buyer to recognise or recall that a brand is a member of a certain product category."* Recognition is the minimum level of brand awareness necessary for a consumer to display brand knowledge. It is measured by the ability of a consumer to identify a brand name as being one from and belonging to a nominated set of brands. The test is referred to as an aided recall test. Brand recall on the other hand denotes the ability of a consumer to name a brand as belonging to a specific product category when the category is mentioned. Unaided recall corresponds to a higher level of brand knowledge and awareness and is characteristically referred to as top-of-mind-awareness. Top-of-mind-awareness (TOMA) is a measure of the position in which a brand is recalled when the category is mentioned. The position of recall is highly associated with brand strength, customer attitudes and intentions towards the brand. The higher the level of awareness-accessibility, the more positive the attitude towards the brand and the more likely a given brand is the regular or main brand of a consumer. Loyal customers are for that reason more prone to name their brand of choice in the first recall position. Brands that are mentioned in second or third place in unaided brand recall questions tend to be "switch-to" brands. This proposition was first introduced by Cohen (1966) in his "level-of-consciousness" theory and is part of a more general psychological model of automatic-unconscious processing.

Numerous researchers have documented additional support for this model over the years. However, two founding studies that support the link between the order of brand mention, brand attitudes and purchase behaviour are noteworthy. The first is Axelrod's study of attitudes that predict purchase (1968). The second is a study by Haley and Case (1979) that tested thirteen attitude scales for brand discrimination and agreement. In a separate but related stream of research, Berger et al. (1994) examined the connections linking attitudes and purchase intent for a durable good (1994). The author concluded that attitude strength is a key intermediary in the relationship between attitude and behavioural intentions. The proposition is put forth that attitudes are strong because they are based on more *knowledge*. This additional knowledge not only differentiates strong and weak attitudes, but also significantly affects subsequent choice behaviour. See Chapter 6 on the effects of knowledge and experience using a quasi-experiment in marketing.

Determinants of customer switching and retention

Customer retention not only expresses the tangible act of repurchase but also includes other indications of brand loyalty. These indicators might be things like word-of-mouth advice and guidance, multiple purchases, changes in patterns of purchase behaviour as well as cross-buying (Homburg, Giering, Hentschl, 1998). Bearing this in mind, customer and brand loyalty does overlap both the concept of customer retention and purchase intention. Purchase intention viewed through the lens of customer satisfaction research describes a conative dimension that corresponds to the concept of customer loyalty (Johnson, 1998). Customer retention on the other hand signifies just how loyal the customer is in reality (Diller, 1996).

Action control

Purchase decisions by consumers are not necessarily straightforward. Weinieck et al. (1983) conclude that a string of variables might come in between the actual purchase and the decision to purchase. One such factor could be the information content of attitude and intent. Alternatively, the "perceived action control" theory introduced by Ajzen (1985) may also explain some mediating factors that occur in between the purchase decision and actual purchase. This concept is an unambiguous measure of situation-specific factors and relates to whether or not a consumer feels he or she can control the conditions surrounding the purchase and thereby impose the intention to exhibit loyal behaviour. This "perceived behavioural control" is defined by Ajzen as "...*one's perception of how easy or difficult it is to perform the behaviour."* The actual carrying out of the behaviour can be affected in two respects – one direct, the other indirect. In the first instance, perceived behavioural control shapes the intentions of the individual. Hence, if an individual accepts as true he or she can control his or her behaviour, an increase in the intention to execute the action will be observed. In the instance in which perceived behavioural control has a direct effect upon behaviour, it acts as a proxy for actual behavioural control. This is for the most part true as long as the person can make an accurate and realistic evaluation of the available control options.

Perceived behavioural control may also be moderated by other factors. These factors as set apart by Ajzen can be either internal or external. In the case of the former, internal factors are associated with the individual. These factors encompass such person-specific items as individual ability, skills, habits, will, self-discipline and the information available (Ajzen, 1985). External factors are not related to the person. To be more precise, they are associated with the environmental conditions in which the person operates. External factors include lack of resources, dependence upon other persons, and inauspicious conditions generally (Ajzen, 1985).

Findings in the field of perceived behavioural control are closely linked to the theory of *action control*. The results of research in this subject track strongly in the convention of social-psychological control theories and can be described by and large from two positions. In the first place the concept explains from the customer's perspective the chance of affecting a state of affairs (Wiswede, 1995). The second perspective follows on from the work of Rotter (1966) in which *action control* is a proxy for the author's *"locus of control"* theory. In this case, action control can be thought of as a personality trait that differentiates individuals according to the extent they accept as true they have power over their own lives.

Because action control acts as a mediating variable between customer loyalty and retention, a case can be made for including the theory in models of bank and financial services customer behaviour. Doing so will likely improve both the prognostic and explanatory power of the models for several reasons. In one instance for example, a customer may in the course of responding to a survey indicate a lack of bank or financial services loyalty. Though the customer may wish to terminate the relationship with the institution, he or she may nevertheless continue to remain loyal because personal circumstances (external) affect perceived action control to change. In a converse example, Internet banking may be expected to usher in a whole new consumer attitude vis-à-vis action control and the ability to switch banks and financial services organisations. When switching financial services institutions is a few mouse-clicks away, consumers will no doubt gain additional control over their lives. As this occurs their perceptions about the extent to which they have command over their lives will change. In this scenario, *action control* is likely to be an even more critical determinant in modelling bank and financial services customer loyalty and retention.

Zone of tolerance

Zeithaml, Berry and Parasuraman (1993) investigated switching intentions of consumers in a work that concluded customer service expectations are characterised not by a single level as in action control theory, but by a range of levels. This range of levels was termed a *"zone of tolerance"* that could be explained as *"...the extent to which customers recognise and are willing to accept homogeneity."* The zone of tolerance (Figure 5.1) therefore stands for the disparity between an ideal criterion and a level of service that is regarded as passable by the consumer. The dimensions of the zone are unique for each consumer and may expand or grow smaller for a variety of reasons that include such things as company controlled variables like price and service attributes. The zone of tolerance may accordingly be thought of as a type of torporific behavioural reaction to dis-confirmation of expectations (Liljander and Strandvik, 1993).

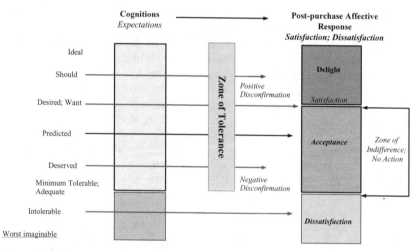

Figure 5.1   Cognitions and Post-Purchase Affective Responses
Source: Adapted from Erevelles & Leavitt (1992, 104)

Precisely why do consumers persist in torporific behaviour when product, brand or service expectations are not corroborated? Morgan and Hunt (1994) discovered a clear-cut association between a customer's commitment to a relationship and the cost of ending it. An individual who looks to establish a new affiliation must terminate the old one. In so doing, that individual acquires switching costs. A switching or termination cost is then the accumulation of those things put into the preceding relationship that cannot be passed on to the new and/or intended one (Morgan and Hunt, 1994). One such switching cost may for example be the cost of educating a new service provider or retailer a propos personal predilection (Bitner, 1995). Another could be the loss of exclusive status or respect derived from repeat patronage surrendered when the affiliation is terminated. Consequently, the consumer who terminates must go through the time and trouble to win this all once again in a new relationship. This proposition is especially germane today in the banking and financial services sector where long-established relationships conceivably bear considerable switching or termination costs. Further complicating the issue for consumers who consider switching is the risk of the unknown and unproven new relationship. For this reason, customers can easily find themselves in a state of torpor with respect to a particular institution. As a result, the customer's zone of tolerance may likely be greater for banks and financial services institutions than for high street retailers and manufacturers of consumer packaged goods like breakfast cereals, canned soups and vegetables and the like. Thus a customer who's expected level of service from the bank has neither been met nor dis-confirmed, may nevertheless remain with the bank and continue to tolerate it because the costs are marginally lower than the costs of termination. Figure 5.1 preceding demonstrates this concept.

Prospect theory

Bank and financial services customers nevertheless do switch institutions. This they do notwithstanding the termination costs and risks associated with establishing a new relationship with a financial institution. Upon further examination though, much of this switching behaviour would breach hypotheses of expected utility theory put forward in early works by Kahneman and Tversky (1981; 1979). To explain this contravention, Kahneman and Tversky proposed a more eloquent model of decision-making under risk (Figure 5.2). The model incorporates the notion of prospect theory whereby a person appraises the product of any choice relative to its apparent departure from a reference point rather than to a level of net assets.

Though the fundamental application of *prospect theory* was intended as a method by which risky decision-processes could be accounted, to a large extent the model can pertain to deterministic decision-processes (Thaler, 1994; Salimen and Wallenius, 1993). From this perspective, three features of prospect theory have emerged which are applicable for the study of deterministic decision-processes:

1. *Reference Point.* A human being appraises the outcome of a judgment in comparison with a negative or positive movement away from a point of

Value

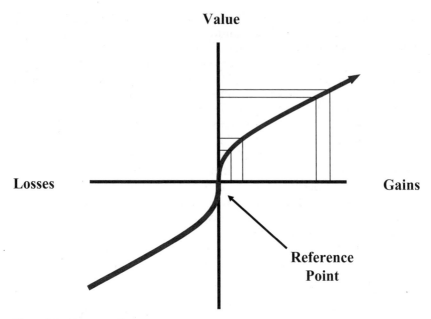

Losses   **Gains**

**Reference
Point**

Figure 5.2   Prospect Theory

reference rather than a level of net assets (Kahneman and Tversky, 1979; Tversky and Kahneman, 1986).

2. *Diminishing Sensitivity.* The marginal value of positive and negative departures from the point of reference will decrease in proportion to the magnitude of that point. For example, an increase in a consumer's wealth from £20 to £30 seems larger to an individual than a raise to £510 from £500 (Kahneman and Tversky, 1979; Diller, 1991). Though both examples demonstrate increases of £10, because the magnitude of the reference point in the former example is smaller than the latter, the increase is perceived to be greater.

3. *Loss Aversion.* An individual's negative evaluation resultant from a diminution in wealth will be larger than the positive evaluation of an increase by the equivalent magnitude (Kahneman and Tversky, 1979; Thaler, 1994).

Prospect theory can be represented graphically by the value function Figure 5.2 depicts. The value function portrays an individual consumer's evaluation of the gains and losses possible from choice alternatives and substitutions. Each alternative is measured proportionate to a reference point that operates as the origin of the value function. The origin or reference point in the value function is therefore the criterion to which an individual compares and evaluates differing outcomes from alternative choices.

Switching decisions by consumers can be analysed by means of the value function. In order to do so however, the reference point or point of origin must be established. This point may be represented by the individual consumer's current preferred product or service. Competing products and/or services serve as choice alternatives that the individual evaluates with reference to the point of origin. The outcome of the decision to either switch or remain is determined by the choice alternative deviations from the reference point. These deviations are the perceived value differences between the point of origin and the personal evaluation of the options presented. Switching behaviour occurs when an option maximises an increase in perceived value over and above the reference point.

Calculative commitment

Commitment between affiliated parties has been demonstrated to be a key gauge of the quality of the relationship (Sheaves and Barnes, 1996; Fournier, 1994). Moreover, it has been verified that commitment can characterise the foundation of strong brand loyalty (Dekiimpe, Steenkamp, Mellens and Abeele, 1997; Bloemer and Kasper, 1995). In these regards, literature from organisational research that contemplates the role of attitude in commitment (*attitudinal commitment*) may be useful. The organisational concept is extended to encompass two main types of commitment – namely, *affective* and *calculative*. *Affective commitment* is described as a "...partisan, affective attachment to the goals and values, and to the organisation for its own sake, apart from its purely instrumental worth (Buchanan 1974)." Then again, *calculative commitment* may be considered to be "...the individual's calculative or instrumental assessment of the perceived quality of remaining with the organisation, relative to leaving (Wallace, 1997; Mathieu and Zajac, 1990; Meyer, Allen and Gellatly, 1990)." Calculative commitment according to Stebbins (1970) is dispassionate. It is a neutral reaction that is swayed by the proximity and/or presence of penalties. These penalties are connected with the individual's plan or resolution to put an end to an affiliation with the organisation. For example, this may occur when a customer regards the costs of switching (breaking the existing relationship and beginning a new one) as too high or when previous versions have reduced the number of appealing options.

Meyer, Allen and Gellatly (1990) report the presence of two sub-dimensions associated with calculative commitment. The first facet is associated with high personal sacrifice while the second is related to a paucity of accessible options. The first dimension – personal sacrifice, is an outcome of economic and/or switching costs. The second dimension is the consequence of the forfeiture of other relationship opportunities. It can be thought of as a sort of "opportunity cost" associated with the maintenance of a single relationship through time. This second dimension – paucity of options, looks as if it is hypothetically and experientially superfluous with its precursors, that is, exit barriers.

The neutral dispassionate aspect of calculative commitment does appear to be less effective than affective commitment when it comes to brands loyalty. In a 1997 study, Samuelson and Sandvik contend that affective commitment denotes a more stable, steadfast and loyal relationship. The research substantiates moreover that increased price tolerance, repurchase intention, and diminished motivation to switch is associated with affective commitment.

Samuelson and Sandvik (1997) argue that *affective* commitment implies a more dedicated, stable and reliable relationship than a relationship based on *calculative* commitment. Their study confirmed that affective commitment increased repurchase intention and price tolerance and decreased motivation to switch. Other research within the same stream (Fornell, 1992; Gremler, 1995) agues the main drivers of customer loyalty are customer satisfaction and switching costs and/or barriers to exit. Muthukrishnan (1993) and Fournier (1994) make the case that commitment is a problematical circumstance for the consumer. Consumers do not have a sense of commitment towards every product, service, store or brand they come across in their every day existence. For that reason, involvement at some level by the consumer with the product or brand may be a precondition to the creation of commitment and then loyalty (Beatty, Homer and Kahle, 1988).

Switching costs and exit barriers

The objective of most marketing actions is to seek means by which the customer can be connected ever more closely to the product or brand. The more intimately the customer is linked to the product or brand, the more difficult it becomes to exit the relationship and look for substitutes. From this vantage point, models of exit barriers and switching costs are a wide-ranging collection of phenomena (Gremler, 1995) that present exceptional opportunities for marketers in search of understanding customer loyalty.

Sources of switching costs phenomena are copious (Fornell, 1992; Gremler, 1995). One of the origins of switching costs could for example be monetary in nature. Monetary switching costs can be thought of as tangible or imaginary losses pecuniary in character that a consumer would experience upon termination of a relationship with the purveyor of a product or service. Examples of monetary switching costs include the loss of out-of-the-ordinary discounts, loyalty points, bonuses and the like. In the banking and financial services arena, monetary switching costs may include such things as standing orders and direct debit instructions, personal relations with the institution's officers and customer services representatives, credit arrangements, prepayment penalties, convenience of branch locations and automatic teller machines, and so forth.

The consumer's appraisal of costless switching and the associated barriers to exit is thought to be a primary trigger of calculative commitment (Mathieu and Zajac, 1990). Research by Fournier (1994) demonstrates the brand may be perceived as a separate relationship partner that plays a role in the give-and-take exchange of a consumer-brand link. Thus the consumer-brand union is not inevitably an affiliation in which the customer is locked in as the dependent party at risk of exploitation. Even if this scenario were to be the case though, negative feelings might not inevitably come to pass. A consumer may observe it is more feasible and significantly less difficult to adjust the attitude towards the object than to end the relationship and invite the switching costs.

Ultimately, perception of risk could be the determining factor in a consumer's propensity to switch. In connection with this, risk probability and risk importance are two facets of the consumer's overall appraisal of risk that are of particular note and importance. Risk probability pertains to the likelihood as perceived by the consumer of a specific outcome as the result of some action (Dowling and Staelin, 1994). Risk importance on the other hand signifies the weight a consumer assigns to the adverse consequences that could come to pass as a result of those actions. Accordingly, commitment and repurchase can be envisaged as a means to diminish when procuring or coping with a product-category the unpleasant feelings associated with the unknown.

Because perception and tolerance of risk is believed to influence loyalty (Cunningham, 1967), a consumer who remains loyal to a brand, product or provider avoids unnecessary risk in so doing. Moreover, loyalty may in part be influenced by the amount of information available to the consumer. A consumer is likely to have more complete information about the loyalty object than its alternatives (Johnson and Fornell, 1991). Thus it is reasonable that the consumer will make risk importance evaluations with a bias in favour of the loyalty object.

Calculative commitment therefore characterises a condition wherein the consumer feels few if any alternatives are available. The risk originating from the product category is perceived to be escalating whenever options are being contemplated. In this situation, the consumer is faced with one of two choices – risk or risk avoidance. In the first instance, the consumer can switch and incur the risks previously detailed. In the second, the consumer can remain with the previous selection, rule out the other options, and as a result increase the level of calculative commitment.

Hypotheses

The hypotheses herein are evaluated using a statistical corroboration approach to explore the role Internet banking may play in current and future banking and financial services customer behaviours – specifically brand choice, loyal and switching behaviours. Seven hypotheses and sub-hypotheses examine such concepts as action control, zone of tolerance, calculative commitment and others previously put forth in connection with customer behaviour within the banking and financial services sectors.

Hypothesis 1

Keller (1993) put forth in the framework of top-of-mind brand awareness research that heightening the level of awareness for a brand will increase the probability the brand will be a member of a handful of brands that gain serious consideration for purchase. Cohen (1966) introduced the level of consciousness concept to argue that earlier unaided brand recall results in a more favourable attitude towards the brand. Regularly used brands and brands with high switch-to-potential are recalled almost exclusively in the first level of consciousness. Cohen argued further that as a result of first level consciousness recall, consumers will engage in any number of favourable actions towards the brand. Accordingly, H1 proposes first mention of a bank and/or financial services institution brand influences the present and/or future probability that a customer will engage in brand switching behaviour. Banks and financial institutions recalled in the highest levels of consciousness are least likely to fall victim to switching behaviour by their customers.

Hypotheses 2, 2a and 3

Brand strength, inimitability and favourability differentiate brand knowledge. These links play an important function in determining the customer response that comprises brand equity. Customer-based brand equity relates to how familiar consumers are with the brand and in what way they hold favourable opinions about the brand.

Keller (1993) demonstrates this particularly with high-involvement brands and decision settings. Consequently, H2 puts forward for high involvement brands like banks and/or financial institutions the more positive the brand image; the less likely a customer is to engage in switching actions. H2a proposes bank and financial services customers are willing to accept negative bank brand attributes so long as they exist alongside positive attributes. More specifically, though a customer may recall his or her bank for some negatively worded bank attributes like poor customer service or most inconvenient location or high rates of interest, this will be not be sufficient to cause switching behaviour so long as some positive bank attributes which are more relevant to the individual exist alongside. Thus a customer may recognise and recall the weaknesses and faults of the institution but trade them off against strengths like personal service and large selection of financial services products to remain with the bank.

Confirmation of H2a launches a related hypothesis. (H3) Bank customers are driven by particular and specific motivations to remain customers and hence show no indifferent attitude in the choice of a bank or financial services institution.

Hypotheses 4 and 4a

Customers who are not indifferent in their attitudes towards their main bank and/or financial services institution are predisposed to high levels of brand involvement. Involvement and commitment with the product or brand leads to extensive information search (Schiffman and Kanuk, 1994). Consequently, customers who take the selection and choice of a financial services institution seriously can be expected to engage in such behaviour. H4 tests the theory that contrary to low involvement brands and products, commitment to and involvement with the brand does not necessarily lead to brand loyalty. Specifically, H4 tests that customers who are committed in choice and selection of a bank and/or financial institution are *more likely* to engage in switching behaviour. If customers are involved they are more likely to engage in extensive information search. Consequently, they are prone to become more knowledgeable about the array of products and services on offer by competing institutions. Switching behaviour will result as they seek to maximise their knowledge to take advantage of available opportunities.

H4a proposes that customers who maintain an assortment of products and services at multiple banks and/or financial services institutions are more likely to engage in switching behaviour over a two to four year period of time.

Hypotheses 5 and 6

Empirical research studies of customer loyalty (cf. Dichtl and Schneider, 1994) corroborate that it is primarily a consequence of a customer's satisfaction with the product, brand and/or service. H5 tests this premise for banks and financial services institutions explicitly. More specifically, H5 investigators postulate that a higher level of overall satisfaction with a bank and/or financial service institution will decrease the likelihood a consumer will engage in switching behaviour. H6 refers the research of Erevelles and Leavitt (1992) and previously discussed models of expectation and satisfaction/dissatisfaction behaviour. Accordingly, H6 proposes to establish that perceived switching costs, pecuniary and other, have an impact on a customer's propensity to switch banks and/or financial services institutions. Simply stated, customers who perceive the costs as well as risks associated with severing the banking and financial services relationship will remain if they are excessively high.

Hypotheses 7 and 7a

Finally, H7 examines the role of Internet banking and customer switching behaviour. Consumers who are familiar with the technology, comfortable in its use, and who maintain Internet accessible accounts will display lower levels of calculative commitment. Consequently, they are more likely to engage in switching behaviour over time. Therefore, H7 postulates that Internet banking as well as access to Internet accessible financial services and accounts is negatively associated with bank and financial services institution brand loyalty. However, not all customers who maintain Internet accessible bank or financial services accounts will engage in switching behaviour. Therefore, H7a posits that account holders who switched are more comfortable with the technology than non-switching loyal customers.

Sample and method

Hypotheses enumerated above were examined through the use of data collected from an in-person survey of bank and financial services customers in London, Egham, Windsor, Staines, Birmingham, Bristol and Bath in the United Kingdom. One hundred twenty nine (129) interviews were collected daily during a three-week period in June of 1999. Sixty (60) interviews were conducted in London alone, with the remaining 69 being evenly distributed throughout Egham, Windsor, Staines, Birmingham, Bristol and Bath. Respondents to the survey were U.K. residents who had been established within the country for at least five years. So that a clear picture of switching behaviour by the general consumer of banking and financial services could be obtained, every effort was made to survey respondents from as many social classifications as possible, with no one category dominating the sample.

Questionnaire

A pilot study of 20 completed in-person interviews was utilised to test a seven-page survey questionnaire. The questionnaire examined brand awareness and accessibility, attitudes toward Internet technology, service level satisfaction, account switching behaviour and more. Numeric codes were assigned to close-ended questions and later to open-ended questions where feasible. A number of changes resulted from the pilot study. Most noteworthy was the change for some questions from a strictly coded agree/disagree format to one that allowed the respondent to comment further. These comments were recorded verbatim as ancillary information to the original coded data and provided a range of insights into the nature of the relationship many respondents had with the bank or financial institution with which they conducted most business.

Respondents were asked an unaided brand recall question at the initiation of the survey. This top-of-mind awareness (TOMA) question asked participants to name all the banks and financial services institutions they could recall. No time limit was set on the recall question. The term financial institution was included along with the term banks to accommodate the emergence of new entrants and non-traditional banks (i.e., Marks & Spencer, Virgin) into Britain's financial services market.

TOMA attitude-accessibility questions on financial services institutions were studied. Questions were designed to assess attribute-to-brand evocations amongst customers of banking and financial services. Concerning this, respondents were asked to name the bank or financial services institution that first came to mind for a series of ten positively and negatively worded bank attribute questions. Bank and financial service attributes examined dealt specifically with customer service and product expectations. Attributes subjected to study emerged from open-ended questions conducted in the pilot study. As a result, bank and financial services attributes of Internet access, price, speed of service, rates, mortgages, credit cards, convenience of location, reliability, friendliness of staff, and image (brand of future or past) were tested with both positively and negatively worded questions. Orders of presentation as well as starting points for the ten positively and negatively worded questions were rotated for each new respondent. Further, each positively worded attribute-to-brand question was followed by a negatively worded question for a different brand attribute. For this reason, the likelihood of a respondent providing a rote answer to each question was reduced.

Woodside and Trappey (1992) demonstrate attribute-to-brand evocation to be an important measure of brand strength, consumer attitude and choice behaviour. When respondents are required to name the brand that first comes to mind for specified brand attributes, the researcher is working back to front from what respondents would normally expect. In doing so, several advantages with respect to understanding a consumer's cognitive processing of brand information can be had. Most noteworthy however is the fact that strategic cognitive processing of brand information by respondents is minimised. As a result automatic-unconscious processes dominate. Attribute-to-brand information retrieved from long-term memory into working memory is more likely to expose a consumer's attitude towards the brand.

Respondents were asked a series of questions regarding the bank and financial services institution with which they transacted most of their business. Questions ranged from the name of the institution respondents currently bank with and the year in which the account(s) was opened, to whether or not they maintained an Internet accessible account and if so, how often they used it. With respect to the Internet, respondents were asked a series of additional questions on Internet shopping and purchase behaviour. Additional questions were asked on a wide range of conventional banking products and services.

Respondents who switched banks and/or financial services institutions during either a two or four year period were asked a separate set of open-ended questions to examine exit barriers and ascertain motivations for switching. Questions specifically examined problems encountered with changing banks or financial services. Respondents were encouraged to comment further on their level of satisfaction with the products and services of the institution with which they currently transacted most business.

Level of commitment towards the choice of bank or financial institution was measured using a five-point Likert scale. The scale ranged from "strongly disagree" (1) to "strongly agree" (5). Compound measures of respondent commitment from previous research by Meyer, Allen and Gellatly (1990) were adapted for bank and financial services research. Items selected for measurement included but were not limited to price-performance, reliability of administration, and friendliness of administrative personnel.

Finally, demographic data that included respondent age, household size, marital status, education, nationality and totally annual household income were also gathered

Analysis and results

Table 5.4 depicts market share percentages for the banks. Responses demonstrate those banks survey respondents declared as their main bank – the bank at which they transact most of their business. The table illustrates that in the sample, NatWest, Lloyds TSB, Barclays and HSBC/Midland cumulatively represent nearly seventy five percent (74%) of the market for financial services amongst the respondents. Because NatWest, Lloyd's,

Table 5.4   Market Shares for Ten Banks

Financial Institution	N	Percent	Cumulative
Nat West	35	27.1%	27.1%
Lloyd's TSB	27	20.9%	48.1%
Barclays	20	15.5%	63.6%
HSBC; Midland	13	10.1%	73.6%
First Direct	12	9.3%	82.9%
Citibank	6	4.7%	87.6%
Abbey National	5	3.9%	91.5%
Halifax	5	3.9%	95.3%
Royal Bank of Scotlar	4	3.1%	98.4%
Co-operative Bank	2	1.6%	100.0%
Total	129	100.0%	

Barclays and HSBC represent such a large proportion of the U.K. financial services market amongst the consumers studied in the survey, data analysis and hypotheses testing are limited to these four banks.

The following cross tabulation (Table 5.5) examines main bank account switching behaviour amongst the survey respondents. Survey participants were asked to name the bank with which they transacted most of their business. Participants were further asked to name the bank with which they transacted most of their business in the previous two years. Customers for whom this relationship changed are considered to be "switchers." Non-switchers are those customers who have remained loyal to the bank during the two-year period and have not moved to another bank for most of their business.

The table indicates relatively stable market shares for each of the four major banks in the study. Some migration between banks has taken place over the period, but for the most part, there has been little net effect on market share. For example, two years ago 28.7 percent of the respondents claimed NatWest to be their main bank. Currently, 27.1 percent of the respondents make the same claim. The small difference falls well within the sample error of the survey, but does demonstrate a trait that is typical amongst the market leaders, i.e., any switching by the customers has not changed the overall market position of the leaders.

Approximately 91 percent of NatWest current customers were customers of the bank two years ago. Those customers of two years ago who did switch banks went primarily to HSBC (5.4%) and First Direct (5.4%). First Direct is a "telebank" subsidiary of HSBC that offers customers the convenience of transacting all bank business at any time solely via the telephone and automatic teller machines. Lloyds bank displays a similar profile. Ninety-three percent (93%) of Lloyds current customers were customers of the bank two years ago. Those customers who did switch went mostly to First Direct and Barclays. Barclays customers who did switch, went mostly to First Direct (9%) and Citibank (13%) while HSBC customers moved to Lloyds (15%) and Barclays (8%).

Most switching behaviour appears to have been from the market leaders to innovators like First Direct and Citibank – a new entrant into the U.K. market that held no market share two years prior to the execution of the study. While First Direct offers "telebanking" as its primary incentive, Citibank offers global reach, higher rates of interest and more customer access to current account funds through the Internet and online banking.

While First Direct's market share can be seen to come from major high street banks within the U.K., the 4.7 percent market share of Citibank currently demonstrated in the table is primarily at the expense of Barclays and Deutsche Bank. Deutsche Bank customers in the survey are fundamentally professionals who are new residents in the U.K. and have moved for work

Table 5.5 Main Bank Switching Behaviour

		Name of the bank with which you had your account two years ago											
Main Account Today		Abbey National	Barclays	Co-op-erative	Deutsche Bank	First Direct	Halifax	Hong Kong Bank of Canada	HSBC Midland	Lloyds TSB	NatWest	Royal Bank of Scotland	UBS	Total
Abbey National	5 100.0% 100.0%													5 100.0% 3.9%
Barclays		17 85.0% 73.9%						1 5.0% 7.7%	1 5.0% 3.7%	1 5.0% 2.7%				20 100.0% 15.5%
Citibank		3 50.0% 13.0%		2 33.3% 66.7%	1 16.7% 12.5%									6 100.0% 4.7%
Co-operative			1 50.0% 100.0%								1 50.0% 20.0%			2 100.0% 1.6%
First Direct		2 16.7% 8.7%			7 58.3% 87.5%				1 8.3% 3.7%	2 16.7% 5.4%				12 100.0% 9.3%
Halifax						5 100.0% 100.0%								5 100.0% 3.9%

Table 5.5 Main Bank Switching Behaviour – *continued*

Name of the bank with which you had your account two years ago

	Abbey National	Barclays	Co-op erative	Deutsche Bank	First Direct	Halifax	Hong Kong Bank of Canada	HSBC Midland	Lloyds TSB	NatWest	Royal Bank of Scotland	UBS	Total
Lloyds TSB								2 7.4% 15.4%	25 92.6% 92.6%				27 100.0% 20.9%
NatWest		1 2.9% 4.3%		1 2.9% 33.3%			1 2.9% 100.0%			32 91.4% 86.5%			35 100.0% 27.1%
Royal Bank of Scotland											4 100.0% 80.0%		4 100.0% 3.1%
Total	5 3.9% 100.0%	23 17.8% 100.0%	1 .8% 100%	3 2.3% 100.0%	8 6.2% 100.0%	5 3.9% 100.0%	1 .8% 100.0%	13 10.1% 100.0%	27 20.9% 100.0%	37 28.7% 100.0%	5 3.9% 100.0%	1 .8% 100%	129 100.0% 100.0%

and changed accounts with the move. It is important to note that these respondents chose an American bank and a new entrant into the U.K. market. This suggests professionals who travel and consider a potential work-related move likely. In the future, online access and global reach are likely to be significant factors in choice behaviour amongst these consumers and American banks are currently leaders in this technology and marketing.

Results – Hypothesis 1 and 2

Does being the bank first mentioned in an unaided brand recall question impact a customer's propensity to switch? How does position of unaided recall vary amongst loyal (non switcher) customers and those customers who have never been a bank customer or who have switched either to or from their main bank? The results of the data analyses support H1. A cross tabulation and chi-square analysis of unaided recall and switching behaviour for the four market leader retail banks, NatWest, Lloyds TSB, Barclays, HSBC/Midland was used to expose relationships that might exist between switching attitude and the position of unaided bank brand recall ability. The table indicates comparable results for switching behaviour and recall position for all four banks. Chi square values of 94.68, 54.02, 54.31 and 84.84 were obtained for NatWest, Lloyds, Barclays and HSBC respectively. Findings were all significant at the 0.000 level.

Switching behaviour

The following cross tabulation (Tables 5.6, 5.7) of switching behaviour demonstrate 84 percent of loyal NatWest customers mention NatWest first in an unaided bank brand recall test. This finding was comparable for Lloyds, Barclays and HSBC loyal customers, ranging from 80 percent for Lloyds to 88 percent and 80 percent for Barclays and HSBC.

New customers – customers who switched from a competitor bank to their current main bank (e.g., a Barclays customer who switched to NatWest) display a profile similar to loyal, non-switching customers. These customers are distinct however from the standpoint they are more likely to recall the present main bank brand across first, second, as well as third positions – reflecting no doubt the residual brand recall from the bank from which they switched. In an unaided recall question of bank brands, defector bank customers – those customers who switched away from their main bank to a competitor (e.g., a NatWest customer who went to Barclays) are likely to not recall the brand at all. If the brand is recalled, it is most often recalled in one of the lower order of mention positions. This reveals that the customer who has switched banks de-prioritises the brand; filing it in long-term memory along with a likely nexus of negative brand attributes associations.

Those respondents who have never been NatWest customers will recall the bank brand name more than half the time in either the third recall position (31.8%) or the fourth position (27.1%). If a respondent reveals no unaided bank brand recall for NatWest, there is 100 percent likelihood the respondent was never a bank customer. This finding is consistent between the other banks studied, with the likelihood ranging from 90 percent for Barclays to 90.9 percent and 95 percent for HSBC and Lloyds respectively.

A very high likelihood exists that those whose respondents recalling the bank brand in first position are either long time loyal customers or customers who have switched to the bank. Lower order positions of recall are highly associated both with respondents who have never been a customer of the bank and turncoat customers switching from the bank.

Positive and negative attribute-to-brand evocations

An additional series of summary variables was created for each bank brand. The summary variables each represent the total number of positive and negative attribute-to-brand mentions for the respective banks. Each time a bank brand was evoked for a positively worded bank attribute, the new variable increased. So for example, if when asked the question "What bank first comes to mind when I say fastest service" a subject responded NatWest, the new variable took on the value of 1. If when asked the question "What bank comes to mind when I say most convenient?" the subject again answered NatWest, the variable cumulated and took on the value of 2. The process was repeated for each bank and each subject for both the positively and negatively worded attributes.

Table 5.8 titled "Mean Positive, Negative, and Total Attribute Recall Varying by Customer" supports H2. It examines the relationship between a portfolio of bank customers, positive and negative attribute-to-brand evocations and switching behaviour. The table displays overwhelming evidence that non-switching, loyal customers primarily evoke the bank when positive brand attributes are mentioned. This lends further credibility to the argument that a positive brand image is associated with bank brand loyalty.

NatWest is a case worth examining. Non-switching loyal customers of NatWest evoke the bank brand on average 2.47 times across both positive and negative attributes. Non-switchers will evoke the bank an average of 1.8 times for positive attributes and 0.66 times for negative attributes. Those customers who recently switched to the bank from a competitor will evoke the NatWest bank brand on average 3.3 times for

Table 5.6 Switching Behaviour of Nat West and Lloyds

Nat West	Position					No Recall	Total
	1st	2nd	3rd	4th	5th		
Non Switcher	27	2	3				32
	84.4%	6.3%	9.4%				100.0%
	90.0%	12.5%	9.1%				25.6%
Switched from Competitor to Main Bank	1	1	1				3
	33.3%	33.3%	33.3%				100.0%
	3.3%	6.3%	3.0%				2.4%
Switched from Main Bank to Competitor	1	1	2		1		5
	20.0%	20.0%	40.0%		20.0%		100.0%
	3.3%	6.3%	6.1%		14.3%		4.0%
Never a Bank Customer	1	12	27	23	6	16	85
	1.2%	14.1%	31.8%	27.1%	7.1%	18.8%	100.0%
	3.3%	75.0%	81.8%	100.0%	85.7%	100.0%	68.0%
Total	30	16	33	23	7	16	125
X^2 94.68	DF 15			Sig. 0.000			

Table 5.6 Switching Behaviour of Nat West and Lloyds – *continued*

Lloyds TSB	Position					No Recall	Total
	1st	2nd	3rd	4th	5th		
Non Switcher	20 80.0% 66.7%	5 20.0% 31.3%					25 100.0% 20.0%
Switched from Competitor to Main Bank	1 50.0% 3.3%					1 50.0% 6.3%	2 100.0% 1.6%
Switched from Main Bank to Competitor	1 50.0% 3.3%			1 50.0% 6.7%			2 100.0% 1.6%
Never a Bank Customer	12 12.5% 35.3%	20 20.8% 80.0%	17 17.7% 100.0%	14 14.6% 93.3%	14 14.6% 100.0%	19 19.8% 95.0%	96 100.0% 76.8%
Total	34	25	17	15	14	20	125
X^2 54.021	DF 15			*Sig. 0.000*			

Table 5.7 Switching Behaviour of Barclays and HSBC

Barclays	Position						Total
	1st	2nd	3rd	4th	5th	No Recall	
Non Switcher	15 88.2% 50.0%	2 11.8% 12.5%					17 100.0% 13.6%
Switched from Competitor to Main Bank	1 33.3% 3.3%	2 66.7% 12.5%					3 100.0% 2.4%
Switched from Main Bank to Competitor		3 50.0% 18.8%		1 16.7% 9.1%	2	6 33.3% 10.0%	66.7% 4.8%
Never a Bank Customer	13 13.4% 44.8%	29 29.9% 80.6%	18 18.6% 100.0%	10 10.3% 90.9%	9 9.3% 100.0%	18 18.6% 90.0%	97 100.0% 78.9%
Total	29	36	18	11	9	20	123

X^2 54.317   DF 15   Sig. 0.000

Table 5.7 Switching Behaviour of Barclays and HSBC – continued

HSBC Midland	Position					No Recall	Total
	1st	2nd	3rd	4th	5th		
Non Switcher	8 80.0% 26.7%	6.1%	2 20.0%			8.0%	10 100.0%
Switched from Competitor to Main Bank	3 100.0% 10.0%						3 100.0% 2.4%
Switched from Main Bank to Competitor				1 33.3% 4.2%		2 66.7% 9.1%	3 100.0% 2.8%
Never a Bank Customer	3 2.8% 21.4%	20 18.9% 100.0%	24 22.6% 92.3%	23 21.7% 95.8%	16 15.1% 100.0%	20 90.9%	106 100.0% 86.9%
Total	14	20	26	24	16	22	122
X^2 84.846	DF 15			Sig. 0.000			

Table 5.8 Mean Positive, Negative, and Total Attribute Recall Varying by Customer

	Total Positive	Total Negative	Total Recall	Overall Mean
Nat West				
Non Switcher	1.81	0.66	2.47	1.65
Switched from Competitor to Main Bank	3.33	1.00	4.33	2.89
Switched from Main Bank to Competitor	0.40	3.60	4.00	2.67
Never a Bank Customer	0.21	0.64	0.85	0.57
df3; F	30.021	7.164	15.358	
Sig.	0.000	0.000	0.000	
Lloyds				
Non Switcher	1.52	0.08	1.60	1.07
Switched from Competitor to Main Bank	0.00	0.00	0.00	0.00
Switched from Main Bank to Competitor	0.50	1.50	2.00	1.33
Never a Bank Customer	0.33	0.55	0.88	0.59
df 3; F	11.295	1.906	1.880	
Sig.	0.000	0.132	0.136	
Barclays				
Non Switcher	1.00	1.12	2.12	1.41
Switched from Competitor to Main Bank	0.67	0.00	0.67	0.44
Switched from Main Bank to Competitor	0.50	3.17	3.67	2.44
Never a Bank Customer	0.40	0.98	1.38	0.92
df 3; F	3.461	5.059	5.530	
Sig.	0.018	0.002	0.001	
HSBC				
Non Switcher	2.60	0.10	2.70	1.80
Switched from Competitor to Main Bank	2.67	0.00	2.67	1.78
Switched from Main Bank to Competitor	0.00	0.00	0.00	0.00
Never a Bank Customer	0.20	0.33	0.53	0.35
df 3; F	44.982	0.667	18.429	
Sig.	0.000	0.574	0.000	

positively worded bank attributes. On the other hand, those customers who left NatWest for one of the competitors will evoke the brand on average an equivalent amount of times (3.6) for negatively worded bank attributes.

In the context of bank brand attributes, it is worthwhile noting a study on personal computers conducted by the author (Trappey, 1999) for Hewlett Packard U.K. This research demonstrates relevant and important findings for marketers with respect to positive and negative attribute-to-brand evocations versus the total number of brands recalled. Results of this study are based on a large-scale survey (n = 672) summarised in the table and charts following. Subjects were asked firstly, "Please name all the brands of personal computers of which you are aware." Both the brands named and the number of brands mentioned were recorded. Next, subjects were asked to name the brand that first-came-to-mind for specific brand attributes, like fastest/slowest, highest/lowest price, and the like. This technique was demonstrated in this chapter and in previous chapters.

Data indicate a definite shift in the positive/negative attribute-to-brand ratio, as customers are able to recall more and more brands. Thus, total brand recall likely reflects more than advertising effects (e.g. product and/or category knowledge and experience – an issue taken up in the next chapter). For example, note in the following chart (Figure 5.3) that as subjects are more able to recall a larger number of brands (knowledge increases), the positive attribute-to-brand evocation bias dissipates.

Customers who can only recall one brand in an unaided brand recall question will evoke the same brand or several brands for an average of 4.11 positive attributes to every 1.22 negative. The following Figure 5.3a and b (table and chart) examines this in more detail. Note in the table following that subjects who can recall between 14 and 17 brands in an unaided recall question evoke an equal number (11) of brands for positive and negative brand attributes. Thus, the positive/negative ratio becomes one (1).

Subjects virtually always evoke more brands for positive attributes than negative ones. Furthermore, as they become more aware of brands, they can recall more brands for specific attributes in attribute-to-brand recall questions. This fact can be seen clearly in both the table and the accompanying chart. The chart however displays some additional interesting

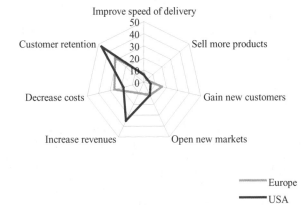

Figure 5.3(a)

Mean No. Brands Recalled for:

Total Brands Recalled	Positive Attributes	Negative Attributes	Ratio of Pos./Neg.
0	0.00	0.00	
1	4.11	1.22	3.36
2	3.75	1.79	2.10
3	5.44	2.76	1.97
4	6.00	3.29	1.82
5	6.29	3.61	1.74
6	7.81	5.13	1.52
7	7.69	5.29	1.45
8	8.37	5.81	1.44
9	9.29	7.06	1.32
10	10.00	6.83	1.46
11	9.75	6.38	1.53
12	10.50	4.50	2.33
13	8.86	7.29	1.22
14	11.00	11.00	1.00
15	10.00	6.00	1.67
17	11.00	11.00	1.00
Overall Mean	7.64	5.23	1.68

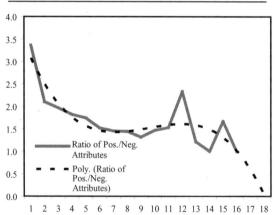

Figure 5.3(b)   Ratio of Positive/Negative Attribute-to-Brand Evocations Varying by Total Brand Recall

properties. Note that the ability to recall brands for both positive and negative attributes is a curvilinear function. The second-order polynomial regressions demonstrate that when TOMA brands approach recall levels of about 19–20 brands, positive and negative attribute-to-brand evocations become equal. Positive attribute-to-brand evocations decline at a faster rate than negative, which show a lingering effect as TOMA brand increases. See Figure 5.4.

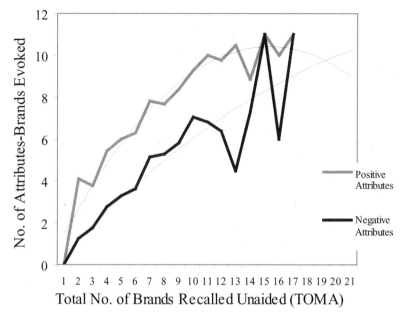

Figure 5.4   Attribute-to-Brand Evocations are Curvilinear as TOMA Brand Increases

Result – Hypotheses 2a and 3

The preceding Table 5.8 indicates more importantly a strong relationship between bank brand image and switching behaviour. Customers who have recently switched from a competitor to their current main bank are likely to evoke their new bank brand for positive attributes 2–3 times more often than loyal customers. The antithesis holds true for customers who have switched away from their main bank to a competitor. These customers are approximately 2–4 times more likely than loyal customers to evoke their previous bank brand when negative bank brand attributes are mentioned.

Support for H2a and H3 may also be found in this table. Non-switching bank customers demonstrate a willingness to remain loyal even though they may evoke their current bank brand for negatively worded bank attributes. A *zone of tolerance* (H2a) whereby customers accept certain shortfalls in the banks expected delivery of services can be observed to varying degrees in each of the four banks. HSBC customers for example will evoke the brand on average 2.6 times for positively worded bank attributes and 0.10 times for negatively worded ones. Barclays loyal customers display a significant amount of tolerance. The bank brand will be evoked 1.12 times on average for negatively worded attributes, but only 1.00 time for those positively worded. The evidence would suggest customers are not indifferent, but are motivated by the brand's positive attributes to remain with the bank (H3). Because of this they are less likely to engage in switching behaviour.

Table 5.9 examines the total number of positive and negative attribute-to-brand evocations varying by the position in which a bank brand was mentioned in an unaided recall question. Just how the order of brand mention affects brand loyalty amongst financial services customers is explored later with regression analysis. The analysis in the following table however lends further support to H1 and confirms H2, H2a and H3.

The evidence in the table connects higher positions of unaided brand recall with a higher probability the bank brand will be evoked for a positive bank attribute in an attribute-to-brand question. Lower orders of brand mention are associated with higher levels of negative bank attribute-to-brand evocations. If a bank has a low level of brand awareness or is unmentioned in an unaided brand recall question it is likely the brand will pop up later in a negatively worded attribute-to-brand question.

NatWest illustrates the case clearly in the table. When NatWest is mentioned first in an unaided recall question, respondents will evoke the brand on average 2.20 times for positively worded bank attributes. If the brand is

Table 5.9 Positive and Negative Attribute-to-Brand Evocations

	1st	2nd	3rd	4th	5th	No Mention	Overall Mean
Natwest							
Positive Attributes	2.20	0.38	0.15	0.39	0.00	0.18	0.55
Negative Attributes	0.83	0.94	0.79	0.35	0.50	0.65	0.68
Total Attributes	3.03	1.31	0.94	0.74	0.50	0.82	1.22
Lloyds							
Positive Attributes	0.91	1.00	0.24	0.25	0.14	0.15	0.45
Negative Attributes	0.43	0.40	1.00	0.19	0.64	0.25	0.48
Total Attributes	1.34	1.40	1.24	0.44	0.79	0.40	0.93
Barelays							
Positive Attributes	0.93	0.50	0.44	0.09	0.33	0.15	0.41
Negative Attributes	1.07	0.89	1.56	1.27	1.22	1.05	1.18
Total Attributes	2.00	1.39	2.00	1.36	1.56	1.20	1.58
HSBC							
Positive Attributes	2.71	0.24	0.19	0.32	0.00	0.14	0.60
Negative Attributes	0.14	0.29	0.31	0.32	0.25	0.18	0.25
Total Attributes	2.86	0.52	0.50	0.64	0.25	0.32	0.85
Mean of Positive	1.69	0.53	0.26	0.26	0.12	0.15	0.50
Mean of Negative	0.62	0.63	0.91	0.53	0.65	0.53	0.65

recalled in the second, third, fourth or fifth positions of unaided recall, the bank will be evoked an average of 0.38, 0.15, 0.39, and 0.00 times. Furthermore, if the bank is unmentioned in an unaided recall question, it is more likely it will be evoked later for a negative bank attribute than a positive one. This detail can be seen not only in NatWest, but also in Lloyds, Barclays, and HSBC as the ratio of positive/negative attribute-to-brand evocations range from 0.27 and 0.60 for NatWest and Lloyds to 0.14 and 0.75 for Barclays and HSBC.

Barclays demonstrates another point in the table. Never is Barclays evoked more for positive bank attributes than for negative ones in an attribute-to-brand question. In every single case, regardless of the position of the bank's order of recall, negative attribute-to-brand evocations outstrip the positive. While the number of positive attribute-to-brand evocations can be seen as in other banks to diminish with the order of mention, the average number of negative do not. For example, Barclays is evoked for approximately one (0.93) positive attribute when a respondent recalled the bank brand in the first position of unaided recall. When the brand was recalled in the second, third, fourth or fifth position, the likelihood of the brand being evoked for a positive bank attribute decreased to 0.50, 0.44, 0.09 and 0.33 respectively. When the brand was not mentioned in an unaided recall question, it was likely to be evoked only 0.15 times for positively worded bank attributes. However, negatively worded attributes are evoked consistently more than once for Barclays, irrespective of the position. When the bank is mentioned first, second and third, on average it will be evoked 1.1, 0.9 and 1.6 times for negatively worded bank attributes. When the bank is mentioned fourth, fifth, or not at all, it is evoked 1.3, 1.2, and 1.1 times. The bank's ratio of positive/negative attribute-to-brand evocations range from a high of 0.87 in the first position of unaided recall, to 0.6, 0.3, and 0.1 for the second, third and fourth positions. In the fifth position and when the bank is unmentioned in an unaided brand recall question, the ratio repeats the similar pattern of 0.3 and 0.1 positive/ negative evocations.

Models of switching behaviour and brand image

Dichotomous indicator variables for bank loyal customers were created. Bank loyal customers were indicated numerically by a code of 1, 0 indicated all others. Similar variables were created for each recall position. If a bank was recalled first in an unaided recall test of bank brand names, the new first-mention variable took on the value of 1; all other mentions took on the value of 0. This process was repeated for order of mention positions 1, 2 and 3. An additional variable was created to test the effect of not being mentioned. If the bank brand was not recalled at all, the variable took on the value of 1. All recall for the bank brand took on the value of 0.

Table 5.10 includes two parts. The first part represents the raw correlations between bank loyal customers, order of mention and total positive and negative bank attribute-to-brand mentions. The second part of the table uses regression analysis to examine how effective these same independent variables are in predicting bank loyalty.

Correlation analysis

Does bank brand recall imply bank loyalty? Correlation analysis demonstrates a strong association between bank loyal customers and first mention of the bank brand in an unaided recall test. Correlation coefficients between bank loyalty and first position recall are highly significant (0.000) and range from 0.89 and 0.87 for NatWest and HSBC to 0.69 and 0.68 for Barclays and Lloyds. Second and third order mention coefficients are, in all but one instance, negatively associated with bank loyal customers. Third order mention correlation coefficients are generally significant at the 0.05 level while second order coefficients are not. Coefficients for second order mention will nearly pass the 0.10 significance test, however.

Customers not recalling a bank brand at all in an unaided recall test are not likely to be loyal bank customers, though they may be competitor customers or new customers. There is a robust and significant negative association between bank loyal customers and no bank brand mention in an unaided recall test. The correlations run from a high of −0.26 and −0.23 for NatWest and Lloyds, to −0.18 and −0.15 for Barclays and HSBC. Customers who cannot recall the name of the bank brand are therefore likely to be either customers who have switched banks recently, or loyal customers of competing banks. Bank loyalty thus has an additional effect. Loyal customers tend to think of their bank only in the prime recall position and in doing so relegate competing bank brands to lower order and no recall positions.

Customers holding a positive image of the bank brand are less likely to switch banks and are therefore more likely to be loyal customers. This case is clearly supported by the correlations between bank loyal customers for each of the four banks examined and the total number of positive attribute-to-brand evocations. The associations vary from 0.78 for HSBC to 0.61, 0.43 and 0.27 for NatWest, Lloyds and Barclays respectively. The results indicate the more frequently a customer evokes a bank brand for positive attributes in an attribute-to-brand recall question, the more likely the customer is to be a loyal bank customer. This association does not hold for competitor customers, switchers, and/or new bank customers. As one would expect, the total number of negative attribute-to-brand evocations is uncorrelated with bank customer loyalty.

Table 5.10   Regression Models of Bank Loyalty and Order of Mention

Correlation Analysis		Nat West	Lloyds	Barclays	HSBC	Overall Mean
Unaided Brand Recall Order of Mention						
1st Mention		0.865 **	0.675 **	0.685 **	0.885 **	0.778
	Sig. (2-tailed)	0.000	0.000	0.000	0.000	0.000
2nd Mention		-0.135	0.003	-0.153	-0.151	-0.109
	Sig. (2-tailed)	0.167	0.979	0.118	0.123	0.347
3rd Mention		-0.208 *	-0.226 *	-0.191 *	-0.020	-0.161
	Sig. (2-tailed)	0.032	0.020	0.050	0.836	0.235
No Mention		-0.257 **	-0.234 *	-0.184 *	-0.151	-0.207
	Sig. (2-tailed)	0.008	0.016	0.059	0.123	0.052
Attribute-to-Brand Evocations						
Ttl. No. Positive Brand Mentions		0.611 **	0.431 **	0.274 **	0.775 **	0.523
	Sig. (2-tailed)	0.000	0.000	0.004	0.000	0.001
Ttl. No. Negative Brand Mentions		0.017	-0.175	0.038	-0.098	-0.055
	Sig. (2-tailed)	0.863	0.073	0.698	0.320	0.489

N = 106

** Correlation is significant at the .01 level (2-tailed)
* Correlation is significant at the .05 level (2-tailed)

Table 5.10 Regression Models of Bank Loyalty and Order of Mention – *continued*

Regression Analysis	NatWest	Lloyds	Barclays	HSBC	Overall Mean
Unaided Brand Recall Order of Mention					
1st Mention	0.902 *	0.668	0.743	0.766	0.770
2nd Mention	0.094	0.129			0.112
3rd Mention	0.108			0.114	0.111
Attribute-to-Brand Evocations					
Ttl. No. Positive Brand Mentions		0.294		0.156	0.225
Ttl. No. Negative Brand Mentions		−0.212			−0.212
Adjusted R²	0.829	0.683	0.547	0.819	0.720

* Standardised Coefficients (β)

Regression analysis

To lend further support to H2, H2a and H3, regression analysis was conducted on each of the four bank brands studied. Bank loyalty became the dependent variable in a step-wise regression equation in which the first three positions of recall and the total number of positive and negative attribute-to-brand mentions functioned as the independent variables.

Cohen (1966) demonstrates that higher levels of recall are associated with more favourable attitudes toward the brand. This was indeed demonstrated to be the case with bank loyal customers, but with some exceptions. High levels of unaided recall do not preclude unfavourable attitudes. Unfavourable attitudes may exist with high levels of bank brand recall. They possibly will also co-exist with favourable attitudes and might even be important in defining a given bank brand's loyal customer base. This does not suggest customers are indifferent to the brand. To the contrary, it implies customers are willing to accept and trade off some of the brand's negative attributes in favour of other positive attributes deemed more important. Just as Zeithaml, Berry and Parasuraman (1993) noted, customers' service expectations from a bank are characterised by a range of levels – a zone of tolerance representing the difference between the ideal level of service from the bank and that which is considered adequate.

The case for a zone of tolerance whereby loyal bank customers are willing to tolerate negative bank attributes as long as they co-exist beside positive attributes can be seen in the regression model for Lloyds. While the regression demonstrates first mention order of recall ($\beta = 0.67$) and total number of positive attribute-to-brand evocations ($\beta = 0.29$) for Lloyds to be important coefficients in determining customer loyalty, the same may be observed for negative attribute-to-brand evocations ($\beta = -0.21$).

Chi-squared automatic interaction detection (CHAID)

CHAID (Chi-squared automatic interaction detection) is a statistical procedure used to classify and categorise data for segmentation purposes. The procedure takes on the properties of decision tree with a root node and branches. Each split or branch is determined by a set of decision rules for identifying groups and subgroups. CHAID uses chi-squared statistics to identify the optimal split. The target or dependent variable as well as the independent variables, can be nominal, ordinal, interval or ratio in nature.

CHAID analysis was conducted on each of the four bank brands. The target or dependent variable was the nominal customer portfolio or switching behaviour variable previously utilised in this section. The independent variables used for defining the splits and categorising groups and subgroups were the previously used bank brand position of unaided recall variables (dichotomous nominal scale) and the positive and negative

132

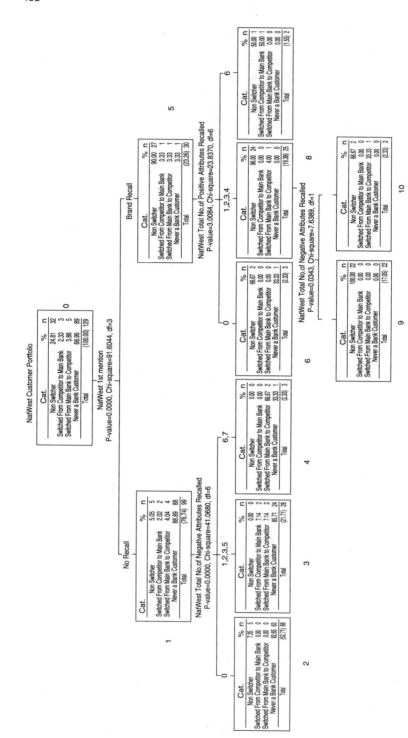

Figure 5.5 Nat West CHAID Model of Switching Behaviour

attribute-to-brand summary variables (ratio or continuous). Similar model results were achieved for each bank. Because it represents the largest segment of the study (27%) NatWest's is the only model presented.

The preceding Figure 5.5 titled "NatWest CHAID Model of Switching Behaviour" demonstrates additional support for H2a and H3. First position unaided recall emerges as the primary node in segmenting customer-switching behaviour. Ninety percent of non-switching bank customers recall NatWest first when asked an unaided brand awareness question. Those persons who have no unaided recall are likely to have never been a customer of NatWest (88.89%), or switched away from the bank (4%). Ninety-six percent of subjects who have recall of the bank and who evoke the brand between one and four times in a positive attribute-to-brand recall question are loyal customers. If they evoke the brand five times or more, they are as likely to be a new customer (50%) as a loyal one (50%).

First order mention and recall of the brand in positive attribute-to-brand recall questions do not preclude the brand from being evoked by loyal customers for negatively worded attributes. Approximately two-thirds (67%) of the subjects who evoke the NatWest brand 3–4 times for negatively worded attributes are loyal customers who also evoke the brand for positively worded bank brand attributes. These same loyal customers are also likely to recall the bank first in an unaided brand awareness recall question.

Table 5.11 refers back to preceding figures and examines the NatWest model in more detail. The table looks in detail at those nodes that contain the highest probability of non-switching behaviour amongst the respondents. Nodes are sorted by gain score from highest to lowest for non-switching behaviour. Node 9 (refer to figure and table) contains 22 non-switchers (loyal) out of the 22 cases in the node – a response rate (gain%) of 100 percent. Subjects in this node are likely to evoke NatWest for both positively and negatively worded attribute-to-brand recall questions. The gain score for node 9 equals the percentage of loyal customers for the node. The index score of 403 percent shows the proportion of non-switchers (loyal customers) for this node is over four times the response rate for the overall sample. Nodes 6 and 10 have response rates of 67 percent and index scores of 269. Node 9 represents 17 percent of the entire sample but comprises 69 percent of loyal customers.

Results – Hypothesis 4

The results support the fourth hypothesis. Customers highly committed in the choice of his or her financial services institution are more likely to engage in switching actions. Two statements in particular were tested as indicators for commitment and/or involvement. Respondents were specifically asked to agree or disagree with the statements 1) "I take the choice of a bank very seriously" and 2) "I choose my bank very carefully."

Table 5.11 Gain Summary of Non Switching Behaviour
Target variable: *NatWest Customer Portfolio*

			Node-by-Node			
Node	Node: n	Node: %	Resp: n	Resp: %	Gain (%)	Index (%)
8.00	22.00	17.05	22.00	68.75	100.00	403.13
6.00	3.00	2.33	2.00	6.25	66.67	268.75
9.00	3.00	2.33	2.00	6.25	66.67	268.75
10.00	2.00	1.55	1.00	3.13	50.00	201.56
2.00	68.00	52.71	5.00	15.63	7.35	29.64
3.00	28.00	21.71	0.00	0.00	0.00	0.00
4.00	3.00	2.33	0.00	0.00	0.00	0.00

		Cumulative			
Node: n	Node: %	Resp: n	Resp: %	Gain (%)	Index (%)
22.00	17.05	22.00	68.75	100.00	403.13
25.00	19.38	24.00	75.00	96.00	387.00
28.00	21.71	26.00	81.25	92.86	374.33
30.00	23.26	27.00	84.38	90.00	362.81
98.00	75.97	32.00	100.00	32.65	131.63
126.00	97.67	32.00	100.00	25.40	102.38
129.00	100.00	32.00	100.00	24.81	100.00

An additional five statements were tested and are listed in the following table.

Table 5.12 illustrates that on average switchers typically choose either of these two statements to summarise their commitment in the choice of financial services institutions. Fifty-four percent of the respondents who agree with this statement are typically loyal. The single largest segment of customers who switch (46%) is found to agree with this statement. The same point can be further demonstrated by observing loyal bank cus-

Table 5.12 Attitude and Loyalty

Attitude towards choosing a bank	% Loyal	N
I choose my bank very carefully	54%	26
I take the choice of a bank very seriously	58%	26
It was important for my choice that if "felt" right	81%	36
I do not feel involved in choosing a bank	84%	19
Personally, the choice of a bank is not relevant for me	86%	7
I do not care which bank I choose	90%	10
I am not at all concerned about which bank I choose	100%	5
$F = 2.481$ $df\ 6$ Sig. 0.027		129

tomers. In examining non-switching behaviour, it is evident a much larger percentage (81%) of loyal customers tend to agree with the statement that the bank choice "felt right." Bank loyal customers also tend to be more lackadaisical and apathetic about their choice of a financial institution than are customers who engage in switching behaviour. Non-switching bank customers are more likely to state they do not feel "involved in choosing a bank," they "do not care" which bank they choose, and that they are "not at all concerned" about bank choice.

Results – Hypothesis 4a

Are bank customers with multiple current accounts across various financial institutions more likely to engage in switching behaviour? The data support H4a. The table titled "Current Accounts and Switching Behaviour" examines this issue in detail.

Bank loyal customers tend on average to maintain 1.4 current accounts over a two to four year period. Approximately eighty-eight percent (88%) maintain only one account over a two-year period, while 78 percent will do so over a four-year period. This number decreases substantially amongst customers who engaged in switching behaviour over the same periods. Customers who switched banks will maintain 2.09 and 1.86 current accounts respectively over a two-year and four-year period. More than two-thirds of customers engaging in switching behaviour maintain three accounts over a two-year period. This number decreases slightly to 60 per-cent over a four-year period.

Table 5.13 reveals bank loyalty is negatively correlated to the number of current accounts a customer maintains. The relationship is significant and robust both for customers who have been loyal for a two-year and four-year period. The coefficient between a bank customer loyal for two-years (–0.32) is as expected slightly larger than the coefficient for a four-year period (–0.24). The table demonstrates further an age-old axiom in marketing – past behaviour is highly predictive of future behaviour. The correlation between bank loyalty over a four-year period and bank loyalty over a two-year period is 0.76.

Results – Hypothesis 5

Bank loyalty tends to be a persistent behaviour. Bank loyal customers are even willing to tolerate some negative aspects of the institution in exchange for some overpowering positive attributes. Nevertheless, main-taining multiple accounts with several institutions tends to influence switching behaviour. This being the case, what can financial institutions do to decrease switching behaviour amongst these customers? Can high levels of satisfaction with the bank offset the likelihood the behaviour will occur?

Table 5.13 Current Accounts and Switching Behaviour

		Mean No. of Current Accounts	
		2 Years	4 Years
Switched Banks		2.09	1.86
Bank Loyal		1.42	1.41
	F	13.97	7.81
df = 1	*Sig.*	0.00	0.01

	Percentage Loyal Varying by No. of Current Accounts		
No. Current Accounts	2 Years	4 Years	N
1	87.80%	78.05%	82
2	82.76%	72.41%	29
3	66.70%	60.00%	15
4	0.00%	0.00%	2
5	0.00%	0.00%	1
df 4 F	5.05	2.727	129
Sig.	0.001	0.032	

Subjects in the study were asked to rate their level of satisfaction with four aspects of the bank with which they maintained their main account. The items rated by respondents were price-performance, reliability of the bank's administration, friendliness of administrative personnel, and friendliness of the bank's advisors. The question used a five-point ordinal rating scale where 5 represented "very satisfied" and 1 represented "very unsatisfied."

Regression analysis was used to test the hypothesis that satisfaction affects bank loyalty. Two dichotomous nominal variables were created for bank loyalty. One variable represented bank loyalty over a two-year period. The other represented the same behaviour over a four-year period. If a subject had not switched banks within two years, the two-year variable took on the value of 1 (loyal, non-switcher), otherwise it took on the value of 0 (not loyal, switched banks). This coding scheme was repeated for bank switching behaviour over the four-year period. The previously listed satisfaction variables consequently became the independent variables in a stepwise regression equation in which the dependent variables alternated between bank loyalty over two and four year periods.

Table 5.14 shows customer satisfaction with the reliability of bank administration to have a major influence on bank loyalty. This is in fact the case for bank loyalty over both a two-year and four-year period of time. Both models are highly predictive and display adjusted R^2s of 0.79 and 0.69 respectively for two-year and four-year bank loyalty.

Table 5.14 Regression Analysis of Satisfaction Variables and Bank Loyalty

Satisfaction with:
Model Summary | **Bank Loyal for 2 Years**

Variables Included	B	SE	β	t	Sig.	R	R²	Adj. R²
Reliability of Administration	0.20	0.01	0.89	21.91	0.00	0.89	0.79	0.79
Variables Excluded								
Price-Performance Ratio			−0.11	−0.62	0.54			
Friendliness of Administrative Personnel			0.09	0.30	0.77			
Friendliness of Advisers			−0.07	−0.32	0.75			
Anova:	df	1	F	480.05	Sig.	0.00	Mean²	83.69

Model Summary | **Bank Loyal for 4 Years**

Variables Included	B	SE	β	t	Sig.	R	R²	Adj. R²
Reliability of Administration	0.18	0.01	0.83	16.95	0.00	0.83	0.69	0.69
Variables Excluded								
Price-Performance Ratio			−0.35	−1.65	0.10			
Friendliness of Administrative Personnel			−0.34	−0.98	0.33			
Friendliness of Advisers			−0.38	−1.38	0.17			
Anova:	df	1	F	287.33	Sig.	0.00	Mean²	65.03

The model includes the independent variables eliminated by the stepwise regression. Excluded from the equation for non-significance are price-performance and friendliness of administrative personnel and advisors. When it comes to loyal customers' money, no amount of friendliness by bank staff can overcome administrative errors. The model demonstrates if a bank is to maintain loyal customers, there is no substitute for getting the details right one hundred percent of the time.

Results – Hypothesis 6

Generally, loyal bank customers expect more problems to be associated with switching financial services institutions than do customers who have switched banks. Respondents who switched during a two- to four-year period indicated they experienced only marginal problems associated with switching. Hypothesis 6 is supported. Perceived switching costs do have an effect on a customer's penchant to move from one financial institution to another.

Table 5.15 illustrates the multiple-response frequencies for four-year bank loyal customers to a question on perceived switching cost. Ease of transfer of direct debits and standing orders comprises a third of all the responses and the majority (51.1%) of the cases. Related to ease of transfer are the perceived switching costs associated with the accuracy of those transfers – 17 percent of the responses and 26.6 percent of the cases.

Table 5.15   Perceived Switching Costs

Perceived Switching Costs	Count	% of Responses	% of Cases
Don't Know	25	17%	26.6%
Ease of Transfer of Direct Debits and Standing Orders	48	33%	51.1%
Accuracy of Transfer of All Payments Direct Debits, Standing Orders	25	17%	26.6%
Slow Initial Start-Up Service	3	2%	3.2%
Waiting Until Check Books Printed and Bank Cards Issued	12	8%	12.8%
Not Having a Cash Card During the Transition Period	2	1%	2.1%
Hassle Generally	7	5%	7.4%
Too Time Consuming	12	8%	12.8%
Administrative Charges	2	1%	2.1%
Loss of Established Relationship With the Bank Staff	11	7%	11.7%

N Responses = 147	100%	
N Cases = 94		

Combined, the issues of ease and accuracy of transfer of direct debits and standing orders comprise half of the perceived costs associated with switching financial institutions in more than three-fourths (78%) of all the cases where loyal bank customers gave answers to the questions.

CHAID analysis

The statistical technique of chi-squared automatic interaction detection (CHAID) previously utilised in testing hypotheses 2a and 3 was again applied to model the perceived switching costs associated with changing financial institutions. Bank loyalty over a four-year period of time was used once more as the target or dependent variable in the analysis. Dichotomous nominal variables were created for each categorical response previously presented in table of multiple-response frequencies of perceived switching costs. The new series of independent nominal variables were coded 0 (not mentioned) and 1 (mentioned as a perceived switching cost) for use in modelling.

Yet again, the analysis (Figure 5.6) demonstrates the perceived switching costs associated with ease of transfer of direct debits and standing orders to be a driving concern amongst bank loyal customers. The first branch of the following model illustrates this point plainly. Forty-one bank loyal customers comprise 100 percent of the second node. Node 2 represents those persons who perceive ease of transfer of direct debits and standing orders to be a major impediment to switching banks. If loyal customers do not mention this switching cost, then loss of an established relationship with bank staff will be. And for those loyal customers who do not mention this cost, 100 percent will mention not having a cash card during the transition period as a obstacle to switching behaviour.

Results – Hypothesis 7

As they become more comfortable with Internet technology, will customers' perceptions of banking evolve into one of costless switching? Will PC banking usher in a barrier-less era where changing banks is as easy as clicking a mouse? Results of Hypothesis 7 indicate this is likely to be the case.

If perceived risk, costly exit-barriers, and fewer alternatives increase calculative commitment amongst bank customers, then a feeling of security and comfort with Internet technology is crucial if customers are to take up competing financial services' offerings. Willingness to conduct purchases routinely over the Internet can indicate how comfortable a consumer is with the technology. So they may avoid the unnecessary risk associated with the Internet, unfamiliar, inexperienced, and non-users are likely to remain with their previously chosen bank, thereby foreclosing other

140

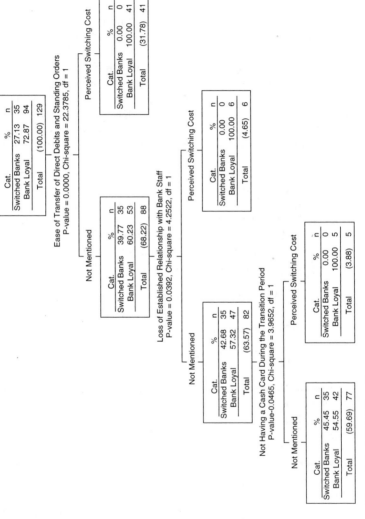

Figure 5.6 CHAID Results

alternatives and increasing calculative commitment. Thus, those consumers who regularly purchase a variety of items over the Internet are likely to associate lower exit barriers and less risk with the technology than those who do so infrequently and/or not at all. Because of this, they are more likely to engage in bank switching behaviour.

Clues to the willingness of Internet bank customers to engage in switching behaviour and take up competing financial services' offerings can be found in the patterns of current account ownership.

Respondents who own an Internet bank account will on average maintain 3.08 other financial services accounts with multiple institutions while non-owners will keep 2.54. Such tendencies demonstrate at the outset that Internet bank account holders have different perceptions of the risk associated with changing banks than do non-holders. This being the case, it can be posited that the perceptions of risk associated with using the Internet for routine transactions as well as attitudes towards Internet technology in general are likely significantly different between the two groups – holders of Internet bank accounts and non-holders.

Internet usage behaviour

Subjects were asked to report on the items purchased via the Internet over a two-year period of time. As demonstrated in (Table 5.16) extracted from the survey questionnaire, items ranged from computer hardware and software to books, CD's, legal and insurance services and real estate.

A summary variable labeled, "Total No. Items Purchased Via Internet," was created from this question. The variable represents the total number of different items purchased by a subject during the course of two years.

Table 5.16   Internet Purchases

	N	Percent		N	Percent
Computer Hardware	9	7%	Clothing, Shoes	4	3%
Computer Software	20	16%	Wine	6	5%
Video, Movies	2	2%	Generic Grocery Items	2	2%
Music, CDs, Tapes	33	26%	Branded Grocery Items	2	2%
Books	54	42%	Jewelry	0	0%
Magazines, Newspapers	9	7%	Flowers	11	9%
Concerts, Plays	12	9%	Stock Market Quotes	9	7%
Travel Arrangements	36	28%	Investment Choices (stocks)	14	11%
Home Electronics	5	4%	Legal Services	0	0%
Autos, Motorcycles	1	1%	Insurance Services	4	3%
Recreational Equipment	3	2%	Real Estate	7	5%

Total No. of Respondents: 129

The findings in Table 5.17 highlight the relation between this summary variable and the dichotomous nominal variables for bank loyalty over a two-and four-year period of time and ownership of an Internet bank account – also a dichotomous variable where 1 represents ownership of an account and 0 represents no ownership.

Table 5.17 Internet Usage and Bank Loyalty

Do You Have An Internet Bank Account	Pearson Correlation Sig. (2-tailed) N
Bank Loyal for 2 Years	Pearson Correlation Sig. (2-tailed) N
Bank Loyal for 4 Years	Pearson Correlation Sig. (2-tailed) N

** Correlation is significant at the 0.01 level (2-tailed)
* Correlation is significant at the 0.05 level (2-tailed)

Clearly the more items purchased via the Internet during a two-year period, the more comfortable the consumer is with conducting financial transactions utilising the technology. The correlation coefficient of 0.59 between items purchased and the ownership of an Internet bank account is significant at the 0.000 level. Rising levels of Internet purchases translate into higher probabilities of Internet bank account ownership.

The findings in Table 5.18 are the proportions of respondents maintaining an Internet bank account varying by quartiles of item purchase. Examination of persons who have made no (0) Internet purchase of any sort reveals that less than four percent (0.04) are likely to have an Internet bank account. Purchase of at least one item over the past twenty-four months more than triples the likelihood of account ownership to 11 percent. Respondents who have purchased five or more items over the two-year period are 5.3 times more likely to own an Internet account than those who have made at least one purchase. The proportion of 57 percent Internet account ownership for this group makes them 16 times more likely to be account owners than those persons who have made no purchases whatsoever. The relationship between the number of items purchased over the Internet during a two-year period of time and Internet bank account ownership is direct and significant ($F = 19.048$; $p < .000$; adjusted $R^2 = .30$).

If conducting routine purchases over the Internet makes a consumer more likely to engage in financial transactions and account ownership,

Table 5.18 Internet Bank Accounts Varying by Internet Item Purchase Frequency

Dependent Variable: Do You Have An Internet Bank Account

Quartiles of Total Items Purchase Over Internet	Mean	Std. Deviation	N
0 Items Purchased	.0364	.1889	55
1 Item	.1111	.3234	18
2–5 Items	.1111	.3203	27
5+ Items Purchased	.5862	.5012	29
Total	.1860	.3907	129

do either or both of these activities tend to make them more or less likely to engage in bank switching behaviour? Data tends to support the fact that respondents who have purchased the largest number of items over the Internet are likely to engage more frequently in switching behaviour. The association between the number of purchases made with two- and four-year bank brand loyalty is negative and direct. The correlation coefficients as demonstrated in the previous table are –0.199 and –0.222 respectively. The table of correlations also reveals consumers with internet bank accounts are less likely to be loyal customers over both two- and four-year periods of time. Once again, this relationship is negative, direct and significant. Variables for two-year and four-year bank loyalty display coefficients of –0.194 and -0.201 respectively with Internet account ownership.

The proportion of bank-loyal customers can be seen to diminish significantly with ownership of an Internet bank account. Table 5.19 shows that 86 percent of all customers with no Internet bank account have not engaged in switching behaviour during a two year period of time. This compares to 67 percent for customers with an Internet account. Similar results can be found for bank loyalty and switching behaviour over a four-year period of time, with non-Internet account owners demonstrating a proportion of 77 percent loyal compared with 54 percent for owners (F = 5.35; p < .0.022).

Attitudes toward internet technology

Not all customers with Internet bank accounts engage in switching behaviour. Some customers take up the electronic offerings of the bank with which they maintain their main account, while others switched – either before their main bank could make the offer, or notwithstanding it. In either case, a question about attitudinal differences between the groups arises. Are holders of Internet bank accounts who switched banks within the past two years different in their attitudes towards the technology than those customers who have not switched? Do customers who switch feel

Table 5.19 Bank Loyal Past 2 Years

Proportion of Loyal Customers

Dependent Variable: Bank Loyal for 2 Years

Do You Have An Internet Bank Accoun	Mean	Std. Deviation	N
No Internet Bank Account	.8571	.3516	105
Internet Bank Account	.6667	.4815	24
Total	.8217	.3843	129

Tests of Between-Subjects Effects

Dependent Variable: Bank Loyal for 2 Years

Source	Type III Sum of Squares	df	Mean Square	F	Sig.
Corrected Model	.709[a]	1	.709	4.948	.028
Intercept	45.360	1	45.360	316.688	.000
Internet Account	.709	1	.709	4.948	.028
Error	18.190	127	.143		
Total	106.000	129			
Corrected Total	18.899	128			

[a] R Squared = .038 (Adjusted R Squared = .030)

more secure with the technology than non-switchers? As a result, do they feel more comfortable and in control with their new bank?

Respondents with bank accounts permitting online Internet access were asked a series of questions concerning their perceptions and attitudes towards the bank they access, the Internet and the world-wide-web (www) in general. Subjects were asked to use a five-point Likert scale to indicate whether they agreed with the statements or not. The highest level of agreement was coded 5 for "strongly agree" and the lowest 1 for "strongly disagree". Table 5.20 lists the means of responses from questions asked of the 24 subjects with bank accounts that allowed online Internet access.

Customers with online Internet accessible accounts who have switched banks in the past four years differ significantly from non-switcher account holders in several respects. Firstly, they are more likely to agree they are more comfortable recommending their current financial institution to friends and family – a mean of 4.00 compared to 3.08 for loyal customers. No doubt this is due in large part to the fact they tend to have a more positive feeling towards the bank (4.2) and perceive it offers increased value for money (4.1). Not only are they more apt than their non-switching counterparts to report increased usage of their bank's services and products (means of 4.1 versus 2.9) but they are more aware of competitor's online bank service offerings. Interestingly, respondents with Internet

Table 5.20 Internet Banking Attitudinal Questions

Attitude	Bank Loyal for 4 Years				
	Switched	Loyal	Overall	F	Sig.
I use their services and products more often	4.09	2.92	3.51	6.92	0.02
My number of transactions has increased	2.54	1.85	2.20	2.43	0.13
I feel more comfortable about recommending my bank to friends and family	4.00	3.08	3.54	7.49	0.01
I perceive that my bank offers increased value for my money	4.09	3.00	3.55	6.81	0.02
I have a much more positive feeling towards my bank	4.18	3.31	3.75	8.07	0.01
I am less willing to switch to another bank with online access	3.90	2.85	3.38	6.55	0.02
I am now more aware of what kind of online banking services other banks are offering	3.36	2.69	3.03	3.41	0.08
I make use of almost all their online banking services	3.00	2.46	2.73	1.98	0.17
The branch as a distribution channel gets for me less and less attractive	4.36	4.00	4.18	0.77	0.39
I am afraid of information security problems	2.73	2.69	2.71	0.01	0.95
I would do more transactions via the Internet if there was no information security problem	3.64	2.92	3.28	2.12	0.16
I am willing to provide credit card and purchase information through WWW and Email	3.00	3.61	3.31	1.60	0.22
I am willing to provide credit card and purchase information that is encrypted	4.64	3.92	4.28	4.95	0.04

1 Strongly Disagree; 2 Disagree; 3 Neither; 4 Agree; 5 Strongly Agree

accessible bank accounts who have changed banks in the past four years indicate they are less willing to switch to another bank with online account access – means of 3.9 and 2.9, respectively. Though the tendency to engage in switching behaviour may be greater for those consumers who have Internet accessible bank accounts than those who do not, it is clear resultant levels of satisfaction and feelings of perceived value for money derived from the account contribute to an increased sense of brand loyalty for the online product.

Classification and regression tree analysis (C&RT) was conducted on the thirteen variables represented by the questions delineated in the previous table. Like CHAID analysis, the target (dependent variable) as well as the independent variables can be nominal, ordinal or continuous in nature. However, unlike CHAID analysis that can generate non-binary trees, C&RT analysis generates binary trees in which each split results in precisely two branches or child nodes. This particular regression method seeks to minimise impurity measures. The resulting model is to a large extent accurate (87%) at generating predictions for both switching and non-switching bank customers with online Internet access to their main accounts. Table 5.21 demonstrates a risk estimate of 0.13 associated with the classifications of switching and bank loyal customers. The standard error is half (0.07) the risk estimate. Overall, the model is slightly better at predicting and classifying loyal customers than customers who switched banks – 92 percent versus 83 percent, respectively. Nevertheless, the results are particularly revealing about attitudes and perceptions held by customers who switched banks in particular and loyal customers in general.

The following classification and regression tree (Figure 5.4) demonstrates 91 percent of respondents (10 out of 11) with Internet accessible bank accounts who switched banks within the past four years feel more comfortable about recommending the bank with whom they have the account to

Table 5.21 Misclassification Matrix

Predicted Category	Actual Category			Percent Correct
	Switched Banks	Bank Loyal	Total	
Switched Banks	10	2	12	83.3%
Bank Loyal	1	11	12	91.7%
Total	11	13	24	87.5%
	Resubstitution			
Risk Estimate	0.1250			
SE of Risk Estimate	0.0675			

friends and family. Persons stating they are more comfortable are over-whelmingly (67%) switchers. Willingness to provide credit card information and purchase information through the world-wide-web and e-mail is a critical variable in the equation with 55 percent of switchers agreeing to the statement. Not only are Internet account customers who have switched banks within the past four years likely to use the banks services and products more often (80%), but also they are more willing to provide encrypted credit card and purchase information than non-switching customers (67% compared to 33%).

Support for H7a can be seen in an examination of bank loyal customers. The case that account holders who switched are more comfortable with the technology than non-switching loyal customers is demonstrated in the classification and regression tree. Bank loyal customers may comprise the larger segment of subjects with online accessible accounts, but they are nearly nine times (89%) more likely to disagree with the statement they feel more comfortable about recommending the bank than customers who switched banks (11%). They are less likely to increase services and products usage as a result of the account (67%), less enthusiastic about providing credit card and purchase information via the web (45%), and totally unwilling (100%) to provide encrypted credit card and purchase information through the electronic medium.

Discussion

The most noteworth aspect of financial services switching behaviour in the U.K. is that the majority of account movements have been from market leaders to market innovators like First Direct and Citibank. Both institutions offer new electronic media as primary benefits for their banking customers. First Direct offers "telebanking" as its primary incentive. Along with higher rates of interest, Citibank offers global reach and more customer access to current account funds through the Internet and online banking. Respondents who switched to Citibank are primarily new professional residents in the U.K. who moved for work. It is important to observe that with the move came a change of banks – most likely to accommodate pay. Moreover, in the changeover these respondents chose a new entrant into the U.K. market – an American bank. This suggests professionals who travel and consider a potential work-related move likely. In the future, online access and global reach are likely to be significant factors in choice behaviour amongst these consumers and American banks are currently leaders in this technology and marketing.

Previous research proves brands that are mentioned in second or third place in unaided brand recall questions tend to be "switch-to" brands. Cohen (1966) first introduced this proposition in his "level-of-consciousness" theory. Research reported herein provides added support for the theory that unaided brand recall can be an indicator of past or future switching behaviour. Moreover, expansion of this theory demonstrates other positions of unaided brand recall should not be overlooked for their information content when it comes to switching behaviour. Position of unaided bank brand recall will vary significantly between loyal (non-switcher) customers and those customers who have never been a bank customer and/or who have switched either to or from their main bank. Customers switching from a competitor bank to their current main bank (e.g., a Barclays customer who switched to NatWest) display a profile similar to loyal, non-switching customers. These customers are distinct however from the standpoint they are equally likely to recall the present main bank brand across first, second, and third positions. This certainly reveals the strength of the enduring brand recall of the bank from which they switched. In an unaided recall question of bank brands, defector bank customers – those customers who switched away from their main bank to a competitor (e.g., a NatWest customer who went to Barclays) are likely to not recall the brand at all. If the brand is recalled, it is most often recalled in one of the lower order of mention positions. This reveals that the customer who has switched banks de-prioritises the brand; filing it in long-term memory along with a likely nexus of negative brand attributes associations.

The results suggest that there is a very high likelihood that subjects who recall the bank brand in first position are either long time loyal customers or customers who have most recently switched to the bank. Lower order positions of recall are highly associated both with respondents who have never been a customer of the bank and turncoat customers switching from the bank.

Evidence here buttresses the fact that a positive brand image is associated with bank brand loyalty. In unaided attribute-to-brand recall questions, non-switching, loyal customers primarily evoke their own main bank or financial services institution when positive brand attributes are mentioned. Customers who have recently switched from a competitor to their current main bank are likely to evoke their new bank brand for positive attributes 2–3 times more often than loyal customers. The antithesis holds true for customers who have switched away from their main bank to a competitor. These customers are approximately 2–4 times more likely than loyal customers to evoke their previous bank brand when negative bank brand attributes are mentioned.

Non-switching bank customers demonstrate a willingness to remain loyal even though they may evoke their current bank brand for negatively worded bank attributes. Unfavourable attitudes may exist with high levels of bank brand recall. They possibly will also co-exist with favourable attitudes and might even be important in defining a given bank brand's loyal customer base. This does not suggest customers are indifferent to the brand but suggests customers are motivated by the brand's positive attributes to remain (H3). Because of this they are less likely to engage in switching behaviour.

High levels of unaided recall do not preclude unfavourable attitudes. To the contrary, it implies customers are willing to accept and trade off some of the brand's negative attributes in favour of other positive attributes deemed more important. A *zone of tolerance* (H2a) whereby customers accept certain shortfalls in the bank's expected delivery of services can be observed to varying degrees in each of the four banks. Just as Zeithaml and Parasuraman (1993) noted, customers' service expectations from a bank are characterised by a range of levels – a *zone of tolerance* representing the difference between the ideal level of service from the bank and that which is considered adequate.

The evidence connects higher positions of unaided brand recall with a higher probability the bank brand will be evoked for a positive bank attribute in an attribute-to-brand question. Lower orders of brand mention are associated with higher levels of negative bank attribute-to-brand evocations. If a bank has a low level of brand awareness or is unmentioned in an unaided brand recall question it is likely the brand will pop up later in a negatively worded attribute-to-brand question.

Correlation results demonstrate a strong association between bank loyal customers and first mention of the bank brand in an unaided recall test – thus bank brand recall does imply bank loyalty. Customers who do not recall a bank brand at all in an unaided recall test are not likely to be loyal bank customers, though they may be competitor customers or new customers. There is a robust and significant negative association between bank loyal customers and no bank brand mention in an unaided recall test. Customers who cannot recall the name of the bank brand are therefore likely to be either customers who have switched banks recently, or loyal customers of competing banks. Bank loyalty thus has an additional effect. Loyal customers tend to think of their bank only in the prime recall position and in doing so relegate competing bank brands to lower order and no recall positions.

Customers who hold a positive image of the bank brand are less likely to switch banks and are therefore more likely to be loyal customers. The results indicate the more frequently a customer evokes a bank brand for positive attributes in an attribute-to-brand recall question, the more likely the customer is to be a loyal bank customer. This association does not hold for competitor customers, switchers, and/or new bank customers. As one would expect, the total number of negative attribute-to-brand evocations is uncorrelated with bank customer loyalty.

Customers highly committed in the choice of financial services institutions are more likely to engage in switching actions. Bank loyal customers also tend to be more lackadaisical and apathetic about their choice of a financial institution than are customers who engage in switching behaviour. Non-switching bank customers are more likely to state they do not feel "involved in choosing a bank," they "do not care" which bank they choose, and that they are "not at all concerned" about bank choice.

Customers with multiple current accounts across various financial institutions are more likely to engage in switching behaviour. Bank loyal customers tend on average to maintain 1.41 to 1.42 current accounts over a two to four year period. Approximately eighty-eight percent (87.80%) maintain only one account over a two-year period, while seventy-eight (78.05%) will do so over a four-year period. This number decreases substantially amongst customers who engaged in switching behaviour over the same periods. Customers who switched banks will maintain 2.1 and 1.9 current accounts respectively over a two-year and four-year period. Two-thirds of customers who engaged in switching behaviour will maintain three accounts over a two-year period. This number decreases slightly to 60 percent over a four-year period. Bank loyalty is negatively correlated to the number of current accounts a customer maintains. The relationship is significant and robust both for customers who have been loyal for a two-year and four-year period.

Bank loyalty tends to be a persistent behaviour. Bank loyal customers are even willing to tolerate some negative aspects of the institution in exchange for some overpowering positive attributes. Nevertheless, maintaining multiple accounts with several institutions tends to influence switching behaviour. Customer satisfaction with the reliability of bank administration was shown to have a major influence on bank loyalty. This is in fact the case for bank loyalty over both a two-year and four-year period of time. When it comes to loyal customers' money, no amount of friendliness by bank staff can overcome administrative errors. The model demonstrates that if a bank is to maintain loyal customers, there is no substitute for getting the details right one hundred percent of the time.

Generally, loyal bank customers expect more problems to relate with switching financial services institutions than do customers who have switched banks. Respondents who switched during a two- to four-year period indicated they experienced only marginal problems associated with switching. Perceived switching costs do have an effect on a customer's penchant to move from one financial institution to another.

As they become more comfortable with Internet technology, customers' perceptions of banking evolve to include the concept of costless switching. Internet and PC banking will in no small sense usher in a barrier-less era where changing banks is as easy as clicking a mouse. If perceived risk, costly exit-barriers, and fewer alternatives increase calculative commitment amongst bank customers, then a feeling of security and comfort with Internet technology and the bank's technology is crucial in the future if customers are to take up competing financial services' offerings.

Willingness to conduct purchases routinely over the Internet can indicate as well as influence the level of comfort a consumer has with the technology. So they may avoid the unnecessary risk associated with the Internet, unfamiliar, inexperienced, and non-users are likely to remain with their previously chosen bank, thereby foreclosing other alternatives and increasing calculative commitment. Consequently, those consumers who regularly purchase a variety of items over the Internet are likely to associate lower exit barriers and less risk with the technology than those who do so infrequently and/or not at all. Because of this, they are more likely to engage in bank switching behaviour. Data tends to support the fact that respondents who have purchased the largest number of items over the Internet are likely to engage more frequently in switching behaviour. The proportion of bank-loyal customers can be seen to diminish significantly with ownership of an Internet bank account.

Internet bank account holders tend to maintain multiple accounts with multiple financial services institutions. Such tendencies demonstrate at the outset that Internet bank account holders have different perceptions of the risk associated with changing banks than do non-holders. This being the case, it can be posited that the perceptions of risk associated with using the Internet for routine transactions as well as attitudes towards Internet technology in general are significantly different between holders of Internet bank accounts and non-holders.

Not all customers with Internet bank accounts engage in switching behaviour. Some customers take up the electronic offerings of the bank with which they maintain their main account, while others switched – either before their main bank can make the offer, or notwithstanding it. In either case, a question about attitudinal differences between the groups arises.

Customers with online Internet accessible accounts who have switched banks in the past four years are more likely to agree they are more comfortable recommending their current financial institution to friends and family. This is due in large part to the fact they tend to have a more positive feeling towards the bank and perceive it offers increased value for money. Not only are they more apt than their non-switching counterparts to report increased usage of their bank's services and products but they are more aware of competitor's online bank service offerings.

Finally, respondents with Internet accessible bank accounts who have changed banks in the past four years indicate they are less willing to switch to another bank with online account access. Though the tendency to engage in switching behaviour may be greater for those consumers who have Internet accessible bank accounts than those who do not, resultant levels of satisfaction and feelings of perceived value for money derived from the account contribute to an increased sense of brand loyalty for the online product.

References

Aaker, D. A. *Managing Brand Equity. Capitalizing on the Value of a Brand Name*, New York: The Free Press, 1991.

Abela, A. S., Jr. "Current Research: Value Exchange: The secret of building customer relationships on line," *The McKinsey Quarterly*, 2 (1997).

Adolf, R., Grant-Thompson, S., Harrington, W. and Singer, M. "Current Research: What leading banks are learning about big databases and marketing," *The McKinsey Quarterly*, 3 (1997).

Ajzen, I. 'Form Intentions to Actions: A Theory of Planned Behaviour," in Kuhl, J., Beckmann, J., *Action Control: From Cognition to Behaviour*, Heidelberg, 1985.

Alpert, F. H. and Kamins, M. A. "An Empirical Investigation of Consumer Memory, Attitude, and Perceptions Toward Pioneer and Follower Brands," *Journal of Marketing*, 59 (1995): 34–45.

Anderson, E., Fornell, C. and Lehmann, D. "Customer Satisfaction, Market Share and Profitability: Findings from Sweden," *Journal of Marketing*, 58 (July 1994).

Axelrod, J. N. "Attitude Measures That Predict Purchase," *Journal of Advertising Research*, 8, 1 (1968): 3–17.

Bearden, W. and Teel, J. "Selected Determinants of Consumer Satisfaction and Complaint Reports," *Journal of Marketing Research*, 10 (1983).

Beatty S. E., Homer, P. and Kahle, L. R. "The involvement-commitment model: Theory and implications," *Journal of Business Research*, 16, 2 (March 1988): 149–167.

Bell, D. E. "Regret in decision making under uncertainty," *Operations Research*, 30, 1982.

Berger, A. et al. "Subjective product knowledge as a moderator of the relationship between attitudes and purchase intentions for a durable product," *Journal of Economic Psychology*, 15 (1994): 301–314.

Bitner, M. J. "Building Service Relationships: It's All About Promises," *Journal of the Academy of Marketing Science*, 23, 4 (1995): 246–251.

Bloemer, J. M., Kasper, H. and Lemmink, J. "The relationship between overall dealer satisfaction with the attributes of dealer service, intended dealer loyalty and intended brand loyalty: a Dutch automobile case," *Journal of Consumer Satisfaction, Dissatisfaction and Complaining Behaviour*, 3 (1990).

Bloemer, J. M. and Kasper, H. "The Complex Relationship Between Consumer Satisfaction and Brand Loyalty," *Journal of Economic Psychology*, 16 (1995).

Booz, Allen and Hamilton. *Internet Banking in Europe: Survey of Current Use and Future Prospects*, Studies 1997.

Buchanan II, B. "Building Organizational Commitment: The Socialisation of Managers in Work Organisations," *Administrative Science Quarterly*, 19 (1974).

Churchill, G. A. and Surprenant, C. "An Investigation into the Determinants of Customer Satisfaction," *Journal of Marketing Research*, 19, 1982.

Cohen, L. "The Level of Consciousness: A Dynamic Approach to the Recall Technique," *Journal of Marketing Research*, Vol. 3, 2 (1966).

Colgate, M. and Stewart, K. "The challenge of relationships in services," *International Journal of Service Industry Management*, 9, 5 (1998).

Cunningham, S. M. "Perceived Risk and Brand Loyalty," in Fox, D. (ed.), *Risk Taking and Information Handling in Consumer Behaviour*, Boston: Harvard University Press, 1967.

Danaher, P. and Matsson, J. "Customer Satisfaction during the service delivery process," *European Journal of Marketing*, 28, 5 (1994).

Dekimpe, M. G., Steenkamp, J.-B. E.-M., Mellens, M. and Abeele, P. V. "Decline and Variability in Brand Loyalty," *The International Journal of Research in Marketing*, 14, 5 (1997): 405–420.

Dichtl, E. and Schneider, W. "Kundenzufriedenheit im Zeitalter des Beziehungsmanagement," in Belz, C., Schögel, M., Kramer, M. (eds), *Lean Management und Lean Marketing*, St. Gallen, 1994.

Diller, H., Preispolitik, 2nd ed. Stuttgart, Berlin: Köln, 1991.

Diller, H. 'Kundenbindung als Marketingziel', *Marketing ZFP*, 18, 2 (1996).

Dowling, G. R. and Staelin, R. "Perceived Risk: The Concept and Its Measurement." *Psychology and Marketing*, 3 (1994).

Engel, J. F., Blackwell, R. D. and Miniard, P. W. *Consumer Behaviour*, 6th ed. Chicago: The Dryden Press, 1990.

Engelhardt, W. and Freiling, J. "Integravität als Brücke zwischen Einzeltransaktion und Geschäftsbeziehung," *Marketing ZFP*, 1 (1995): pp. 26–35.

Ennew, C., Wright, M. and Thwaites, D. "Strategic marketing in financial services: retrospect and prospect," *International Journal of Bank Marketing*, 11, 6 (1993).

Erevelles and Leavitt. "A Comparison of Current Models of CS/D," *Journal of Consumer Satisfaction*, Dissatisfaction and Complaining Behaviour (1992).

Ernst & Young, *Technology in banking*, Survey 1998.

Financial Times. Sainsbury's Banking Boom, The *Financial Times Newspaper* (23) October 1997.

Fornell, C. "A national Customer Satisfaction Barometer: The Swedish Experience," *Journal of Marketing*, 56 (January 1992).

Fotheringham, S. A. "Consumer Store Choice and Choice Set Definition," *Marketing Science*, 7 (1988): 299–310.

Fournier, S. *A Consumer-Brand Relationship Framework for Strategic Brand Management*, PhD. Dissertation, University of Florida, 1994.

Foxall, G. R. "Theoretical Progress in Consumer Psychology: The Contibution of a Behavioural Analysis of Choice," *Journal of Economic Psychology* (1986): 393–414.

Goldsmith, R. E., Emmert, J. and Hofacker, C. "A causal model of consumer involvement: replication and extension," *Proceedings Winter Educators' Conference* (1991).

Gummesson, E. "The new marketing: developing long term interactive relationships," *Long Range Planning*, 20 (1987).

Gremler, D. D. "*The Effects of Satisfaction, Switching Costs, and Interpersonal Bonds on Service Loyalty*," PhD. Dissertation, Arizona State University, 1995.

Gronroos, C. "Value-driven relational marketing: from products to resources and competencies," *Journal of Marketing Management*, 13 (1997).

Haley, R. I., and Case, P. B. "Testing Thirteen Attitude Scales for Agreement and Brand Discrimination," *Journal of Marketing* 43, 4 (1979): 20–32.

Henning-Thurau, T. and Klee, A. "The impact of customer satisfaction and relationship quality on customer retention: a critical assessment and model development," *Psychology & Marketing*, 1997.

Herrmann, A. *Produktmanagement*. München, 1998.

Hermanns, A. and Sauter, M. *Management-Handbuch Electronic Commerce*. Verlag Vahlen, 1999.

Holmsen, C. A., Palter, R. N., Simon, P. R. and Weberg, P. K. "Retail banking: Managing competition among your own channels," *The McKinsey Quarterly*, 1 (1998): 82–93.

Homburg, C., Giering, A. and Hentschl, F. "Der Zusammenhang zwischen Kundenzufriedenheit und Kundenbindung," forthcoming in *Die Betriebswirtschaft*, 1998.

Homburg, C. and Rudolph, B. "Theoretische Perspektiven zur Kundenzufriedenheit," in Simon, H., Homburg, C. (eds), *Kundenzufriedenheit*, Wiesbaden, 1995.

Johnson, M. D. *Customer Orientation and Market Action*, New Jersey, 1998.

Johnson, M. D. and Fornell, C. "A Framework of Comparing Customer Satisfaction Across Individuals and Product Categories," *Journal of Economic Psychology* (1991).

Johnson, M. D., Anderson, E. W. and Fornell, C., "Rational and Adaptive Performance Expectations in a Customer Satisfaction Framework," *Journal of Consumer Research*, 21 (March 1995).

Jones, J. "Branding and loyalty: Key issues for retaining the customer," *Journal of Financial Services Marketing*, 1, 3 (1996)

Kahneman, D. and Tversky, A. "Prospect Theory: An Analysis of Decision under Risk," *Econometrica*, 47 (March 1979).

Keller, K. "Conceptualising, Measuring, and Managing Customer-Based Brand Equity," *Journal of Marketing*, 57, 1 (1993).

Korte, C. *Customer Satisfaction Measurement: Kundenzufriedenheitsmessung als Informationsgrundlage des Hersteller- und Handelsmarketing am Beispiel der Automobilwirtschaft*, Frankfurt, 1995.

Kotler, P. "Marketing management: Analysis, planning, implementation, and control," Prentice-Hall, 1995.

La Barbera, P. A. and Mazursky, D. "A longitudinal assessment of consumer satisfaction/dissatisfaction," *Journal of Marketing Research*, 20 (1983).

Liljander, V. and Strandvik, T. "Estimating Zones of Tolerance in Perceived Service Quality and Perceived Service Value," *International Journal of Service Industry Management*, 4, 2 (1993).

Lingenfelder, M. and Schneider, W. *"Die Kundenzufriedenheit Bedeutung, Meßkonzept und empirische Befunde,"* Institut für Marketing, Arbeitspapier Nr. 80, Universität Mannheim, 1990.

Loomes, G. "When Action Speaks Louder than Prospects," *American Economic Review*, 78 (1988): 463–470.

Loomes, G. and Sudgen, R. "Regret Theory: An Alternative Theory of Rational Choice under Uncertainty," *The Economic Journal*, 92 (1982).

Mathieu, J. E. and Zajac, D. M. "A Review and Meta-Analysis of the Antecedents, Correlates, and Consequences of Organizational Commitment," *Pschological Bulletin*, 118, 2 (1990).

Meyer, J. P., Allen, N. J., and Gellatly, I. R., "Affective and Continuance Commitment to the Organization: Evaluations of Measures and Analysis of Concurrent and Time-Lagged Relations," *Journal of Applied Psychology*, 75, 6 (1990).

Meyer, A. and Oevermann, D. 'Kundenbindung', Handwörterbuch des Marketing, Stuttgart 1995, Sp. 1340–1351.

Mittal, B. and Lee, M. S. "A causal model of consumer involvement," *Journal of Economic Psychology*, 10 (1989).

Morgan, R. M. and Hunt, S. D. "The Commitment-Trust Theory of Relationship Marketing," *Journal of Marketing*, 58 (July 1994): 20–38.

Mulhern, F. J. "Retail marketing: From distribution to integration," *International Journal of Research in Marketing*, 14 (1997): 103–124.

Muthukrishnan, A. V. *"Decision Ambiguity and Consumer Brand Loyalty,"* Ph.D Dissertation, University of Florida, 1993.

Oliver, R. L. and Swan, J. E. "Consumer Perceptions of interpersonal Equity and Satisfaction in transactions: a field survey approach," *Journal of Marketing*, 53 (1989).

Olshavsky, R. W. and Granbois, D. R. "Consumer Decision Making – Fact or Fiction," *Journal of Consumer Research*, 6 (September 1979): 93–100.

Peter, S. *Kundenbindung als Marketingziel*, Wiesbaden, 1997.

Peter, J. P. and Olson, J. C. *Consumer Behaviour and Marketing Strategy*, 4th ed., Howewood, IL: Irwin, 1996.

Piller, F. T. *Kundenindividualle Produkte–von der Stange*. Harvard Business Manager, 3 (1997).

Rotter, J. B. "Generalized Expectancies for Internal versus External Control of Reinforcement," *Psychological Monographs*, 80, 1 (1966): 27–56.

Salimen, P. and Wallenius, J. "Testing Prospect Theory in a Deterministic Multiple Criteria Decision-Making Environment," *Decision Sciences Journal*, 24, 2 (1993).

Samuelson, B. M. and Sandvik, K. "The Concept of Customer Loyalty," Proceedings of the Annual Conference – European Marketing Academy, 26, 3 (1997): 1122–1140.

Schiffman, L. G. and Kanuk, L. L. *Consumer Behaviour*. London: Prentice Hall, 1994.

Sheaves, D. E. and Barnes, J. G. "The Fundamentals of Relationships: An Exploration of the Concept to Guide Marketing Implementation," *Advances in Service Marketing and Management*, 5 (1996).

Sheth, J. N. and Parvatiyar, A. "Relationship Marketing in Consumer Markets: Antecedents and Consequences," *Journal of the Academy of Marketing Science*, 23, 4 (1995): 255–271.

Shimp, T. A. "Advertising, Promotion, and Supplemental Aspects of Integrated Marketing Communications," 4th ed., Fort Worth: Dryden Press, 1997.

Solomon, M. R. *Consumer Behaviour*, Massachusetts: Allyn and Bacon, 1994.

Solomon, H. *Virtual Money*, New York & London: Oxford University, Press, 1997.

Spectrum. "Moving into the Information Society," *DTI Information Society Initiative*, London: Publisher?, 1996.

Stebbins, R. A. "On Misunderstanding the Concept of Commitment: A Theoretical Understanding," *Social Forces*, 48 (1970).

Thaler, R. H. "Towards a Positive Theory of Consumer Choice," in Thaler, R. H. (ed.) (1994): *Quasi Rational Economics*, New York, 1994.

Tversky, A. and Kahneman, D. "The Framing of Decisions and the Psychology of Choice," *Science*, 211 (January 1981).

Tversky, A. and Kahneman, D. "Rational Choice and the Framing of Decisions," *Journal of Business*, 59, 4 (1986).

USWeb/CKS Strategies for Growing Your Business through E-commerce. Proven Techniques for Expanding Your Business with a Successful E-commerce Initiative (1999).

USWeb/CKS Success in the Internet Economy. Which companies will ride this wave successfully and which will be overturned (1998).

USWeb/CKS Mastering Change. Four Ways to Survive and Thrive in the Digital Economy (1998).

Wallace, J. E. "Becker's Side-Bet Theory of Commitment Revisited: It is Time for a Moratorium or a Resurrection?" *Human Relations*, 50, 6 (1997).

Webster, F. W. "The changing role of marketing in the corporation," *Journal of Marketing*, 56 (October 1992).

Wiendieck et al., "Konsumentenentscheidungen – Darstellung und Diskussion konkurrierender Forschungsansätze," in Irle, M. (ed.), *Methoden und Anwendungen in der Marktpsychologie*, Göttingen, 1983.

Wiswede, G. *Einführung in die Wirtschaftspsychologie* München, 1995.

Woodside, A. and Trappey, R. "Finding out why your customers shop your store and buy your brand ACP Models of Primary Choice," *Journal of Advertising Research* (November/December 1992).

Woodside, A. G. and Trappey, R.J. "Customer Portfolio Analysis Among Competing Retail Brands," *Journal of Business Research*, 35, 189–200 (1996).

Woodside, A. G., Frey, L. L. and Daly, R. T. "Linking service quality, customer satisfaction and behavioural intention," *Journal of Health Care Marketing*, 9 (1989).

Yi, X. "Memory & Cognition," Dept. of Phonological Recoding in Short-Term Memory, 19, 3 (May 1991): 263–273.

Zeithaml, V. A., Berry, L. L. and Parasuraman, A. "The Nature and Determinants of Customer Expectations of Service," *Journal of the Academy of Marketing Science*, 21, 1 (winter 1993).

Reports:

NatWest Annual Report, 1998.

Morgan Stanley, *"The Internet Retailing Report"*, May 1997.

Morgan Stanley, *"The European Internet Report"*, June 1999.

PriceWaterhouseCoopers: *Building tomorrow's leading retail bank*, The Economist Intelligence Unit Limited and Coopers & Lybrand, 1996.

PriceWaterhouseCoopers: *European Private Banking Survey*, 1996/97.

PriceWaterhouseCoopers: *Consumer Electronic Access Project*, Final Report, Overview and demand/supply findings (Volume I), Application scenarios and winning strategies (Volume II), October 1998.

PriceWaterhouseCoopers: *Information Management and the Future of Banking*, 1998.

PriceWaterhouseCoopers: *E-Commerce Initiative*, Internet Based Financial Services Results of Telephone Survey Executive Summary, March 1999.

PriceWaterhouseCoopers: *Online Banking*, January 1999.

PriceWaterhouseCoopers: *Electronic Business Outlook*, 1999.

Trappey, R. J. *Modelling Personal Computer Purchase Behaviour – Hewlett Packard, U.K.*, 1999.

6
Learning How Linkage Advertising and Prior Experience Affect Customer Behaviour

Background

Linkage advertising is the literature and related materials given to customers who respond to advertisers' offers of these materials (Woodside, 1994). Linkage advertising "links the up-front advertising to the sale with additional arguments and benefits which the up-front advertising [i.e., the print or broadcast advertisement that includes the linkage offer] didn't have space or time to include" (Rapp and Collins, 1987). In the United States in the 1990s most advertising expenditures include allocations for creating and sustaining direct links with customers, including such actions such as linkage-advertising, learning and referring to customers by their names in a database marketing programs, and creating "frequency marketing" customer clubs (Cappo, 1992; Frequency Marketing, 1993).

Rapp and Collins (1987, 1990, 1994), who have been the most outspoken advocates of linkage-advertising, say that,

> Too often awareness advertising leaves the prospect dangling, with no idea of what to do next, where to buy, or how to obtain more information. At the very least, the ideal advertising and marketing process should bridge this gap between the advertising and the sale by offering – and providing – additional information. We call this "linkage" (Rapp and Collins, 1987, p. 17).

The use of linkage advertising may be more valuable in some industries than in others. State/province tourism is a good example of such an industry. In this field, "[in creating image advertising] advertising agencies are thoroughly briefed on all tourism wonders a state has to offer... and then are forbidden to mention them.... Presumably due to the political minefield of highlighting individual cities, much less individual attractions, state tourism advertising is a bizarre enterprise wherein states attempting to lure visitors find themselves being ludicrously vague about why" (Garfield,

1994, p. 32). Rapp and Collins's proposal of linkage-advertising may be useful for solving this dilemma. The following two-step advertising strategy is used often by some destinations (e.g., states and provinces): (1) image advertising in scheduled media that includes heavy emphasis on the availability of linkage-advertising with several easy ways to acquire it, and (2) very detailed linkage-advertising with both lots of reason-why and procedural information about how to go about doing it (e.g., travelling to and inside the destination area; attractions; things to do; specific accommodation by region; restaurants; and shopping and what to buy).

While in later books Rapp and Collins (1990,1994) provide many exciting and insightful case histories of the sales impacts of linkage-advertising strategies, these fail to include formal comparisons or discussions about drawing valid causal inferences of the impact of linkage-advertising. Knowledgeable senior executives are likely to require stronger evidence than one-group case studies with no formal comparisons of sales impacts. A substantial of literature is available on how to use true experiments (i.e., randomly assigning subjects to test and control groups to achieve comparability within known limits of sampling error) to examine causal propositions on advertising's impact on sales (e.g., Banks, 1965; Caples, 1974; Raymond, 1974). However, substantial practical difficulties and expense are usually associated with meeting the design requirements of using true experiments (see Banks, 1965; Cook and Campbell, 1979, chap 8).

Greater awareness and use of quasi-experiments in advertising research with nonequivalent, but comparable, groups to examine causal relationships between linkage-advertising and multiple, dependent customer variables is advocated. Quasi-experiments are tests of the effects of changing levels of outcome variables (e.g., sales levels) caused by treatment variables (e.g., advertising and linkage-advertising) when random assignment has not been used to create equivalent comparison groups from which treatment-caused change is inferred (Cook and Campbell, 1979, p. 6). Described herein is a field study application of a quasi-experiment on the impact of linkage-advertising on several dependent variables; the method and results presented support the use of quasi-experiment designs in advertising research and the general proposition that linkage-advertising likely causes substantial changes in multiple consumer variables. We also describe how the results from the field study can be used to estimate the return on investment of the linkage-advertising program.

We first describe two quasi-experimental designs: a one-group post-test-only design and a quasi-experimental design with predicted higher order interaction effects. The first is used widely in assessing the effects of linkage-advertising, but it is not recommended. The second one is used sparingly, but it is recommended highly. Second, the method and results from a field study are applied to the data. Third, net revenue analysis is conducted on the linkage-advertising program. This chapter closes with conclusions and suggestions for using quasi-experiments in advertising research.

Quasi-experimental designs in advertising

The research design used most often for assessing the impact of advertising (and a design that should be used less often) as the one-group post-test-only design. Also described is a less known, but more useful, research design: the post-test-only design with predicted higher-order interactions. Given the excellent literature available on the topic (Banks 1965; Cook and Campbell 1979), the purpose is not to present a detailed review of the use of experiments and quasi-experimental designs.

Banks (1965) and Cook and Campbell (1979) provide detailed discussions on validity and research design threats to internal and external validity (see also Churchill 1991; Campbell and Stanley, 1966).

The one-group post-test-only design

Most reported case studies on the influence of linkage-advertising on increasing sales, or generating contacts by customers, are best categorised as examples of the one-group post-test-only design. This design may be displayed with an X standing for the treatment and O standing for observation or measurement of effect.

$$X \qquad O$$

A basic deficiency of this design is the lack of pretest observations from people who will be exposed to the advertising treatment. Cook and Campbell (1979, p. 96) describe the deficiencies thus:

> As a result, one can not easily infer that the treatment is related to any kind of change. A second deficiency is the lack of a control group of persons who did not receive the treatment. Without this control it is difficult to conceptualise the relevant threats (to internal validity) and to measure them individually. In most contexts one needs time-relevant data from pretest measurement to check on maturational trends. One also needs information from groups that have not had the treatment to check on any causally irrelevant factors that could affect post-test scores (e.g., branding purchases) and prevent one from inferring what the post-test mean would have been in the treatment group where there had been no treatment.

While these telling weaknesses are well known and reported widely in the scientific and practitioner advertising literature (e.g., Caples, 1974; Raymond, 1976), the one-group post-test-only design still appears to be the research design used most often to assess linkage-advertising effects (e.g., Rapp and Collins, 1987, 1990, 1994). In North America, a majority of the competitive submissions of linkage-advertising impacts for the Direct Marketing Association's annual Echo Awards Program are based on the one-group post-test-only design (cf. Woodside, Beretich and Lauricella, 1993). It is possible that advertising managers may select the invalid research designs to assess advertising effectiveness because of time constraints. However, it is more likely that the central reasons for the poor choice of research design are lack of knowledge and experience of working with true and quasi-experiments.

By not formally examining results (i.e., comparing the Os) with and without advertising, advertising managers cannot respond adequately to the most often asked question about advertising by senior executives: "How much did the advertising influence changes in dependent variables, such as brand awareness, attitude, image, and purchases, that would not have occurred without the advertising?" Without such specific comparative evidence of impact, the credibility and need for continuing with the advertising program and employing the advertising manager are weak; advertising becomes an activity to do during good times and to eliminate during business downturns. Thus, advertisers often become their own worst enemy by continuing to measure and report the effectiveness of advertising based on the one-group post-test-only design.

The post-test-only design with non-equivalent groups and predicted higher-order interactions

In higher-order interactions, the hypothesised interaction relationship includes a positive (or negative) relationship between two variables for one group (e.g., a group exposed to X, where X is advertising), and a zero or negative (positive) relationship between the same two variables for the other group (a second group not exposed to X, advertising nonexposure). A significant difference in two positive (negative) correlations between the two variables represents a lower-order interaction. In terms of sources of internal invalidity (other causes that could be responsible for the observed difference between the treatment and the control group), it is much easier to think of reasons why the members of the experiment and control groups should be maturing at different rates in the same direction than it is to think of reasons why one group should be changing in one direction and while the other group is not changing at all, or changing in the opposite direction.

Post-test only, nonequivalent group research designs with predicted higher-order interaction effects look complex, but they will probably provide more accurate estimates of the impacts of advertising on customer behaviour and sales. Cook and Campbell (1979, pp. 134–136) illustrate how, in the absence of pretest information, interaction predictions can be used with intact groups to provide relatively strong inferences about cause. A food-shopping study of overweight and normal-weight people (Nisbett and Kanouse, 1969) may have been the best-known example of a higher-order interaction of two nonequivalent groups facilitating cause-and-effect interpretation. Nisbett and Kanouse tested the hypotheses that overweight people lack the ability to discriminate the internal body cues that indicate hunger. They found a higher-order interaction effect: among people with normal weight there was a strong positive correlation between the time they last ate and their supermarket grocery bills, while among overweight people there was a weak negative correlation. Alternative hypotheses were not plausible for explaining such a higher-order interaction effect.

From their review of Nisbett and Kanouse and their case studies with multiple outcomes of several dependent variables strongly following the predictions of one set of hypotheses, Cook and Campbell (1979, p. 135) emphasise that the moral is clear:

> casual interpretation tends to be facilitated and the predicted interaction between nonequivalent groups grows more complex. But the chance of obtaining so many data points in the predicted order decreases with the number of data points predicted. There are many reasons for this, including chance, selection differences in the intact groups which influence data patterns but are irrelevant to theory, and theories that are partially or totally incorrect. Replication is crucial when making higher-order interaction predictions.This helps control for chance fluctuations.

General higher- and simple-order interaction advertising hypotheses

The general following hypotheses are the higher-order and simple-order interaction hypotheses applied to linkage advertising that are tested empirically in this chapter. H1A: Within a given period (buying season), repeat customers exposed to a brand's linkage-advertising will participate in more activities promoted in the linkage-advertising than new customers exposed to the linkage-advertising, while (H1B) repeat customers who are not exposed will participate less in these promoted activities than new customers who are not exposed and all customers who are not exposed will participate in fewer promoted activities than linkage-advertising exposed customers. (H1A and H1B are illustrated in Figure 6.1, panel A.)

H2A: Within a given time period (buying season), a positive interaction effect on brand-affect (i.e., positive image about the brand) and HB2: intentions-to-but occur between exposure to linkage-advertising and a level of prior experience (e.g., prior visits) with a product-service (see Figure 6.1, panels B and D).

H3: Within a given time period (buying season), repeat customers who are exposed to and brand's linkage advertising will spend more money on the

162

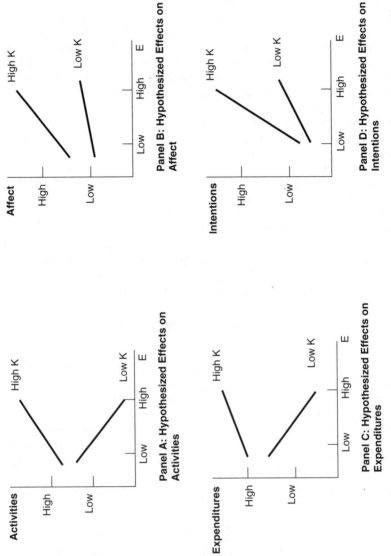

Figure 6.1 Hypothesised Effects of Knowledge (K) and Experience (E) on Customers' Activities, Affect, Expenditures Intentions

brand than new customers who are exposed to the brand's linkage-advertising, while repeat customers who are not exposed will spend less than new customers not exposed, and all customers not exposed will spend less money than linkage-advertising exposed customers (see Figure 6.1, panel C).

H1, H2 and H3 are higher-order interaction hypotheses that are particularly relevant in tourism-destination marketing where a destination, such as the State of Texas, is an analogous to a given brand. Advertising of such "brands" often include a free catalogue offer; that is, a detailed visitor's information guide (VIG), usually consisting of 100–300 pages of promotional information on local tours, attractions, accommodations, festival events, restaurants, and other information.

The rational for these higher-order advertising interactions includes the following points. Repeat visitors (customers) who are not exposed to such advertising can be expected to engage in fewer activities and spend the least because they focus their visiting time on repeating activities they enjoyed on prior visits, not do repeat marginally enjoyable activities or activities found previously enjoyable, and have not been exposed to advertising promoting many additional activities. New customers who have not been exposed to advertising can be expected to participate in more activities, tour the destination area more fully, and spend more money than repeaters who have not been exposed to advertising, the many new customers come to explore the destination-unique sights and events for the first time. Repeat visitors who have been exposed to advertising are likely to spend the most money, partly because the advertising increases their knowledge of the things to do at the destination area, they have the most positive attitude about the activities available at the destination (based on the learning theory of preferences; see Krugman, 1962; and the knowledge-based affect: Woodside, 1994), and they are most efficient in doing more activities compared to new customers exposed to advertising. The new customers who have been exposed to the advertising will learn about and do more activities and therefore spend more money than new customers who have not been exposed, because the exposed customers know about more activities.

Linkage-advertising may be particularly effective in increasing brand-affect and intentions to return to the destination among visitors with prior visits to the destination because it stimulates deeper mental processing of current and former experiences by the visitor. Thus, destination linkage-advertising may serve as an album that helps to build, maintain, renew, and strengthen mental connections of places/events and outcomes experienced, in some ways comparable to a family photograph album.

Basic research plan

The basic plan for the post-test-only design with nonequivalent groups is shown in the first two rows below. This design can become more complicated than that shown if observations (os) are collected from several sets of two nonequivalent groups exposed versus not exposed to the treatment (rows 3 and 4). Including additional sets of nonequivalent groups meets Cook and Campbell's (1979) requirement of replication being crucial for making higher-order interaction predictions.

Group	1A	X	O
Group	1B	X	O
Group	2A	X	O
Group	2B	X	O

The broken line between each set of nonequivalent groups indicates that they were not formed randomly. For building replications into the design, each group could represent brand buyers from different (geographic) markets. For the tourism advertising example, Group 1 night visitors to Texas from nearby markets, Group 2 from more distant U.S. markets, and Group 3 from foreign markets. Analogous to Nisbett and Kanouse (1969) asking each subject about the time since she or he had last eaten and classifying each according to whether they were normal or overweight, each subject in the advertising quasi-experiment would be asked about the number of previous purchases of the brand (i.e., previous visits to the state) and their exposure to the recent advertising brochure (the VIG), as well as their origin, other demographic information, and additional buying behaviour information.

If the predicted higher-order interaction pattern is found consistently across groups, the case for strong inference that the advertising was responsible for additional customer expenditures is strengthened; and it is possible to estimate from the overall interaction effect how much additional customer expenditure was due to advertising. Consequently, a profit and loss statement can be prepared based on the revenues and costs associated with the advertising/marketing program.

A word of caution

Cook and Campbell (1979, p. 96) caution that while results from a one-group post-test-only design and related designs are "generally uninterpretable, the reader is urged not to conclude that studies using them are invariably uninterpretable." The one-group post-test-only design and the post-test-only design with nonequivalent groups without specifying higher-order interactions can be made more complex; degrees of freedom (Campbell, 1975) can be built into the design by adding many dependent variables that are expected to behave at different levels based on theory. When data on many variables are collected carefully from one group following exposure to a treatment variable, then the one-group post-test-only design may be better classified as a one-shot case study. Consequently, contextual knowledge is rich, even if impressionistic, as Cook and Campbell said, "intelligent presumptions can be made about what this [one] group would have been like without X [the treatment]" (1979, p. 96). In such rich, post-test contexts, predictions of different levels of the multiple dependent variables from competing theories can be compared with empirical observations (see Wilson and Wilson, 1988, for an industrial buying behaviour example of testing competing theories by building in degrees of freedom). Thus, the researcher can sometimes function as a detective (see Schulman, 1994) noting the levels of different variables, using this information to rule out some threats to both internal and construct validities, and conclude that one theory is supported while at the same time refuting a competing theory. This caution and advice was followed by building in multiple dependent variables and prediction from the theory of linkage-advertising effects on these variables.

Method

The use of post-test-only design, with nonequivalent groups and predicted higher-order interactions, was made possible by Prince Edward Island's (PEI) marketing strategy and the research method used for the province: an island tourist exit survey. Each year, most of PEI's tourism marketing strategy is focused on creating and advertising the free offer of a high-quality linkage-advertising. Advertising is placed in scheduled media vehicles in selected Canadian (English and French), U.S., and European markets offering a free copy of PEI's annual *Visitor's Information Guide*.

The linkage-advertising, that is, the *Visitor's Information Guide* (referred to as the VIG in the following discussion), consists of a 170 page, glossy, soft-covered book in magazine format. For the 1992 marketing campaign, a total of 280,000 VIGs were published: 250,000 in English and 50,000 in French. A total of 96 percent of the VIGs were distributed during 1992; 84 percent of the distributed guides (267,860) were sent to customers (and potential visitors) who requested the guide in response to advertised free offer. The remaining 16 percent were distributed at PEI provincial information centres.

To test the three hypotheses, the data collected for the 1992 PEI exit survey were used. These data and detailed marketing/advertising expenditure data were provided to us on a computer disk and in reports prepared by the marketing agency, a PEI government-sponsored organisation. The only use of the data made by the marketing agency was to profile visitors' demographics, attitudes toward PEI, behaviours – including expenditures – while in PEI, according to their origins, the data were not analysed to measure the impact of the linkage-advertising on the attitudes and behaviours of PEI customers.

The questionnaire

The questionnaire used to collect the data for the study consisted of 12 pages of questions. Data were collected on the purpose of the current trip; the number of previous trips and their purposes; the length of time since the last trip to PEI; visitors' reception of the VIG and whether or not they received the guide before or after entering PEI; their awareness and extent-of-use of the VIG; their evaluations of the visual appeal, ease of use, and amount of information in the VIG; their mode of entry into PEI (e.g., ferry, air, cruise ship); the type of accommodation they chose in PEI; their evaluation of the accommodation they chose in PEI; their participation in 15 activities while in PEI and evaluations of it; information on visiting 10 attractions in PEI and evaluations of these attractions; the areas visited in PEI and overnight stays there; the perceived quality of PEI's road signage; their evaluations of PEI on 0 image items; their expenditures in Canadian dollars while in PEI (including credit-card purchases and spending by children); the proportions of total PEI expenditures by 8 categories; the travel-party size and description; and demographic information (age; marital status; education; employment outside the home; life-cycle stage; annual household income; and origin by province, state and country).

Specific operationalisations

Knowledge

Increased consumer knowledge about PEI is the result of customer search-acquisition-use of external information and previous experience. However, in operationalising knowledge it is necessary to separate external information from previous experience and empirically define knowledge as acquiring the province's VIG. An aided-recall question was asked, respondents were shown the cover of the VIG and were given five options: "Did you receive a Visitor's Guide a) prior to entering PEI; b) when you arrived in PEI; c) both prior and upon entry into PEI; d) did not receive a Visitor's Guide; e) don't know/don't remember."

Data of the degree-of-use of the VIG were collected: "To what extent would you say you used the Visitor's Guide during your trip to PEI?" Four options were read to each respondent from "I completely depended on it to plan what we would do while on PEI" to "I did not use any portion of the Visitor's Guide."

Previous experience

The following two questions were asked to learn about previous experience: "Is this your first visit to PEI as an adult or have you been here on either pleasure or business travel or both before?" and "About how many times have you been to PEI as an adult before, for either business or pleasure?"

Activities

"Yes" and "no" responses were collected on participation in 15 activities while on PEI the activities included going to the beach, golfing, harbour cruises, attending live theatre, and enjoying nightlife. Also, using a 4-point scale ranging from "very disappointed" to "very pleased," the respondents were requested to evaluate the activities they participated in.

Attractions

"Yes" and "no" responses were collected on visiting 10 attractions. The attractions included the historic home of William Henry Pope, Cavendish Beach, and PEI National Park, among others. A 4-point scale was used to collect data on visitors' evaluations of the 10 attractions.

Regions visited

PEI has 3 counties (Prince , Queen, and King) consisting of 11 distinct regions. Data were collected on visiting and staying overnight in the 11 regions. The regions included Cavendish, Charlottetown (the provincial capital), Eastern Kings, Southern Kings, West Prince, and Summerside, among others.

Image

A total of 10 questions on visitors' associations of PEI with specific attributes and benefits was used to collect data on the perceived image of the province. The 10 questions included the following: "There's more to do in PEI than I had imagined," "PEI's people are friendly," "It's boring on PEI," "PEI's beaches are superior," and others, Four-point scales were used with these items, ranging from "strongly agree" to "strongly disagree."

Behavioural intention

Two items were used to assess the behavioural intention: "I would recommend PEI to friends and relatives" and "I would definitely come to PEI again." Four-point scales were used with items, ranging from "strongly agree" (scored as +2) and "strongly disagree" (scored as –2)

Expenditures

Data were collected on amounts (in Canadian dollars) and proportions of expenditures for seven expense categories (including accommodation, meals, purchases of food and alcohol in stores, day-time recreation and entertainment, night-time entertainment, handcrafts and souvenirs, and others).

Demographics

Data were collected on 7 demographic related variables: age (5 categories); marital status (3 categories); formal education completed (6 categories); work outside the home (7categories); total household income before taxes and deductions (in Canadian dollars) for 1991 (5 categories; and home province, state, or country.

Procedure

The interviews were completed during the seasonal period (May 22 to October 5, 1992) when over 95 percent of leisure travellers visit PEI. The questionnaire was administered person-to-person at all points of exit from PEI. Partly because PEI was an island with no fixed link at the time the data were collected, over 93 percent of all the province's visitors arrived via one of two ferries; 6 percent via the airport, and less than 1 percent via cruise ship. (With the opening of the bridge connecting PEI to the mainland, collecting data involving visitors to the island will be more complex). The interviews were conducted orally at both ferry locations, the province's major airport near Charlottetown, and selected cruise ships. The team of nine interviewers worked on a three-day-on, two-day-off schedule to ensure that week days and weekends were covered equally.

The proportions of completed interviews of leisure-travel visitors by their origins were very similar to previous empirical estimates of visitors by origin. For example, 65 percent of completed interviews were with Canadians residing in other provinces and 31 percent were with respondents from the U.S.: two-thirds of PEI leisure visitors were previously estimated to be Canadian residents each year during 1990 and 1991 and one-third Americans.

The only exception to this procedural rule involved Japanese visitors. In order to obtain a profile of Japanese visitors and their visiting behaviour, of the selected total respondents nearly 1 percent were Japanese; this segment of customers is estimated to represent less than 0.2 percent of total leisure visitors. To ensure a high cooperation rate (88%), the interviews with Japanese respondents were conducted in Japanese by native Japanese interviewers.

Results related to data collection

Possibly because some delays and waiting at the exit points is involved in leaving PEI, the substantial majority of visitors requested to participate in the study did comply. A total of 2,239 interviews of PEI leisure visitors were completed. The overall cooperation/completion interview rate was 94 percent. In addition, a total of 453 business travellers were interviewed briefly; the data for these visitors are not included in this report.

Due mainly to some nonresponses to some of the questions, the useable number of responses to test the hypotheses was around 88 percent of the completed interviews. In the following section, sample sizes are reported in the tables of findings for specific issues.

Assessment of the data collection model

Visitor recall of acquiring and using the VIG, length of stay, activities participated in during the visit, expenditures, places stayed at overnight, and other destination-travel events is likely to be minimised by the exit-intercept method used. Also, the very high cooperation rate is a positive feature of the method; reported response rates in advertising, effectiveness research studies to assess "inquiry conversion" are below 70 percent (for example, Messmer and Johnson, 1993, report a 67 percent response rate in a telephone study). Inquiry conversion is the proportion of inquiries requesting the linkage-advertising who converted into customers (e.g., destination leisure visitors).

The most important advantage of the exit-intercept method may be the opportunity it provides to compare buying behaviour of visitors acquiring linkage-advertising. A quasi-experimental design, in the form of a post-test-only design with high-order interactions, can be used to provide relatively strong inferences about cause and effect. Two negative features should be noted about the the exit-intercept model. First, the cost per completed face-to-face interview is substantially higher than mail surveys; the difference for this study was estimated to be three times that of a mail-survey response.

Second, as an island with limits entry-exit access, PEI provides a somewhat unique natural laboratory for leisure-travel research. It should be easier to collect substantial amounts of trip data per travel party in such circumstances compared with provinces and states with many entry-exit points such as Ontario, South Carolina, and California. However, the method described can probably be modified successfully to permit useful data collection in those circumstances by, for example, interviewing leisure travellers at representative gasoline service stations and convenience stores.

Findings

Figure 6.2 summarises the findings relating to the three hypotheses. Experience (E) in Figure 6.2, represents two levels of prior visit experience to PEI: new and repeat visitors. In Figure 6.2, knowledge (K) includes two customer levels: acquiring versus not acquiring the VIG. Data were analysed in several ways, for example, including not only respondents receiving the guide and reporting "some use" and "complete use" (81 percent of receivers of the guide) versus people reporting no exposure to the guide; the results were more supportive of the hypotheses using this restrictive sample of respondents versus comparisons for all respondents receiving versus not receiving the VIG. No main effect was found receiving the VIG before versus after arrival on PEI. Reported here are the more conservative findings based on the total respondents; thus, in the following results, the 20 percent of the respondents reporting very limited or no use of the VIG are included in the overall high-K group, because they did receive the VIG.

Also, comparisons were made of respondents having 0,1.5, 3.5, 5.5, 7.5, 9.5, and 13.0 (mid-point values on possible responses) previous visits among those receiving the guide and not receiving the guide; the patterns and statistical significance of the results were not different from the following results not based on two levels experience.

H1: Higher-order interaction effect of knowledge and experience on destination activities. The results summarised in panel A of Figure 6.2 and statistical tests of main and interaction effe ects provide strong support for Hypothesis 1. Using multiple regression analysis, increasing K is associated with increasing numbers of destination activities (p, .0000); and the interaction effect shown in panel A of Figure 6.2 is highly significant (p < .0002).

The results for the test of main and interaction effects model include an adjusted R^2 equal to .09. Here is the model showing the influences by K, E. and K by E:

Nonstandardised model: $A = 6.03 + .81(K) - 1.06(E) + .81(K)(E)$

The betas in the standardised model (transforming all raw scores for each variable into standardised scores) indicate that all three variables are important influences on changing the number of activities, and that E has a stronger influence than the interaction of K by E.

The standardised model: $A = .17 (K) - .22(E) + .14 (K)(E)$

Additional findings support the proposition that increasing the number of destination activities leads to increasing destination-related expenditures. In fact, several path analyses for predicting destination expenditures indicated that the increasing number of destination activities is associated more strongly with increases in destination expenditures compared with the direct influence of any other variable, such as acquiring the guide, the number of regions visited, and the number of previous trips to the destination. More specific findings on this issue are described later.

Thus, high-versus low-K, that is, acquiring versus not acquiring the guide, is associated directly (and indirectly via increasing activities) with increases in destination expenditures (Table 6.1). More important, the strong support of the proposed second-order interaction effect of K and E on increasing participation in destination activities facilitates the causal interpretation that acquiring the guide is responsible for increasing activities of visitors.

H2A: Single-order interaction effects of K and E on positive image and (H2B): intentions-to-return to the destination. The two parts of the second hypothesis were not supported by the results: a positive interaction effect of K and E on positive image and intentions to return to the destination was not supported. The results are summarised in panels B and D in Figure 6.2.

171

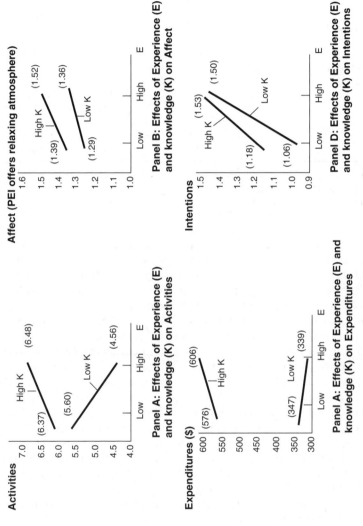

Figure 6.2 Observed Effects of Knowledge (K) and Experience (E) on Customers' Activities, Affect, Expenditures and Intentions

Table 6.1   Expenditures by Acquiring Guide and Experience

	Expenditures ($)		
	Average	*SD*	N
Acquired Guide?[a]			
Yes	588	633	1313
No	345	414	804
Previous experience[b]			
Novice	509	516	1183
Repeat	480	638	793
Acquired Guide?[c]			
No			
Novice	347	394	344
Repeat	339	339	375
Yes[d]			
Novice	576	545	839
Repeat	606	784	418

[a] $F = 91.8400$ df = 12115 $p < .0000$, $w^2 = .04$
[b] $F = 1.3000$ df= 11974 $p < .2545$, $w^2 = .00$
[c] $F = 0.0753$ df = 1717 $p < .7838$, $w^2 = .00$
[d] $F = 0.6100$ df= 11255 $p < .4337$, $w^2 = .00$

Psychometric Properties of the Image Scale Items. One of the limitations of the empirical study is that a systematic approach as described by Churchill (1979) was not followed in developing the image and behavioural intention scale items. The ten items that were used to assess visitors' images of PEI were selected by the PEI Department of Tourism, Parks, and Recreation based on the results of several previous image studies. Before testing the third hypothesis, the psychometric properties of the 2 items in the behavioural intention scale were also examined. Several factor analyses were performed, both using only the 10 image items and using these 10 items along with the 2 behavioural intention items (the same 4-point scale was used for each of the 12 items: "strongly disagree" to "strongly agree"). The review of several varimax rotations of the factor matrices led to the conclusion that a 4-factor solution provided the most useful interpretation of meaning for the image and behavioural intention scale items; 59 percent of the total variation in response was explained by the 4-factor solution. The construct names, coefficient alphas, and correlations among the 4 scales are summarised in the following table.

Based on the results summarised in Table 6.2, it was concluded that the nomological validities (cf. Peter, 1981) of these scales were useful for further analyses. The 2 behavioural intention items loaded in a separate factor in the rotated factor analysis; the correlation coefficient (.61) for this 2-item scale is substantially higher than the four correlations among the four scales formed from the data analysis, as shown in Table 6.2. Two general image items, which were named Atmosphere, loaded in the same factor in the rotated factor matrix with a correlation of .68. The three negatively worded items among the ten image items loaded on one factor, named Complain (Table 6.2), with a coefficient alpha of .51. The finding that these three negative worded items all loaded on the same factor may reflect a response style (see Babakus and Boller, 1992, pp. 261–262). Only 1 item loaded heavily in the rotated factor and was named Delight. The limitation should be recognised that in factor analysis, a single item does not constitute an unobservable construct that this entire analysis is limited

Table 6.2 Coefficient Alphas for Three Constructs

Construct	Item		Coefficient alpha
Atmosphere	1	PEI's people are friendly	0.68
	2	PEI offers a relaxing atmosphere	
Complain	1	PEI is too old-fashioned for me	0.51
	2	There's not enough nightlife	
	3	It's inconvenient to reach PEI	
Delight	1	There's more to do in PEI that I had imagined	–
Behavioural Intention	1	I would definitely come to PEI again	0.61
	2	I would recommend PEI to friends and relatives	

	Correlation of Matrix Scales[a]			
	Atmosphere	Complain	Delight	Behaviour
Atmosphere	1.00			
Complain	–0.27	1.00		
Delight	0.21	–0.11	1.00	
Behavioural Intention	0.46	–0.33	0.24	1.00

[a] All correlations are significant ($p < .01$)

because it follows, when it should precede in pretests, the collection of the data.

As suggested by Churchill (1979) and Nunnally (1978), alphas of .50 to .60 suffice for early stages of basic research. Thus, it was concluded that the three image scales and the behavioural intention scale shown in Table 6.2 were useful for examining the second hypothesis.

Note that the results in panel B in Figure 6.2 are for one item representing Atmosphere in Table 6.2. The results for Delight and Complain are consistent with the results shown for this Atmosphere item in panel B, as well as the total factor score average values for Atmosphere: the main effects of both K and E on these dependent variables are positive and significant. The visitors acquiring the VIG (the high-K group) had a significantly lower Complain average and those with high prior experience (E) had lower Complain average than low experience visitors. The interaction effects of K and E on Delight and Complain were not significant (these results are not illustrated).

H3: **Higher-order interaction effect of knowledge and experience on expenditures.** In panel C of Figure 6.2, the pattern of the results supports the third hypothesis in direction. As summarised in Table 6.1, the main effect of knowledge (acquiring the VIG) on expenditure was not highly significant; the main effect for experience was not significant. While supported in direction, the hypothesised higher-order interaction effect of K and E on expenditures was not statistically significant (p. .05, using multiple regression test with dummy codes for K, E, and K by E interaction, results not shown). However, examining the results for the grouped data does indicate that a net positive $38 interaction effect occurred between K and E, from Figure 6.2: (606 – 576) – (339 – 347) = 38. The $38 represents 11 percent of the average expenditures ($343) reported for the total sample of respondents. The increased customer knowledge (via the VIG) is associated with the increased expenditures substantially among both novice and repeat customers; and to some limited extent, such knowledge may help reverse the decline in expenditures as customers move from novice to repeat buyers (e.g., visitors).

Analysis of revenues, costs, and net return on investment

In this section further analysis of the total number of visitor parties, visitor party expenditure estimates, and cost data for the linkage-advertising program is presented. From these analyses estimates are made for net revenue and return on investment of the program. These estimates are summarised in Tables 6.3 and 6.4.

Calculations of revenues, costs, and net contribution were completed for three separate markets for PEI (Canada, U.S., and other foreign visitors) and for the total leisure visitor market. Other foreign visitors include leisure visitors mainly from European countries and a very small proportion of Japanese visitors. Because of the limited modes of entry/exit for PEI, highly accurate estimates of the total number of visiting parties from the three origins are believed to be achieved (row 1 in Table 6.3). The average party size for U.S. residents of 5.62 is substantially higher than those of Canadian and other foreign visitors because there is a greater proportion of bus tours from the United States to PEI (row 2). Row 3 in Table 6.3 is calculated by multiplying rows 1 and 2. The estimates in rows 3 and 5 are based on the proportions of acquiring the VIG for each of the three markets.

Note that the estimated total leisure visitor expenditure (row 8) is close to $54 million based on the total travel party numbers for the three markets (75 percent of PEI leisure visitors are residents of other Canadian provinces and spend less in PEI than U.S. and other foreign visitors).

Table 6.3   Visitors, Estimated Revenues and Costs

Market size, revenues, cost variable	Customer Segments			
	Canada	USA	Other Foreign	Total and Weighted Average
Visitors (N)				
(1) Number of parties	88,947	25,790	3,371	118,108
(2) Average party size	3.42	5.62	4.16	3.92
(3) Total visitors	304,199	144,940	14,023	463,162
(4) Parties acquiring VIG	51,110	17,795	2,010	70,915
(5) Parties not acquiring VIG	37,837	7,995	1,361	47,193
Revenues and Costs ($)				
(6) Average Revenue with guide	581	589	715	588
(7) Average Revenue without guide	320	315	632	345
(8) Total revenue (000s)	38,578	12,999	2,297	53,874
(9) Total Revenue with guide (000s)	26,470	10,481	1,437	38,388
(10) Total Revenue without guide (000s)	12,108	2,518	860	15,486
(11) VIG mailings	176,234	47,602	2,383	226,219
(12) Total unit cost	5.10	4.10	4.10	4.43
(13) Total mailing cost (000s)	899	195	10	1,104
(14) VIG's distributed at visitors' centres	50,196			50,196
(15) Total unit cost at visitors' centres	3.00			3.00
(16) Total cost of VIG at centres (000s)				151

A total of 226,219 VIGs were distributed via mail and 50,196 were distributed at visitor centres. The estimated unit costs (rows 12 and 15 in Table 6.3) of the VIG include postage and handling, publication costs of the VIG, and the envelope expense. In Table 6.4 the total cost of the VIG linkage-advertising campaign includes the advertising expenditures in the three markets (row 3) and the total costs associated with publishing and distributing the VIG (rows 4 and 5). Considering the two revenue streams for each of the three markets (visitors acquiring nor acquiring the VIG), the total net revenue (row 12) is presented in Table 6.4.

For the remaining analysis reported in Table 6.4 the most conservative viewpoint that acquiring the VIG influenced only visitors' total expenditures and not in their decision to visit PEI was assumed; thus, acquiring the VIG did not "convert" any inquirers into visitors, but those acquiring the VIG did spend more in PEI than they would otherwise. Row 13 in Table 6.4 includes revenue estimates that would have resulted from visitors acquiring the VIG, assuming the VIG had not been available (multiplying row 4 by row 7 in Table 6.3).

The total revenue estimates (row 15, Table 6.4) are based on estimated total revenues without the execution of the linkage-advertising program. The additional net revenue attributed to executing the linkage-advertising program (row 16) is calculated by subtracting row 15 from row 12.

Table 6.4   Net Revenue Analysis

Variable	Canada	USA	Other Foreign	Total
Revenue ($ 000s)				
1 Vistors using guide	26,470	10,481	1,437	38,388
2 Advertising and VIG costs				
3 Advertising	774	276	55	1,105
4 VIG mailing costs	899	195	10	1,104
5 VIGs at visitors' centres	151	0	0	151
6 Total cost of VIG marketing	1,824	471	65	2,360
7 Net Revenue	24,646	10,010	1,372	26,028
11 Revenue without VIG marketing	12,108	2,518	860	15,486
12 Total net revenue	36,754	12,528	2,232	51,514
Total revenues ($ 000s) from visitors using VIG assuming:				
13 No VIG available	16,335	5,605	1,270	23,230
14 Parties not using VIG	12,108	2,518	860	15,486
15 Total revenue	28,463	8,123	2,130	38,716
16 Additional net revenue because of VIG marketing	8,291	4,405	102	12,798
17 Provincial tax revenue on additional net revenue ($ 000s)	829	441	10	1,280

Note: Provincial sales tax (PST) is 10% of revenues; federal government tax (GST) is 7% of the selling price. PST is calculated on the combined selling price plus GST, e.g., a product or service priced at $1.00 would incur a $0.07 PST. The payment due is $1.177 or $1.18.

Given the provincial sales tax of 10 percent on all products and services, row 17 is calculated by multiplying row 16 by .10. The estimates in row 17 represent the net return in additional tax dollars generated from the linkage-advertising program. Before considering conservative estimates of multiplier effects of expenditures (e.g., 3.0 to 3.5), the net additional tax revenue to the province from linkage-advertising program ($1,280,000) is below the estimated total cost of the program ($2,360,000). Using a conservative expenditure multiplier of 3.0, the net additional provincial tax generated from the linkage-advertising program is $3,840,000, a net return on investment of $1.63 per dollar invested.

In addition to assuming the linkage-advertising program did not cause a share of VIG requesters to convert into visitors, this analysis assumes no carry-over effects of future visitors keeping and referring to their copy of the VIG when planning future trips to PEI.

The additional total expenditures of $12,798,000 likely to represent the difference between life and death for several PEI tourism-related enterprises. Additional analysis of the behaviour of visitors who acquired versus those who did not acquire the VIG indicates that acquiring the VIG is associated with substantial increases in visitor traffic to outlying destinations

Table 6.5 Rate of New and Repeat Customers Visiting Destination Areas

Destination Area	New Customer			Repeat Customer		
	VIG	No VIG	Total	VIG	No VIG	Total
Brackley; Stanhope; Dalway	49	24	42	47	25	36
Cavendish	92	86	90	77	49	64
Charlottetown	95	95	95	89	74	82
Eastern Kings	32	16	28	29	24	27
Evangeline	16	11	15	11	6	9
Kensington	52	51	51	46	24	36
New London	50	50	50	38	16	28
Southern Kings	29	14	25	27	16	22
South Shore	36	24	33	30	19	25
Summerside	52	38	48	46	31	38
West Prince	21	13	19	19	13	16

Note: Declines in visit rates occur often in this table from VIG to no VIG segments for both new and repeat customers. Both main effects are significant for most destination areas.

in PEI (e.g., Eastern Kings and West prince regions), without decreasing visitor traffic to the two most popular destinations (Charlottetown and Cavendish). Details of this association with the VIG of a spreading movement of the visitors throughout the province are summarised in Table 6.5.

For some of the relatively low-income outlying PEI areas, such as West Prince, tourism is a vital industry for a substantial share of residents' income, even though the tourism expenditures in these areas represent a small share of total tourism expenditures in the province. Without the VIG program, it is estimated to be substantially less without the linkage-advertising program (these estimates are available upon request).

Discussion

The pattern of results presented provides strong support that the linkage-advertising program was a substantial influence on changing destination behaviours and increasing the expenditures of visitors to PEI. This is one of the unique features of the presentation of the post-test-only design with predicted higher-order interactions of the influence of linkage-advertising. Previous studies have reported the use of formal quasi-experimental designs to measure the effects of marketing and advertising on customer behaviour variables (e.g., Ehrenburg, 1972; Lilien and Ruzdic, 1982; Weinburg, 1960). Unfortunately, the vast majority of reported studies on the influence of advertising on customer expenditures and other customer behaviours do not include attempts to substantiate the interpretation of cause-and-effect relationships between advertising and customer behaviour. Greater effort is needed to use "procedures that reduce the uncertainty about causal connections even though this uncertainty can never be reduced to zero" (Cook and Campbell, 1979, p. 11).

Advertising researchers and strategists need more knowledge about telling weaknesses of research designs that do not permit reasonable causal inferences of the effect of advertising on customer behaviour, such as the widely used one-group post-test-only design. The continued use of weak tests of causal hypotheses of the effects of advertising on sales likely perpetuates the low faith in advertising among many senior managers.

Equally important, marketers all need to learn about using generally interpretable, nonequivalent control-group designs and actual applications of such designs in advertising aids such learning. A substantial increase in knowledge and application of these designs will increase the credibility of the idea that advertising sometimes has an influence on sales and profits; and marketers can usefully estimate sales and profit levels with and without advertising.

The specific findings described in this report support Davidson's (1985, 1994) axiom that visitors to a destination may use linkage-advertising for help in planning where to go and what to do while in the destination area. This may be the primary benefit of linkage-advertising to customers and could lead to substantial increases in customer expenditures among visitors who have already made their destination choices. The results described for PEI lead us to conclude that the increases in customer expenditures and the resulting return on investment justifies the province's linkage-advertising program, even when the very conservative viewpoint is adopted that the program was not a factor in converting inquirers (persons requesting the linkage-advertising) into visitors.

References

Babakus, E. and Boller, G. W. "An empirical assessment of the SERVQUAL scale," *Journal of Business Research*, 24, 3 (1992): 253–268.

Banks, S. *Experimentation in Marketing*, New York: McGraw-Hill, 1965.

Campbell, D. T. "Degrees of freedom" and the case study. *Comparative Political Studies*, 8 (July 1975): 178–193.

Campbell, D. T. and Stanley, J. C. *Experimental and quasi-experimental designs for research*, Chicago: Rand NcNally, 1966.

Caples, J. *Tested Advertising Methods*, Englewood Cliffs, NJ: Prentice-Hall, 1974.

Cappo, J. "Agencies: change or die," *Advertising Age*, 16, Nov 1992: 52.

Churchill, G. A. "A paradigm for developing better measures of marketing constructs," *Journal of Marketing Research*, 16 (February 1979): 64–73.

Churchill, G. A. *Marketing Research*, Chicago: Dryden Press, 1991.

Cook, T. D. and Campbell, D. T. *Quasi-experimentation*, Chicago: Rand McNally, 1979.

Davidson, T. L. "Strategic planning: A competitive necessity," in C. R. Goeldner (ed.), *The battle for market share: Strategies in research in marketing, travel and tourism research association*, Salt Lake City, UT: University of Utah, 1985: 103–108.

Davidson, T. L. "Assessing the effectiveness of persuasive communications in tourism," in J. R. Brent Ritchie and C. R. Goeldner (eds), *Travel, tourism and hospitality research* (2nd ed.). New York: Wiley, 1994: 537–543.

Ehrenburg, A. S. C. *Repeat-buying,* Amsterdam: North Holland, 1972.

Frequency Marketing, *Colloquy,* 1993.

Garfield, B. "There's catch to States' 'come hither' approach," *Advertising Age,* 65 (June 1994): 32.

Krugman, H. E. "The learning of consumer preferences," *Journal of Marketing,* 24 (Fall 1962): 621–631.

Lilien, G. L. and Ruzdic, A. A. "Analysing natural experiments in industrial markets," *TIMS/Studies in the Management Sciences,* 18 (1982): 241–269.

Messmer, D. J. and Johnson, R. R. "Inquiry conversion and travel advertising effectiveness," *Journal of Travel Research,* 14 (Spring 1993): 14–21.

Nisbett, R. E. and Kanouse, D. E. "Obesity, food deprivation, and supermarket shopping behaviour," *Journal of Personality and Social Psychology,* 12 (1969): 289–294.

Nunnally, J. C. *Psychometric theory,* New York: McGraw-Hill, 1978.

Peter, J. P. "Construct validity: A review of basic issues and marketing practices," *Journal of Marketing Research,* 17 (May 1981): 133–145.

Prince Edward Island Department for Tourism, Parks, and Recreation, *1992 Tourist entry/exit survey,* New York: Wiley, 1992.

Rapp, S. and Collins, T. *Maximarketing,* New York: McGraw-Hill, 1987

Rapp, S. and Collins, T. *The Great Marketing Turnaround,* New York: McGraw-Hill, 1990.

Rapp, S. and Collins, T. *Beyond Maximarketing,* New York: Mc Graw-Hill, 1994.

Raymond, C. *The Art of Using Science in Marketing,* New York: Harper & Row, 1974.

Raymond, C. *Advertising Research: The State of the Art,* New York: Association of National Advertisers, 1976.

Schulman, D. "Dirty data and investigative methods." *Journal of Contemporary Ethnography,* 12 (1994): 214–253.

Weinburg, R. S. *An Analytical Approach to Advertising Expenditure Strategy,* New York: Association of National Advertisers, 1960.

Wilson, E. J. and Wilson, D. T. "'Degrees of freedom' in case study research of behavioural theories of group buying," *Advances in Consumer Research,* 5 (1988): 587–594.

Woodside, A. G. "Modeling linkage-advertising: Going beyond better media comparisons," *Journal of Advertising,* 34 (July/August 1994): 22–31.

Woodside, A. G., Beretich, T. M. and Lauricella, M. A. "A meta-analysis of effect sizes based on direct marketing campaigns," *Journal of Direct Marketing,* 7 (Spring 1993): 19–33.

7
The Role of Human Cognitive Ability (g) in Consumers' Automatic and Strategic Processing of Brands

Notwithstanding a number of widely held claims to the contrary, it is held in the main by scientists, academicians and practitioners that a single measurable factor corresponding to human general intelligence does exist. The factor – Spearman's *g*, is a gauge of human cognitive ability generally assessed with standardised IQ and other psychometric tests that have been developed in over a century of research and testing. Such tests of human cognitive ability, irrespective of substance or structure, time and again provide evidence that the *g* factor influences all aspects of human cognition. For a comprehensive review of the discovery of *g*, cognitive abilities, testing and competing theories to *g*, see Carroll's (1993) work.

Human differences in *g*

Over the past decade, studies in the fields of differential and cognitive psychology, psychometrics, neuroscience and human genetics (Bouchard, 1993; Eysenck, 1993; Jensen, 1987; McGue et al., 1993; Plomin et al., 1994) continue to dispel popular nurture, socio-economic, and environmental effects propositions of *g* by offering more proof that individual human differences have a substantially neural and genetic basis.

Recent research emanating from the Medical Research Council Cognition and Brain Sciences Unit of Cambridge University in the United Kingdom (Duncan et al., 2000) utilised positron emission tomography (PET) scans of human brains involved in high- and low-*g* tasks to examine the neural basis of Spearman's *g*. In the research, investigators conducted a series of PET scans on subjects throughout the execution of high-*g* spatial, verbal and perceptuo-motor tasks. High-*g* scans were then compared with matched PET scans of low-*g* tasks executed by the same subjects in the study. Investigators discovered that contrary to the widely held view that *g* reflects a broad sample of cognitive functions, high-*g* tasks are primarily associated with selective conscription of the lateral frontal cortex in one or both hemispheres of the human brain. As a result, the research demonstrates that high-*g* tasks do not exhibit a diffuse recruitment of multiple regions of the brain, but instead conscript the same frontal region of the brain utilised in a diverse range of cognitive requirements. This same lateral frontal recruitment is displayed for both high- and low-*g* tasks irrespective of the fact that high-*g* and low-*g* comparisons utilised tasks with substantially different content. The results of these tests demonstrate that general intelligence as measured by Spearman's *g* does in fact originate from a precise frontal system. Moreover, this frontal system and its neural basis are central in the control of various types of human behaviour.

Further research studies in the separate but related area of human genetics confirm that the proportion of the population variance in test scores of intelligence attributable to all sources of genetic variability (coefficient of heritability) nearly doubles during the lifespan of a human. For example, heritability of *g* ranges from .40 to .50 when measured in children. In teens and young adults, the coefficient of heritability ranges from about .60 to .70. In later years, shared and between-family environmental effects most noticeable in children and adolescents virtually disappear for adults. A coefficient of heritability of .80 becomes the norm for this age group.

Thus, supported by hundreds of research studies conducted over the decades across all ethnicities and cultures, investigators today continue to prove that not only is there a neural basis for Spearman's *g*, but that humans are also disparate in their intellectual potential. Moreover, they are born that way. Therefore, just as each person is born with a different potential for size, height, athletic ability and the like, so too are they each born with a different potential for cognitive ability.

The role of *g* in life

In recent years, much of the debate over intelligence and intelligence testing has focused on the issue of whether or not it is beneficial to assess individuals on a single key dimension such as *g*. After all, even if *g* is really a general measure of human intelligence and cognitive ability, how can such a measure be of use or benefit in the business of an individual's day-to-day life? Furthermore, of what practical use (or for that matter, misuse) could it be to institutions, business, government and the general public?

Human cognitive ability characterised by *g*, has been established as the single most effective predictor of an individual's performance at school and on the job. Furthermore, *g* has been confirmed to have considerable influence on a person's quality of life – foretelling aspects of health and well-being, probability of divorce, unemployment, and more.

Writing for the *Financial Times* (October 8, 1999), professor of psychology Adrian Furnham at University College, London makes reference to

Cattell's theory of fluid and crystallised cognitive abilities with regard to managerial and entrepreneurial success in the information economy. Cattell's theory of g takes the form of a truncated hierarchy comprised of two components, namely crystallised intelligence (Gc) and fluid intelligence (Gf). The model lacks the apex of the third order factor g, displaying instead twin-peaks of Gf and Gc. Gc is most accurately described as consolidated knowledge arising from opportunity and motivation in applying fluid intelligence. Gf or fluid intelligence is theorised as the ability to solve novel problems in which specific prior knowledge is of little or no use.

Furnham asserts that managers today who possess high levels of fluid intelligence (Gf) as designated by Cattell (cf. Horn, 1986) are most likely to reap the rewards of success in the quickly changing technologically driven environment of the new millennium. Managers' on-the-spot reasoning ability as characterised by Gf, which is independent of prior knowledge or skill is of particular value in an Internet economy. Furnham suggests that in the context of the new Internet economy, managers' perspectives on how problems were solved in the past are useless. It is significant to note that research by Jan-Eric Gustafsson (1988) on the Cattell-Horn theory demonstrates Gf to be perfectly correlated with g. Furthermore, Gf is subsumed into a higher-order variable (g) when all second-order factors in the model, including Gf, are residualised. Thus the proposition put forth by Furnham that Gf is of particular value in the fast-paced, technology-driven Internet economy of the 21st century, is in reality, an argument in favour of managers and entrepreneurs today with the highest levels of cognitive ability (g).

Cognitive processes and ability

Despite a close interest in the subject matter of cognitive processes by academicians, psychologists and marketers, a number of issues critical to managing brands have yet to receive the full attention they deserve. Concerned with a study of the interaction between a range of human factors, both cognitive and physical, this research offers insights into the field of marketing that have yet to be comprehensively addressed – namely the role of human cognitive ability or general intelligence (g) in consumer automatic processing of brands.

Cognitive processes, as defined by Hilgard (1980), involve "the acquisition, storage, and use of information to direct behaviour." Carroll (1993, p. 10) in his comprehensive work is most specific when he states:

A cognitive process is therefore one in which mental contents may be representations or encodings either of external stimuli or of images, knowledges, rules, and similar materials from short-term or long-term memory. The response may be either covert (generally unobservable) or overt (observable).

While both definitions are in agreement in the main, they differ in two key aspects. Firstly, Carroll's definition proposes cognitive processes act either upon input from the senses – external stimuli; or stimuli, deriving from short-term or long-term memory. Although Hilgard's definition does not conflict with this principle, it differs from it in that it proposes cognitive processes act upon information. Since all information can be thought of as value-added data, this slight nuance in the use of the word might imply some other process by which meaningless stimuli are attended to. It might also mean that all stimuli, whether they initiate from the senses, short-term and/or long-term memory, are significant in that they are "information." Secondly, Carroll's process ends with a human response, which may be either observable or unobservable. Thus one can observe that bright sunlight will cause the pupil of the human eye to constrict, but one may not be able to readily observe the degree to which a parent's thoughts may race when the prodigal child returns home. In contrast, Hilgard's definition of cognitive processes specifies that the information (stimuli) direct human behaviour.

Consequently, with specific regard to cognitive processes, Carroll's definition is for the most part appropriate. Hilgard's proposition appears more closely linked to that of an information process. More particularly, it resembles the process proposed later by Jensen (1998). As in Hilgard's definition of cognitive process, Jensen's definition of an information process stresses that the processes "govern the person's decisions and behaviour in a particular situation."

Information processing

There is little disagreement that information processing is at the root of performance scores for IQ and other psychometric tests that are *g* laden. Nonetheless, understanding the basic nature of information processes in human cognition is fundamental for an appreciation of the correlation between the ability to process information and *g*. Despite the fact that information processes are much-studied phenomena in the field of cognitive psychology and other scientific and medical disciplines, competing theories all tend to rely upon a common definition like that proposed by Jensen:

> Information processes are essentially hypothetical constructs used by cognitive theorists to describe how persons apprehend, discriminate, select and attend to certain aspects of the vast welter of stimuli that impinge on the sensorium to form internal representations that can be mentally manipulated, transformed, related to previous internal representations, stored in memory (short-term or long-term), and later retrieved from storage to govern the person's decisions and behaviour in a particular situation (Jensen, 1998, p. 7).

Further to a common definition, two basic tenets of how information processes function have emerged. In the first, it is proposed the processes happen in stages. The stages may come about serially, but at other times they may occur in parallel. In the second tenet, it is agreed information processes occur in real time with each step of the process requiring a discrete amount. As a consequence of both tenets, time is the natural scale for measurement when the processes are studied (Jensen, 1998).

Information processing elements

Though previous theories on human memory structures made analogy to the manner in which computers manipulate, store and retrieve information (cf. Broadbent, D. E., 1957; Atkinson and Shiffrin, 1968), Newell and Simon (1972) first put forth the concept of "human information processing" in a work titled "Human problem solving". In this study the authors proposed that performance of cognitive tasks come about through the function of integrated "programs." The sole purpose of these programs or "production systems" is to process information made available from the senses through sensory channels and/or from memory stores that exist in the central nervous system.

The communications, psychology, and marketing literatures provide several models of human information processing. Most models have some elements in common with one another. No formal model is accepted universally. Jensen (1998) offers a simple straightforward model as demonstrated in Figure 7.1. The model incorporates common elements from numerous proposals. Even though it is understood most information processes originate from physiological and/or structural aspects of the human brain, much of what is agreed is represented by analogy as a series of boxes and flow diagrams in the model. Comparable to most all flow diagrams, lines in the model represent the directional flow of information to and from boxes that stand for processes that act upon the information. In Jensen's model, stimuli from the outside world act as the initial inputs into the information processes. Stimuli may be as mundane as a fall in glucose that sets off the urge of hunger or as complicated and vague as the feeling of loneliness of spirit. Differing stimuli like the two previously mentioned cause unique responses. The responses in turn direct individual behaviours, which may or may not be restricted to a particular response and/or stimulus. For example, the behaviour involved in the act of eating a chocolate bar may be governed by the urge of hunger (response) resulting from a fall in glucose (stimulus). Alternatively, eating a chocolate bar may relate with a feeling of loneliness of spirit. In each case the observed behaviour may be the same, but the stimulus and response that controls it is unique.

Sensory buffer

Sensory stimuli all enter the brain in an undifferentiated form as a torrent of neurons firing along a specific path. Incoming sensory stimuli follow

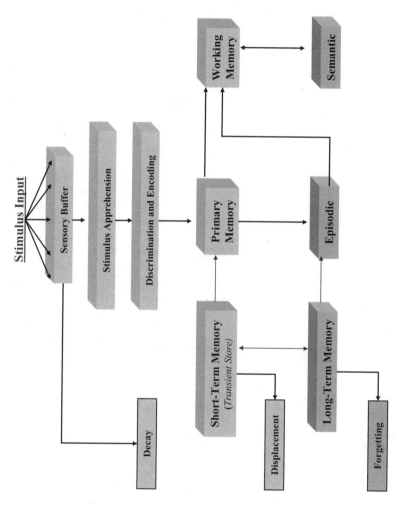

Figure 7.1 Human Information Processing Model

timeworn neural paths from the sensory organ to precise brain destinations. Thus, the determinants for vision, smell, hearing and so forth depend not only on the sensory organ receiving the input and the pathways neurons follow, but also on which exact neurons are stimulated.

To accommodate this constant barrage of stimuli, it is theorised that humans have a sensory buffer to protect the information processing system from an overload of sensory stimulation. This buffer is displayed as the top of the human information-processing model in the previous diagram. The sensory buffer functions as a filter of sorts. Its primary purpose is to insure only specific stimuli are relevant to consciousness at any one particular time. The need to limit stimuli is a fundamental element of the mental state of attention. Without attention or focused awareness no particular portion of the total amount of stimulus input through the senses could possibly be salient.

Stimulus apprehension, discrimination and encoding

When there is a perceived change in salience, stimuli are captured for further processing. The complementary processes of discrimination and encoding later act upon stimuli that have been detained in the stimulus apprehension phase of the model. Responses which consistently vary with dissimilar stimuli indicate which should be singled out for selection or discrimination. Encoding, a process that transforms one sort of input into another, occurs automatically with discrimination. Encoding stage input transformation might be compared with the analogue to digital processes that occur each time a telephone is utilised. Voice emissions vibrate a diaphragm (analogue) in the microphone of the telephone handset. The analogue vibrations are converted to electrical pulses that are converted later by switching computers to a unique series of ones and zeros (digital signals) for transmission by light through fibre optic cables and other electronic means. The reverse of the process occurs on the receiving end of the transmission.

Only information that has been stored can be retrieved. Moreover, the manner in which it is stored affects how and where it will be retrieved (Tulving and Thomson, 1973). Thus, during the encoding process each stimulus is assigned a unique identifier or mark for future retrieval. Encoding of stimuli may or may not complement the discrimination process. For instance, the awareness of well-known stimuli will more often than not engage both discrimination and encoding. The perceptions of stimuli such as familiar brands like Coke, Ford, Marlboro and IBM will typically involve both discrimination and automatic encoding (Tulving and Schachter, 1990). Stimuli such as ЧШФҍ will be discriminated but not encoded. On the other hand, repeated exposure to ЧШФҍ will in the end normally cause idiosyncratic encoding.

Short-term memory

Short-term memory (STM) is also identified as transient store. Though the memory may be very transient, lasting only a fraction of a second, short-term memory in some form nevertheless appears essential for consciousness. The aspect of transience – namely rapid decay of the information input, represents a primary characteristic of STM. Limited processing capacity is another characteristic that is strongly associated with short-term memory. Numerous studies on the transient nature of STM have been conducted. Peterson and Peterson (1959) and Glazner and Cunitz (1966) conducted two outstanding early works.

Primary Memory (PM) and Working Memory (WM) are theorised to encompass the whole of short-term memory. The first component Primary Memory (PM) functions as a short-term staging area. PM does not act upon information, but merely passes it on to Working Memory (WM). WM will review, rehearse, manipulate, convert and operate upon information it receives from PM. However, some complex processing functions of WM may be bypassed altogether via use of automatic-unconscious processes that result from extensive practice of invariant tasks. Like Primary Memory, Working Memory will also act as a staging area from which information may be transferred to long-term memory, specifically Semantic Memory. The actual operation of filing and storing information consumes some of the available capacity of WM. This in turn diminishes the capacity of WM for processing incoming information.

Long-term memory

Though short-term memory (STM) is limited by the transience of the information input, long-term memory appears to have practically unlimited storage capacity. This unlimited storage capacity of LTM is a function of the fundamental nature of memories. LTM is what is normally associated with the term "memory" or "memories." Memories are collections of neurons that fire synchronously in the same pattern each time they are triggered. The links, which connect individual neurons together, are created through the process of long-term potentiation (LTP). The faster a neuron fires, the greater its electrical discharge. Thus, when a single cell receives a stimulus that causes it to fire, it will cause its neighbour cell to fire if it fires fast enough. This action will change the chemical nature of the second cell such that it will remain in a stand-by state for hours or perhaps days. Should the first cell fire again within this time, even a weak response will trigger the second cell. Each time the cells fire in synchrony the chemical link between the two is strengthened so that eventually they become bonded. Consequently, when one cell fires, so too does the other. Should these two linked cells fire rapidly enough to fire a third cell to which they are both weakly attached, the three cells will become bound together to comprise a distinctive firing pattern. This distinctive firing pattern is what makes a memory.

Long-Term Memory (LTM) like Short-Term Memory is theorised to consist of two parts, Episodic Memory and Semantic Memory. Both parts are accessible to Working Memory (WM). Information and experiences that are destined for long-term memory are moved to the hippocampus region of the brain where they may be initially stored for 2–3 years. During this time the hippocampus will replay the experiences back to the cortex region of the brain.

Episodic Memory comprises personal spatial-temporal experiences. These experiences or episodes are recorded in a fashion analogous to film. Thus, episodic memories are neither abstract nor symbolic depictions of personal experiences in time and space. Episodic memories are encoded by the hippocampus region of the human brain and stored in its cortex. The frontal cortex accomplishes retrieval of these memories, which are scattered about the cortical areas of the brain. Because of this specific structure and functioning, episodic memories are more accessible to recognition than to recall. Recognition is the ability to correctly identify previously encountered perceptions or internal experiences as familiar. Occasionally emotional experiences may also play a significant role in episodic memory. Extremely dramatic and/or emotional experiences enter episodic memory directly, completely bypassing (as depicted in the model) Working memory involvement altogether. Consequently, the recognition of a previously encountered person, place, experience, emotion or scent is considered the specific domain of episodic memory.

Semantic memory is the register of facts. These facts are catalogued by the cortex and end up encoded and disseminated throughout the cortical areas of the temporal lobe. Retrieval is carried out by the brain's frontal lobes. Like a library, Semantic Memory holds information that has been abstracted and encoded. The substance of this information is wide-ranging and diverse. For example, Semantic Memory may include information on relationships, rules and previously learned meanings. In may also include strategies for operating on specific categories of information. Strategies for managing chess moves, mathematics operations, statistics, grammar, language and musical notation are specific examples of procedures that may be held in Semantic Memory.

Semantic Memory can be brought into stark relief by certain cases of amnesia – particularly the state of "fugue". This specific state of amnesia involves the loss of episodic memory (EM) but retention of semantic memory. Semantic memory is retained because unlike EM – its complementary portion of long-term memory, information is recorded therein devoid of context (decontextualised). No specific recollection of the occasion or experience associated with the act of acquiring the information is necessary for recall of information from semantic memory.

Information processing speed and response latency

Information processing speed has been demonstrated in numerous tests (Richardson, Eysenck and Piper, 1987; P. C. Kyllonen, 1993; P. C. Kyllonen and R. E. Christal, 1990) to be highly associated with working memory capacity and human general intelligence – *g*. This association is principally accounted for by the processing capacity of the working memory (WM) portion of short-term memory (STM).

Processing capacity of WM is a function of both the speed of information processing and the duration of neural traces occurring in the brain (Lehrl, S. and Fischer, B., 1988; Kline et al., 1994). Filing and storage tasks, as previously mentioned, consume a portion of the available processing capacity of WM and as a consequence diminish it proportionately. Thus, given that short-term memory is transient, it is essential any operation performed by WM on new incoming information take place before it disappears and is lost. For example, when engaged in a simple task of counting objects, most people will make errors if forced to attend to an interruption – especially if the interruption involves the concurrent recital of numbers by a second party. The need to record phone numbers during a directory enquiry and the use of pencil and pad for simple sums are further examples of both the transience of STM and the need to free WM capacity when performing certain tasks. The object therefore of using such aids is to limit the amount of newly input information with which WM has to contend. Thus information can be conveyed to and from LTM in consecutive phases for use in problem solving and the like. Because the actual transmittal of information from WM to LTM consumes a portion of information processing capacity, an essential and constant trade-off occurs in WM between processing and recording information received. Should the amount of incoming information overload WM capacity, processing will collapse and some information will be lost. The result of this loss will cause either output or response related errors. It is for all the reasons previously stated that rapid processing of information is beneficial.

Response times and elementary cognitive tasks

Research studies on information processing ability originating in the field of cognitive psychology confirm that subject response latencies or response times (RTs) to elementary cognitive tasks (ECTs) are effective measures of the speed of human information processing and *g*.

Virtually all ECTs are concerned in some manner with the measurement of the speed of information processing component. Moreover, it is this speed of information processing factor that is so specifically and highly correlated with human intelligence that makes ECTs dissimilar from other measures of psychometric *g*. Because of this, ECTs are typically dissimilar to conventional cognitive ability tests in that test items require no reasoning or problem solving actions by the subject. Since ECTs are unlike IQ tests, which incorporate test items based on previously acquired knowledge, psychometric g can be systematically and independently studied. ECTs are designed to generate data from which individual differences in discrete processes such as stimulus apprehension, discrimination, choice, visual search, and information retrieval from short-term memory scan (STM) and long-term memory (LTM) can be ascertained. The tasks are typically so uncomplicated that each person in the study can execute them effortlessly with few if any errors. Test errors, if any, should not be the result of a lack of understanding of the task requirements by the subject in the study.

Because ECT individual performance is typically measured in terms of response time (RT) or latency, the primary source of individual differences in test scores is therefore generated not by the correctness or accuracy of the responses, but by the time (RTs) required to complete each of the item actions in the test. Response times (RTs) typically reveal something about the cognitive process involved. If for example, a response requires the use of information in memory, the response time will reveal something about the information retrieval process (Sternberg, S., 1996; 1975). Consequently, the response time of about 10 milliseconds required to retrieve the referent of a symbol reveals something about the cognitive processes involving memory. Decisions processes which entail manipulation of knowledge require RTs of about 100 milliseconds. Compositional processes which reflect the time needed to build actions, require RTs of about 1 second. Execution level processes which call for time to perform actions can demand RTs in the vicinity of 10 seconds.

Variations in the speed and efficiency of information processing as reflected by RTs for cognitive processes not only reflect something about the nature of the processes, but also individual differences in cognitive ability. This is consistent with findings from numerous research studies (cf. Jensen, A. R., 1988) that demonstrate RTs to ECTs, particularly those that strain the capacity of working memory, have typical correlates of between –.50 and –.70 with g. Individuals with greater levels of ability, demonstrate significantly lower RTs when processing information than those with lesser. With respect to these scores, individual motivation, test taking strategy and speed-accuracy trade-offs do not explain the correlation range of –.50 to –.70 between RT and g.

Though the correlation between RT and speed and efficiency of information processing has been shown to reliably reflect individual differences in g, just what physiological properties of the human brain account for the speed and efficiency of information processing aspect of g are not fully understood. Recent medical research using advanced technologies – namely PET and MRI scans reveal some likely causes. PET scans for rate of glucose metabolism and MRI scans for degree of myelination of nerve fibres. Nerve conduction velocity (NCV) appears to be one such source for individual differences in speed of information processing. Further studies also reveal random biological "noise" in the neural transmission of information to be another source of variation. Noisy transmission of information causes slower speeds of information processing. NCV and biological "noise" in neural transmission have both been shown to be associated with the level of nerve fibre myelination which is itself currently considered to be the main physical source of variation in g.

Response latency in consumer research

Separate but related studies (Fazio et al., 1989) in the field of consumer behaviour and psychology demonstrate that response latency is a highly predictive measure of the consumer's attitude towards the brand. Response latency utilised in this research is the amount of time measured in milliseconds it takes a subject to indicate a feeling of like or dislike towards an object upon viewing it. Top-of-mind-awareness (TOMA) measured by order of brand mention to an unaided brand recall question (Cohen, 1966) is yet another measure of response latency used by consumer psychologists and marketers. Both measures support the general theory that response latency to brand recognition and recall is an indicator of brand strength and favourability. MacLachlan (1977) and colleagues (e.g., Aaker et al., 1980) verify that response latency – defined by MacLachlan as the length of time taken by a respondent to make a paired-comparison choice, is a valid measure of strength of preference. Aaker et al. (1980) found that the combination of measuring response latency and paired comparisons is superior to constant sum measures.

Grunert (1996) and other researchers (cf. Woodside and Trappey, 1992) argue human information processes – specifically automatic-unconscious processes are crucial for understanding brand recall, strength and favourability. With respect to this, Grunert has emphasized in consumer research that two kinds of cognitive processes are significant and discernible. The first are automatic-unconscious processes. The second are strategic. Automatic processes are mostly unconscious, learned and change very slowly and are not subject to the capacity limitations of working memory. Conversely, strategic processes (or conscious thinking) are subject to human working memory capacity limitations (cf. Kyllonen, P. C. and Christal, R. E., 1990) and can be easily adapted to situational circumstances.

A crucial distinction exists between conscious processing and processing without awareness. "Automatic processes are; mainly unconscious, parallel (more than one can occur simultaneously), are learned and changed slowly, are not subject to capacity limitations of working memory and are always triggered in response to a certain cognitive input. In contrast, strategic processes are conscious, serial, and subject to capacity limitations.

However, strategic processes can easily be adapted to situational circumstances" (Grunert, 1996, p. 88).

Based on this concept, Fazio (1986) and his colleagues (Fazio, Powell, and Herr, 1983; Fazio, Powell, and Williams, 1989) proposed and empirically supported a model of the process by which attitudes guide behaviour. Predating the more recent work in social psychology (Fazio et al., 1983; Fazio et al., 1989), several researchers in associated but separate studies from the marketing and consumer research literature, using other expressions of the same concept, have hypothesized automatic-unconscious processing as a moderating link between the relation of attitude and behaviour (cf. Axelrod, 1968; Cohen, 1966; Gruber, 1969; Haley and Case, 1979; MacLachlan, 1977; MacLachlan, 1979; MacLachlan, Czepiel, and LaBarbera, 1979; Aaker, Bagozzi, Carman, and MacLachlan, 1980).

Cohen (1966) is specific in providing a theoretical rationale for a "level of consciousness concept" as an important determinant of "the amount of brand strength." Axelrod (1968; 1986) demonstrated that top-of-mind-awareness (TOMA) of a brand is a sensitive and stable measure of an automatic-unconscious process that can serve as an intermediate criterion for predicting brand-choice and brand-switching behaviour. Previous research by Trappey and Woodside (1992) used automatic-unconscious processing models to demonstrate a strong link between (unaided) attitude-accessibility and primary brand choice behaviour. The research supported by previous studies (Gruber, 1969; Burke and Schoeffler, 1980) offers the conclusion that managers can utilise this aspect of human cognition as a strategic marketing tool.

Prior research underscores the fact that countless consumer decisions do not employ a substantial amount of conscious and/or controlled processing. Largely, the information processing is automatic and unconscious. In daily life for example, the cognition of outside stimuli and the decision to select or deselect them for conscious attention or not, is in itself an unconscious process. The retrieval of information from long-term memory into working memory is an unconscious process. So too is the assimilation of new information with information already stored in memory an unconscious process. Thus, unconscious automatic information processing sets the limits within which conscious strategic information processing can occur (Grunert, 1988).

Automatic-unconscious processes

In 1890 William James put forward the idea that certain human processes were automatic. In so doing, he opened up a debate among theorists that was later to be discussed mainly in connection with the acquisition of motor skills. Consequently, numerous ordinary motor processes (walking for example) have been demonstrated to be the result of automatic processing. Over a period of time however, the notion of what comprises an automatic process has expanded. Simultaneously, a consensus has emerged amongst investigators with respect to the two main features that appear to distinguish and characterise the processes. Firstly, no conscious attention (controlled or strategic processing) is needed. Secondly, a person who is engaged in the process is not prevented from doing other things simultaneously.

Notwithstanding the fact that conscious attention is not required for automatic processes, it is nevertheless undeniably linked with automation. Grunert (1988) makes reference to one such example given by the psychologist James (1950):

> When we are learning to walk, to swim, fence, write, play, or sing, we interrupt ourselves at every step by unnecessary movements and false notes …

Nevertheless, with practice:

> A glean in his adversary's eye, a momentary pressure from his rapier and the fencer finds that he has instantly made the right parry and return. A glance at the musical hieroglyphics, and the pianist's fingers have rippled through a cataract of notes.

Long-term practice – a process that requires conscious and controlled processing – is in most instances fundamental to the development of automatic processes. Controlled information processing demands focused attention from the individual. Moreover, controlled processing requires expenditure of a conscious mental. The processes are relatively slow when compared to automatic processes because input information processing occurs sequentially. Controlled processes are able to deal only with a limited amount of information at one time. Thus the processes are not capable of executing multiple mental operations simultaneously. The association of controlled processing of information with working memory (WM) means that at times WM may become overwhelmed by the volume of information input. This "overload" occurs specifically when the rate of input exceeds the speed at which the information can be processed. Under these circumstances, WM will either breakdown or shutdown. This causes errors and/or a loss of information. Johnson (1984) provided further evidence to support this statement in his studies of motor skills:

> Automation develops slowly with practice and eases responses in those situations in which learning took place but makes it more difficult to respond to new situations.

Current research studies continue to confirm this proposition. Persons who display truly exceptional performance in a particular field depend upon a greater than ordinary amount of automatic processing of crucial knowledge and expertise in their field of achievement. True mastery requires automatic processing of motor and/or non-motor functions. This can only come about through the accurate over-learning of the task's regular aspects. Therefore, practice must continue long beyond the point of initial mastery – to the point that the precise routine is thoroughly "entrenched" (Sternberg, 1977). Few people truly appreciate or understand this fact. The great Spanish violinist Pablo Sarasate (1844–1908), when on being acclaimed as a genius by a music critic, made the point clearly and humorously when he stated: *A genius! For thirty-seven years I've practiced fourteen hours a day, and now they call me a genius!*

While not all tasks are candidates for automatic processing, others are fully so. The degree to which this can be the case varies primarily with the regularity, predictability and routine associated with the information processing requirements of the task. Tasks that require frequent use of a sequence of operations are primary contenders for automatic processing. All the same, though some skills may require little or no automatic processing, others can *never become fully mastered or mastered at all* without it.

Proficiency with a musical instrument is a case in point of a skill that can never be fully mastered without a high degree of automatic processing. When an orchestral violinist sight-reads a piece of music for the first time, the undertaking requires both a high degree of controlled and automatic processing. Highly skilled players are capable of reading several measures ahead of what is actually being played – particularly during fast passages. Simultaneity of different processes or "pattern thinking" occurs as the reading of notes, dynamics and tempo markings on a printed page are automatically translated into precise muscular movements without any thought whatsoever. Upon seeing an arpeggio, scale, or familiar pattern of notes on the page, fingers will automatically undulate across the strings up and down the fingerboard as the bow makes it progress. Concurrently, working memory and controlled information processing capacity are available for managing musical interpretation and the needs of the conductor and ensemble.

Piloting an aeroplane is another example that requires both controlled (conscious) processing and automatic processing of information. Controlled flight involves coordinated, and at times uncoordinated, movements of the elevator, rudder, and ailerons. With practice, an experienced pilot can perform straight and level flight, climbs, descents, turns, climbing and descending turns, turns about a point, steep turns, chandelles and aerobatic manoeuvres without thinking. Automatic processing of these tasks free the pilot to concentrate on other aspects of flight – namely communication, navigation, management of onboard systems and, under visual flight regulations, avoiding other aircraft!

Instrument flight in particular, demands an extremely high degree of automatic processing with respect to both physical movements and monitoring of aircraft systems. Pilots who are beginning to learn instrument flight quickly become overwhelmed as working memory and information processing capacity are strained to the limits. Novices concentrate on "flying" the aeroplane. Typically they will focus their instrument panel scan chiefly on flight attitude instruments such as the artificial horizon, turn-and-slip and vertical speed indicators. In so doing, they neglect navigational, engine, communications, and aircraft systems information. Things go quickly awry. Usually the instructor is required to take control. Little by little however, with hours of practice, instrument scan becomes an automatic process. The experienced instrument pilot will utilise flight attitude instruments to initiate and terminate manoeuvres and periodically check them to monitor progress. In the meantime, the pilot's scan will be expanded to supervise navigation, engine, communications and flight systems instrumentation. Working memory and processing capacity are released from routine flight manoeuvres, scanning and monitoring tasks to carry out the actual requirements of communications and navigation. Thus, were it not for automatic processing of certain regular aspects of piloting an aircraft both under visual and instrument flight conditions, crucial tasks would be neglected. The results of this scenario are nearly always catastrophic.

Automatic processing may also occur with respect to non-motor skills. For example, automatic-unconscious processing occurs amongst persons who are highly skilled at translating messages coded in Morse. Still, perceptual skills that do not lead (or in any case not straight away) to a motor response are perhaps the most well researched examples on the subject. Automatic processing of perceptual skills is concerned primarily with recognising and categorising stimuli as well as determining a fitting reaction to them. These non-motor skills involve cognitive processes in the sense of Hilgard's definition, namely: "... processes concerned with the acquisition, storage and the use of information to direct behaviour."

Non-motor perceptual skills that invoke automatic-unconscious processing have direct relevance for marketers. This is particularly the case when modelling consumer brand recognition and the decision processes involved with further attention towards the brand. In this respect, both automatic and controlled or conscious processes may play a combined role. Strategic or controlled processing of brand stimuli can lead to increased automatic-unconscious processing. Furthermore, once an automatic-unconscious process has been established, strategic or controlled processing may nevertheless play a significant role in the process of information retrieval. Though prior research minimised the interrelation between strategic and automatic-unconscious processing of brand information, over recent years there has been a considerable shift in thinking. Researchers like Grunert have been most notable in this change of position. Contrary to his theory that the vast majority of consumer decisions "...are not based on strategic cognitive processing" (Grunert, 1988: 178), more recent thinking by this researcher posits, "...retrieval is determined by both automatic and strategic processes" (Grunert, 1996: 91).

Attention and perception

Research on automatic and controlled cognitive processes invariably connects to facets of attention and perception. Automatic processes, as previously stated, require neither attention nor conscious effort (most people can walk and chew gum). On the other hand, controlled cognitive processes, thinking, and possibly even consciousness absolutely require the focused awareness associated with attention.

Controlled or conscious processing links

Since controlled information processing demands focused attention from the individual, a conscious mental effort is expended. Conscious processes are relatively slow when compared to automatic processes because information processing occurs sequentially. The processes therefore are able to deal only with a limited amount of information at any one time. Consequently, controlled information processes are not capable of executing multiple mental operations simultaneously. The strong operational association of controlled processing of information with working memory (WM) means that at times WM may become overwhelmed by the volume of information input. This "overload" occurs specifically when the rate of input exceeds the speed at which the information can be processed. Under these circumstances, WM will either fail or shutdown. This causes errors in response and/or a disintegration and loss of information, concentration and focus. Thus, while automatic processes are linked to attention by conspicuous absence, controlled processes, thinking, and even consciousness itself have absolute need of it. But what exactly is attention and how did human information processing systems become linked to it?

The origins of attention

In theoretical models attention comprises three main elements, namely: arousal, orientation, and focus. However, the neurological basis for attention is firmly rooted in human evolutionary biology and development. It is theorised that in early humans attention acted as a warning system for the brain – shutting down some processes and activating others when in danger. Early humans, like their descendants today, were inundated with a barrage of stimuli. While today's humans may cope with an onslaught of stimuli ranging from the mundane to the sublime, our primitive ancestors' selective attention focused primarily on threats to survival. The sensory buffer previously delineated in the diagram of human information processing described how this element protected the information processing system from sensory system overload. Consequently, only the most important bits of information were channelled for attention and thereby relevant to consciousness.

Limiting stimuli is a basic component of attention and focused awareness, and in man's early predecessors, this characteristic would have been critical. For out of the silence and din of the ancient earth, in primal man, movement in the periphery of vision, a cracking twig, the rustle of leaves or the snort of an unseen animal would have immediately engaged the reticular activating system (RAS) of the brain. In present-day man, this assemblage of nerve fibres radiating throughout the thalamus, hypothalamus, cerebral cortex and brain stem continues to be responsible for controlling levels of consciousness, attention and concentration. Many war veterans recollect how their near-death experiences had a mysterious way of heightening their awareness, crystallising their thoughts and focusing their attention in a way that they've never since experienced.

Once activated, this system (RAS) releases a current of adrenaline throughout the brain. Instantly, segments of modern man's primal brain are put on alert, and others closed down. In the brain stem, the reticular formation in the pons (which plays a role in arousal, attention, muscle movements and vital reflexes like the heartbeat) is put on standby. When this occurs, the heart rate slows and breathing typically becomes shallow and quiet. Midbrain tectrum structures – which comprise visual and auditory systems principally involved with reflexes and quick reactions to moving stimuli, come into play. All other unnecessary activity in the brain would cease.

During this phase, the brain waits for incoming stimuli towards which it can react. Its parietal cortex, superior colliculus and a portion of the thalamus known as the lateral pulvinar, maintain the brain in standby-alert mode. These three specific areas of the brain (namely the parietal cortex, superior colliculus and lateral pulvinar) are primarily occupied in sustaining orientation and focus. Any incoming stimuli will trigger immediate reaction in the brain in areas specific to the type of stimulus received. Then, those areas of the brain previously inactive while in standby-alert mode will suddenly light up with neural activity promulgated by the activation of two neurotransmitters – dopamine and noradrenaline. Alpha brainwaves in the 20–40 Hertz range in this portion of the brain are associated with alertness.

Activation of neurons in the superior collicus and parietal cortex in turn will initiate orientation. The eyes directed by the superior collicus, turn to engage the new stimulus. At that moment, the parietal cortex will disengage the brain's attention from any other present stimulus. Focus is then finally instigated by activity in the lateral pulvinar. The lateral pulvinar acts like radar by lighting up and locking on to a target stimulus. Once this occurs, it will transmit information to the brain's frontal lobes, which in turn will fix on the stimulus and maintain attention.

Explaining attention by spreading activation

Human attention is selective. Capacity limitations of the human information processing require it. (Johnston and Dark, 1986, p. 57) Consequently, in daily living amidst an onslaught of constantly changing stimuli, humans focus only upon a small subset. Given this fact, it is no small wonder brands can go unnoticed. In consumer and advertising research, considerable debate has centred on which the level selection of incoming brand stimuli occur. Do consumers screen out stimuli on the basis of past experience or does some substantive processing occur before the selection is made. If this is so for either case, then the nature of the processing reflects an underlying automatic-unconscious process with respect to stimulus recognition. Automatic stimulus recognition is more fully explained by the theory of spreading activation first put forth by Collins and Loftus (1975) in connection with their work on semantic memory. Later Anderson and colleagues used the proposition as a basic mechanism to explain unconscious processes in the cognitive system (Anderson, 1983; Anderson and Pirolli, 1984).

Spreading activation processes assume a neural network in which memory is regarded as a nexus of nodes and links. In this network, neural activation spreads from node to node(s) via links in the nexus. The strength of individual links between nodes determines the range and extent of activation throughout the network (Grunert, 1996, p. 82). Nodes represent cognitive categories or pieces of information that have been stored in memory. Links between nodes represent bi-directional associations between cognitive categories. The strength of the links between nodes may vary from node to node. According to Collins et al. (1975: 408) "...a concept can be represented as a node in a network with properties of the concept represented as labelled relational links from one node to other concept nodes. These links are pointers and usually go in both directions between the two concepts." Moreover, activation can result from external and internal stimulation.

The following figure examines a hypothetical network with regard to application of spreading activation theory when conducting a marketing analysis for a familiar food product – the American hot dog brand Oscar Mayer. Nodes in the network represent bits of information in a constellation associated with the brand name Oscar Mayer. As is demonstrated in the model, the strongest link (illustrated by the width and boldness of the line) can be found between the brand name and the food category hot dogs. Similarly the brand name has strong connections with drinks and baseball – both of which connect with summer.

Other nodes in the constellation demonstrate interconnectedness that ultimately links them back to the brand nucleus. Such a neural network demonstrates that people have a content addressable memory in which memory search is initiated at or near the location of the concept being searched for.

It is important to note with reference to spreading activation that strength of the links between nodes is determined primarily by two factors. In the first case, strength is a function of the amount and quality of processing the information receives. How much a person actually thinks about the information being processed affects the future spread of activation throughout the memory network. Thus, high quality thought processing with respect to information results in stronger links between nodes. This in turn causes a more robust network to be constructed. Secondly, strength is a function of the nature and quality of processing that occurs when information is encoded.

In the "level-of depth-of processing" approach (Craik and Lockhart, 1972; Craik and Tulving, 1975; Lockhart, Craik and Jacoby, 1976) it is proposed that the more the meaning of information is attended to during encoding, the stronger the associations in memory will be. Consequently, the manner in which a person thinks about the information can affect the nature and potential of the connecting links in the network (Grunert, 1996, p. 86). This strength in turn increases not only the likelihood that information will be accessible but also the ease with which it will be recalled. .

The following figures demonstrate varying types of hypothetical neural network schema. These examples demonstrate a few examples in range of the infinite possibilities for the spread of activation throughout memory networks. The first example (Figure 7.2) from Johnston and Dark (1996) illustrates networks comprised of a minimum of three nodes to those of nine. The second example (McClelland and Rumelhart, 1981, p. 61) noted in Figure 7.3 illustrates a network of all possible connections between sixteen nodes. Each letter represents a single neuron in the network. The strength of the connections is not explicitly shown.

Every node in the network can be activated to some greater or lesser degree. Furthermore, activation in the network may result from external stimulation. For example, when a phoneme is heard, the memory node corresponding to that phoneme will become activated. If the nodes related to specific phonemes are externally activated, and if these nodes are strongly linked with higher-order cognitive categories such as a brand name, then the node corresponding to the brand name will also be activated. Activation is an automatic-unconscious process; unconscious, and not subject to capacity limitations. Moreover, activation spreads

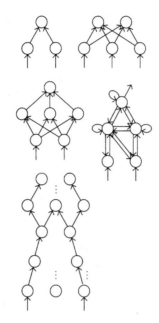

Figure 7.2   Three to Nine Node Networks

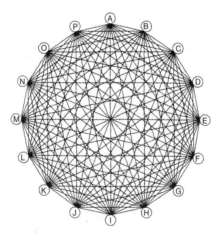

Figure 7.3   A 16-Unit Neural Network Showing All Possible Interconnections

throughout the network in parallel (Balota and Lorch, 1986, p. 64). Because of this parallel process, activation radiates simultaneously from all activated nodes passing through all connections. Consequently, the level of activation for any given node is the sum of all activation it receives from other nodes in the network. Therefore, if during the process activation is lost, such loss is inversely proportional to the strength of the link between two nodes. Within the neural network, patterns of activation will quickly move towards some asymptote in the absence of new sources of activation.

Top-down versus bottom-up cognitive processing

Theories on automatic-unconscious processing ultimately lead back to the nature of human general intelligence and its measure as signified by g. Previous discussion detailed the fact that response times (RTs) to elementary cognitive tasks (ECTs) are highly correlated with the general intelligence factor g. Further discussion laid the groundwork in the case that the ability of working memory (WM) to access, manipulate and process information swiftly and efficiently reveals the fundamental nature and measure of g. To the extent that certain motor and non-motor tasks can become automatic processes, available WM capacity is released from routine tasks to perform operations and manipulate incoming information.

Each and every one of the aforesaid premises ultimately lead full-circle to a question pertaining to the possible effects that automatic processing of elementary cognitive tasks (ECTs) might have on response times (RTs); and thereby the measurement of g. More specifically, if sufficient rehearsal leads to automatic processing of certain motor and non-motor tasks, could response times (RTs) to elementary cognitive tasks (ECTs) be improved through training and practice?

Systematic improvement of performance over the course of practice is evidence of learning. The learning hypothesis of the RT-g correlation is contradicted by evidence that shows that the RTs incertain ECTs are correlated with g, yet show either no improvement with practice, or so slight a degree of improvement as to account for only a fraction of the individual differences variance. After prolonged practice, improvement in ECT performance still shows reliable individual differences between subjects at the asymptotic level of performance (that is, at the point beyond which the effects of practice have nearly leveled off and will show little further improvement for a given individual) (Jensen, 1987).

A study (Neubauer and Freudenthaler, 1994) expressly designed to investigate the effects of prolonged practice on the RT-IQ correlation measured two kinds of RT on a sentence-picture verification test in sixty university students over the course of more than 2,500 trials and nine hours of practice. The authors concluded, "If RTs in an ECT still correlate with psychometric intelligence after more than 2,000 trials of training (as was demonstrated), then top-down explanations of this relationship on the basis of metaprocesses ... or controlled vs. automatic processing ... seem largely implausible. Instead, from our findings we infer a strong support for the biologically based bottom-up explanations of the 'mental speed' theory of intelligence."

In cognitive psychology

Top-down versus bottom-up distinguishes between two theoretical possibilities: (1) Top-down means that the causal direction of the RT-g correlation arises from individual differences in "higher," or more complex, mental processes, which are deemed responsible for individual differences in the "lower," or less complex, speed of processing reflected in RT. (2) Bottom-up means that individual differences in the speed of processing, reflected in RT, are the causal basis of individual differences in the higher, more complex mental processes of the kind involved in abstract reasoning, problem solving, and knowledge acquisition. WM may in fact be g, see Kyllonen and Christal (1990).

The top-down theory holds that higher mental functions, such as the subject's ability to fully grasp the task requirements, to discover and use more effective strategies, to transfer past learning and allocate the most appropriate "cognitive resources" to the particular task, and the like, all determine the person's RT in any ECT. As these kinds of complex mental functions are what are assessed by IQ and the most highly g-loaded tests, and as these higher mental processes influence RT, it is little wonder that we should find a correlation between RT and g. There is an operational distinction between speed and efficiency. Efficiency refers to the moment-to-moment consistency of speed of processing information, as reflected by the amount of variability (measured by the standard deviation) of a person's RT over a number of trials.

The bottom-up theory, on the other hand, holds that individual differences in performance of these higher mental functions are themselves a manifestation of individual differences at a simpler, more basic, and more general level of brain activity, namely, neural and synaptic attributes that determine the speed and efficiency of information processing.

In consumer research

In retail store image research, Tigert (1983) successfully applied what might be identified as top–down (versus bottom-up) models of automatic-unconscious processing to discover which retailing attributes were determinant in customer primary store choice behaviour. Determinant store attributes are store characteristics that lead to choice of particular store to shop (cf., Alpert, 1971; Tigert, 1983).

Tigert (1983) asked retail store shoppers to mention the reasons first and second most important in choosing the store (e.g., supermarket) where they shopped most often. He found that shares of mentions for the determinant attributes using this direct questioning technique were directly correlated highly with logit coefficients in modelling primary store choice. The approach taken by Tigert (1983) is top-down, because he began his questioning with attitude-object, by asking for the name of the primary store, and then asking the respondent for the first and second store attribute that the respondent associated with his/her primary store.

However, the argument may be valid that Tigert's open-ended questioning procedure caused strategic cognitive processing by the respondents, because the respondents were asked to report the first and second store attributes most important to themselves that came to their minds in choosing the store where they shop most often. Such a question requires two steps in answering: first, a network of several store attributes related to the respondent's primary store would be created from long-term memory and entered into working memory; second, the respondent would need to evaluate which of the associations between these store attributes and his/her primary store was determinant of his/her primary store decision. Thus, elements of both automatic and strategic cognitive processing are present in answering the question posed to shoppers by Tigert.

In contrast with Tigert's (1983) approach, Trappey and Woodside (1991) used a bottom-up questioning procedure to measure automatic-unconscious processing of the linkage of store attributes and store names. Using a telephone survey, respondents were asked to name the store that "first comes-to-mind" when hearing each of 14 possible store evaluative attributes, for example, "lowest overall food prices," "most convenient location," and "best quality produce." Both logit and multiple regression models were tested of respondents' primary store choices based on their TOMA responses of store names linked with each of these 14 attributes. These results supported an attribute-accessibility hypothesis of the association of primary store choice based on evaluative attributes and TOMA of store name, and what Hauser (1986) defines as bottom-up consumer agenda of selecting among choice alternatives (cf., Trappey and Woodside, 1991).

Both top-down and bottom-up research approaches to measure attitude-accessibility used by Tigert (1983) and Trappey and Woodside (1992), respectively, indicate direct relationships between store image and the store's ability to attract and maintain patronage exist. Prior research on store image using rating scales (e.g., 5-point or 7-point, "strongly disagree" to "strongly agree" scales) has been criticised severely for its inability to account for only small proportions of the variance in store patronage (cf., Doyle, 1977; Doyle and Gidengil, 1977; Corstjens and Doyle, 1989).

Hypotheses

Though specific linkages between response latency (RTs), attitude and behaviour towards the brand have been previously established (cf. Cohen; Fazio, Powell, and Herr, 1983; Fazio, Powell, and Williams, 1989; Grunert, 1988, 1990; Woodside and Trappey, 1992), research in the consumer behaviour and marketing disciplines continue to ignore the role that human cognitive ability may play in the process. Attitude-to-behaviour, attitude-accessibility and attribute-to-brand research conducted heretofore use measures of response latencies (RTs and TOMA) but fail both in the research method and in the results to account for individual differences in speed of information processing and WM capacity. In so doing, previous research has neglected a possible significant cause for variability in the brand problem-solving, selection and decision processes – namely human differences in cognitive ability – g.

Research presented here into the role that g may play in brand recall and brand choice behaviour has important consequences. More specifically, discovery that answers to unaided brand recall questions under limited response time restrictions proxy RTs to ECTs and/or are affected by individual differences in WM capacity, information processing speed and g, may unearth methodological flaws in previous research. For example, response latency measures used in previous research to measure brand like/dislike utilise a variation of the memory-scan paradigm ECT developed by Saul Sternberg of Bell Labs. Other researchers, most notably Frearson and Eysenck (1986) use the same device

This test measures the time taken to scan short-term memory for a particular item of information and utilises a binary response console (see Figure 7.4) interfaced with a computer that runs trials automatically and records RTs from subjects. Reaction stimuli are programmed in a computer and appear typically in each trial for 3 seconds on a computer monitor display in back of the binary response console. For each trial, the subject responds by depressing either the left or the right button, which may be labeled yes-no, true-false, same-different, or as in research by Fazio et al., like-dislike.

In this research, time and again two remarkable effects are observed in practically all subjects. In the first instance, RT is seen to escalate in a linear fashion. The slope of the line is a function of set size where set sizes vary randomly from 1 to 7 digits in memory scan ECTs. In the second instance, and most importantly, it takes some 30 to 50 msec longer to respond "No" in the experiments than to respond "Yes" (Jensen, 1987). Therefore, because previous research on the attitude-to-behaviour and attitude-accessibility cognitive processes in consumer brand behaviour utilise such devices and contain such measures as RTs to stimuli presented on a computer monitor (cf. Fazio, Powell, and Herr, 1983; Fazio, Powell, and Williams, 1989) there is a distinct possibility they may contain a 30 to 50 msec bias with respect to unfavourable attitudes (like-dislike). Furthermore, previously reported studies have been conducted on university students and do not control for individual human cognitive ability when assessing RTs. Even had the studies done so, because there is a range restriction with respect to cognitive ability (i.e., approximately IQ 110 plus amongst university students), it is difficult to explain how and if such results may be extrapolated to the larger range of a population with normally distributed abilities.

Although research by the author and others has demonstrated that attitude-to-brand accessibility is an automatic-unconscious process (as such, it is not subject to capacity limitations), no previous research in this area has explored to what degree unaided brand recall could be affected by the speed of human information processing and by implication working memory (WM) capacity. Several hypotheses tested herein address this issue and the previously related matters.

Firstly, (H1) because WM has limited capacity, it is hypothesised for any given product category (soft drinks, fast foods, cars, banks) that there is a positive direct relationship between total unaided brand recall measured in a 60-second test and human cognitive ability – g. It follows therefore that (H1a) for highly learned items such as brand names, consumers with higher levels of g have ability to retrieve from long-term memory (LTM) and access in WM significantly more brand information than consumers with lower levels. This extra capacity displayed by individuals with higher levels of g is a function of both the speed and efficiency of information processing. Thus, consumers with greater cognitive ability, who are demonstrably more capable of retrieving (LTM) and processing larger amounts of information at faster speeds, are likely to have more information available in WM during the strategic processing phase of brand choice decision-making. Furthermore, H1 and H1a raise a question with respect to the role human cognitive ability as measured by g, may play not only in brand recall, but also in directing certain consumer behaviours.

H2 asserts that certain consumer behaviours, explicitly the number of hours of television viewing engaged in on a daily basis, will vary according to the individual's cognitive ability. H2a proposes that total unaided brand recall is more dependent upon cognitive ability than advertising. More specifically, the ability to recall a given number of brands within a limited timeframe is less a function of the total media and advertising to which a consumer is exposed – measured by the total number of hours of TV watched daily, than it is the general cognitive ability of the consumer.

Here are the results of the two hypotheses tested. At a fundamental level, both hypotheses and their subparts propose that a subject's ability to recall brand names in long-term memory (LTM) and access and process them in working memory (WM) to answer a timed unaided brand recall test is governed largely by the subject's information processing ability as reflected by g. It is hypothesised in this research that at a elementary level, the recognition of advertising stimuli, the retrieval of information, the provision of a heuristic for brand evaluation, and the ultimate relevance decision that determines further higher-level processing, are all ultimately governed by human cognitive ability or general intelligence (g). The purpose of the research presented herein is to offer preliminary evidence to the effect that 'human variables' controlling for consumer behaviour necessarily include, together with age and gender, human cognitive abilities as well.

Method

Following a pilot test on children reported next herein, seven hundred twenty three interviews were conducted throughout London over a twelve month period of time beginning in the summer of 1998. All interviews, including those in the pilot test, took place in a controlled environment (i.e., the author's university offices, school offices, or rented offices). With the exception of the pilot test, interviews were limited to persons eighteen years of age and older. Each interview included two sets of tasks: (1) a test of the respondent's cognitive ability (*g*) measured by the Kaufman Brief Intelligence Test, and (2) an interviewer administered consumer-based marketing survey. Approximately half of the marketing surveys included a timed (60 seconds) unaided brand recall test in which the respondent was asked to name all brands he/she could recall within a specific product category (detailed later). Apart from this, all respondents were asked to answer additional behavioural, demographic and attitude and lifestyle questions. Attitude and lifestyle questions varied from concert, theatre, art gallery, cinema, and museum attendance to books read and TV viewing habits, as well as hobbies and other activities.

In the first component of the interview, the Kaufman Brief Intelligence Test (K-BIT) Test 2, Matrices was administered, with all its procedures being meticulously adhered to (Kaufman and Kaufman, 1990). K-Bit Test 2, Matrices, is a 48-item noverbal measure consisting of a variety of items involving visual stimuli. Visual stimuli are relegated to two categories – meaningful stimuli are represented by people and objects. Abstract stimuli are depicted as designs and symbols. The Matrices test is carefully planned as a measure of mental processing ability or intelligence. It an especially good measure of simultaneous information processing.

Abstract matrices were made prevalent by Raven (1965) as a means of appraising the intelligence of children and adults. The matrices test were considered more "culture-fair" than the popular IQ tests used at that time. Raven's tests are still universally applied (Raven, Court and Raven, 1996) today. Raven's procedures and tests have received international approval within the discipline of psychology and have been employed in research concerned with general intelligence, race differences in IQ scores, as well as left-brain versus right-brain mental processing, crystallised (*Gc*) opposed to fluid intelligence (*Gf*), remediation of modifiable cognitive skills, and development of theories of information processing (Kaufman and Kaufman, 1983, pp. 46–47). The capacity to solve visual analogies, particularly those with nonfigurative stimuli, has been demonstrated as an very reliable measure of general intelligence (*g*), simultaneous information processing, nonverbal reasoning, and fluid thinking. The capacity for fluid-thinking (Gf) first propagated by Horn and Cattell (1966) in their theory of crystallised (Gc) and fluid intelligence (Gf), signifies the capacity of an individual when encountering novel problem-solving conditions to adapt. All items in the test require understanding of the relationships among the stimuli, and all are multiple choice, requiring the person either to point to the response or say its letter. For the easiest items, the individual selects which one of five pictures goes best with a stimulus picture (e.g., a car goes with a truck, a bone goes with a dog). For the next set of items, which also uses meaningful stimuli, the person chooses which one of six or eight pictures best completes a 2 × 2 visual analogy (e.g., a hat goes with a head just as a shoe goes with a foot). The majority of Matrices items involve abstract stimuli and require the individual either to solve a 2 × 2 or 3 × 3 matrix or to complete a pattern of dots. Each abstract item demands nonverbal reasoning and flexibility in applying a problem-solving strategy. Many items also assess the ability to handle several variables simultaneously.

In the concluding half of the interview, subjects were asked to quickly name all the brands that come to mind for high- and low-involvement products. Two categories of products comprised each of the involvement criteria. Banks and cars represented high involvement criteria while soft drinks and fast foods represented low involvement. Each of the unaided recall/response latency tasks was allocated the limit of 60 seconds and was preceded by the statement "Please name for me as quickly as possible in the next 60 seconds all the fast food (rotate categories) brands of which you are aware. Begin." Elapsed time was kept by the interviewer who recorded the brands mentioned and the order of mention. The order of execution of the four product tasks was randomly rotated from subject to subject.

Pilot test: the role of cognitive ability in brand recall amongst children

There is no surprise in the fact that the human category 'age' has received a great deal of attention on the part of marketers and the behavioural and cognitive sciences. Age is among the most fundamental variables that shape the needs, attitudes and strategies of humans. Apart from gender there are, perhaps, only a few sources of variation that could be used to categorise consumers as clearly. Children's cognition deserves close attention not merely because it is different from that of adults but also because, by being basic to adult's cognitive development, it provides a better insight into the behavioural and communication patterns typical of the more mature consumers.

The enquiry reported in this work was based partially on previous research into automatic-unconscious processing of brands by the author (Woodside and Trappey, 1992; 1996). Further grounding (cf. Grunert, 1996) emanates from the earlier mentioned work on attitude-accessibility of Fazio et al.

(1989) and studies on the psychometric testing of *g*. Several hypotheses, of which only òne is reported herein, were tested using data collected in the course of a specially designed experiment.

The study was confined to a total number of 34 girls between the ages of 11 and 17 years who share similar socio-cultural and educational backgrounds. The research followed the requirements for an experimental design with randomised blocks and repeated measurements from test units. In-person interviews and testing were conducted by the author in the course of two simultaneous sessions scheduled on the 24th of June 1999, at an all-girls boarding school in Eastbourne, East Sussex, England. Girls were allocated to interviews by the Deputy Principal with respect to further acknowledgement of their willingness to co-operate in the study. Each girl was interviewed in isolation in a separate study room. A total number of 32 useable interviews were obtained in the course of the research.

The decision to study responses of girls was driven in part by the evidence that girls display more rapid maturation in verbal expression, absorb irrelevant information more readily, and perform better in tests of perceptual speed and short-term memory than boys do (Jensen, 1999). With regard to the age of the girls studied, Piaget's (1954) theory of cognitive development suggested stratification of subjects into blocks of 11–12, 13–14, and 15–17 years of age to guard against major intra-strata variance. Subject levels of cognitive ability were assumed to be normally distributed.

Results of pilot test

K-BIT Matrices test scores were obtained for a total of 32 subjects. The distribution of the scores displayed a mean IQ score of 99.55 and a median and mode of 99. The scores overall approached that of a normal distribution. Scores for the entire sample were further divided into quartiles. The first quartile comprised Matrices test scores in the range of 19–27 correct items. The mean level for this quartile was a score of 23.77 items. The second quartile included scores in the 28–31 range with a mean of 29.12. The third quartile comprised scores of 32–34 while the fourth included scores of 35 and greater. Mean scores for the third and fourth quartiles were 33.22 and 37.00 respectively.

Table 7.1 indicates Matrices test raw scores to be highly and significantly correlated (coefficient of 0.492 at the .007 level of significance) with the number of fast food brands recalled within sixty seconds. This correlation demonstrates that the ability to recall a higher number of fast food brands within a limited timeframe (i.e., 60 seconds) is associated with greater working memory capacity, higher levels of simultaneous information processing, fluid thinking (G*f*) and ultimately human general intelligence (*g*).

The number of soft drinks (0.130; sig. 0.464) automobiles (0.243; sig. 0.180) and banks (0.031; sig. 0.863) recalled within sixty seconds display

Table 7.1 Children: Matrix Raw Score x No. of Brands Recalled (60 seconds) by Product Category

		Correlations				
		Matrix Raw Score	Drinks	Fast Foods	Cars	Banks
Matrix Raw Score	Pearson Correlation Sig. (2-tailed) N					
Drinks	Pearson Correlation Sig. (2-tailed) N	.130 .464 32				
Fast Foods	Pearson Correlation Sig. (2-tailed) N	.492** .007 32	.107 .582 32			
Cars	Pearson Correlation Sig. (2-tailed) N	.243 .180 32	.396* .025 32	.579** .001 32		
Banks	Pearson Correlation Sig. (2-tailed) N	.031 .863 32	.237 .184 32	.411* .027 32	.643** .000 32	

**. Correlation is significant at the 0.01 level (2-tailed).
*. Correlation is significant at the 0.05 level (2-tailed).

low levels of correlation at best and are not statistically significant. Perhaps the only case worth considering for possible further comment is that of automobile brand recall – a correlation coefficient of 0.243 and a 0.180 level that approaches statistical significance.

Though fast food brands were the only product category significantly correlated with Matrices test raw scores, 60-second brand recall tests indicate some brand categories to be intercorrelated. Automobiles were significantly correlated with soft drinks (0.396; sig. 0.025) banks (0.643; sig. 0.000) and fast foods (0.579; sig. 0.001). Banks showed an additional correlation – 0.411 at the 0.027 level of significance with fast foods. Thus individual girls in the study who were able to recall the highest number of fast food brands within the 60-second timeframe demonstrate not only higher Matrix test raw scores, but also the ability to recall a greater number of high-involvmement product brands – specifically, automobiles and banks.

The following Table 7.2 examines the average number of brands a subject was able to recall with a 60-second timeframe for each of the individual categories soft drinks, fast foods, cars, and banks. This examination is grouped by quartile of raw scores achieved on the Matrices test. The initial quartile represents those girls who correctly assessed 19–27 items in the 48-item test. On average, girls in this quartile correctly assessed 23.77 items out of 48. The second and third quartiles comprise those girls who correctly assessed 28–31 and 32–34 items. The mean number of items correctly assessed for each of these quartiles was 29.12 and 33.22 respectively. The last quartile represents scores of 35–40 correct responses on the 48-item scale. The mean score for this quartile is 37 items correctly assessed.

Table 7.2 No. Brands Recalled (60-seconds) Varying by Product Category and Quartiles of Matrix Raw Score

Mean

Quartiles of Matrix Raw Score	Drinks	Fast Foods	Cars	Banks
19–27 (mean 23.77)	6.56	3.00	7.00	3.88
28–31 (mean 29.12)	5.63	3.60	6.86	3.75
32–34 (mean 33.22)	7.44	4.75	5.75	3.22
35–40 (mean 37.00)	7.50	5.13	9.25	4.13
Total	6.79	4.17	7.22	3.73

Examining the table demonstrates a clear relationship between the matrices test raw scores and the number of brands recalled unaided within a specific product category within a 60-second limited timeframe. For drinks the average number of brands recalled ranges from a low of 6.56 within 60-seconds for the lowest quartile of Matrices raw scores to a high of 7.50 in the highest quartile. This pattern repeats itself for each of the product categories. A mean of 3.00, 7.00 and 3.88 brands are recalled for fast foods, cars and banks respectively in the lowest quartile. The means can be seen to increase steadily through each of the Matrices test raw score quartiles and culminate with 5.13 for fast foods, 9.25 for automobiles and 4.13 for banks.

Note the overall means for each of the product categories. Banks and fast foods (high- and low-involvement products) with overall means of 3.73 and 4.17 respectively, display the smallest number of brands mentioned within the 60-second test. Despite the fact that banks and fast foods represent significantly different levels of consumer involvement in purchase decisions, the observation they are similar with respect to the overall number of brands recalled within the 60-second test is likely due to the reality that both product categories are highly concentrated and contain only a handful of major competitors who advertise heavily. Soft drinks and cars display similarly high overall means of 6.79 and 7.22 respectively and represent the opposite end of the competitive and advertising spectrum. These two product categories are filled with many different brand competitors, some of which are parent-child and/or endorsed brands, all of which engage heavily in advertising and promotional efforts. Automobiles demonstrate the highest overall brand recall amongst the product categories at each level irrespective of Martices test raw score quartile. This can be attributed to the fact that in day-to-day life exposure to differing brands occurs frequently outside of any advertising medium as individuals come into contact with them in transportation and normally observe numerous models, makes and types during the process.

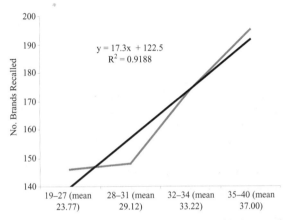

Figure 7.4 Total Brands Recalled (60 seconds) Varying by Quartiles of Matrix Raw Score

The total number of brands mentioned in sixty seconds for each of the four products (soft drinks, fast foods, automobiles and banks) was summed across all subjects. Figure 7.4 demonstrates a strong linear relationship between the total number of brands recalled within a 60-second unaided brand recall test and the general cognitive ability of subjects as meausured by quartiles of Matrices test raw scores in the experiment. Subjects in the lowest quartile of cognitive ability (Matrices test scores) were able to recall a total of 146 brands across both high- and low-involvement product categories while subjects in the highest quartile were able to recall nearly 200.

The sums for the four products were further collapsed into their respective high and low involvement product categories and the sums carried forward. The mean number of brands recalled for each product category was calculated for each quartile of cognitive ability. Table 7.3 pertains to the question and summarises the variation in the total number of brand mentions by product involvement category and cognitive ability. The observed patterns for both product categories demonstrate a steady increase in the number of brand mentions relative to an increase in the level of a

Table 7.3   High and Low Involvement Brand Recall

| Quartiles of Matrix Raw Score | No. of Brands Recalled in 1 Minute | | | | Total Recall |
| | Low Involvement | | High Involvement | | |
	Sum	Mean	Sum	Mean	
19–27 (mean 23.77)	68	9.71	78	9.75	146
28–31 (mean 29.12)	69	9.86	79	11.29	148
32–34 (mean 33.22)	94	11.75	80	8.89	174
35–40 (mean 37.00)	92	13.14	103	14.71	195
Total; Overall Mean	**323**	**11.14**	**340**	**10.97**	663
F		*4.027*		*2.046*	
Significance F		*0.056*		*0.164*	

subject's cognitive ability. Subjects in the lowest quartile of cognitive ability demonstrated a total 68 brand mentions for low involvement products and 78 brands for high involvement products. On average, they were able to recall 9.71 and 9.75 brands per minute respectively for low and high involvement categories. Summing across categories, 146 unaided brand mentions in total are attributed to the lowest quartile.

Conclusions from pilot test

The pilot test provides cautious support for the proposition that children's ability to recall brands is correlated with K-BIT Matrices test scores and thereby with levels of individual cognitive ability provides reason for further study. Results from a further large-scale study are reported in the following section.

Large-scale study of role of cognitive ability in brand recall

Previously it was mentioned in the research methodology that a large-scale study of seven hundred twenty three interviews conducted throughout London over a twelve month period of time beginning in the summer of 1998 followed the pilot test on children. Each interview included the same two sets of tasks: (1) a test of the respondent's cognitive ability (g) measured by the Kaufman Brief Intelligence Test (K-BIT), and (2) an interviewer administered consumer-based marketing survey. Nearly half of the marketing surveys included the 60-second timed unaided brand recall test in which the respondent was asked to name all brands he/she could recall within a specific product category (detailed later). All respondents were asked to answer additional behavioural, demographic and attitude and lifestyle questions.

The following Figure 7.5 highlights the distribution of K-BIT Matrices test raw scores for the 723 subjects who participated in the study. The figure demonstrates a near standard normal curve with respect to the K-BIT Matrices test raw scores. The mean, median, and modal scores for the subjects are nearly identical – 34.67, 35.00, and 34.00 respectively. The mean, median, modal test scores correspond to a range of IQ scores between 100 and 102 for the age groups studied in this sample. It can be seen further in the descriptive statistics that the minimum test score was 15 correct items. The maximum number of items correctly responded to was 48 and represents all items on the K-BIT Matrices test being correctly completed.

H1: For any given product category (soft drinks, fast foods, cars, banks) there is a positive direct relationship between total unaided brand recall measured in a 60-second test and human cognitive ability – *g*.

Approximately half, 332 of 723 subjects studied, participated in the 60-second timed unaided brand recall test. Bear in mind, these 332 subjects, like the subjects in the pilot test and the remainder of the sample, first participated in the K-BIT Matrices test before being asked to name for specific product categories (i.e., soft drinks, fast foods, cars and banks) all the brands they could recall within a limited 60-second timeframe. Respondents were instructed all answers would be recorded. No effort was made to restrict replies by the subject, but subjects were instructed they should try to answer as accurately as possible with as many brands as they could recall within the timeframe. Product categories were rotated from respondent to respondent. The product category mentioned by the interviewer served as the cue for the subject to begin. Thus, subjects were instructed to name all brands within the specific product category within the timeframe immediately upon hearing the product category cue. Consequently, when subjects heard the word "cars," the stopwatch was initiated and they began to enumerate all brands of which they were capable of recalling within the 60-second timeframe. If a subject exhausted the memory search before the limits of 60-seconds, the remaining time was allowed to expire in silence with no further prompting from the interviewer.

Table 7.4 is a correlation matrix that displays Matrices test raw scores by the number of brands subjects were able to recall for each of the specified product categories within the 60-second timeframe. Table 7.4 supports H1 and demonstrates a strong direct association between recall for all product categories and Matrices test raw scores that is statistically significant. More specifically, the data indicate that the number of brands a subject is able to recall within a specified 60-second timeframe is associated with the subject's cognitive ability or *g* as measured by K-BIT Matrices test raw scores. Pearson correlation coefficients range from .311 and .291 for soft drinks and fast foods to .381 and .345 for banks and automobiles. All correlations are highly significant at the .000 level.

Matrix Raw Score

N	*Valid*	723.00
	Missing	5.00
Mean		34.67
Std. Error of Mean		0.24
Median		35.00
Mode		34.00
Std. Deviation		6.37
Variance		40.56
Skewness		-0.34
Std. Error of Skewness		0.09
Kurtosis		-0.30
Std. Error of Kurtosis		0.18
Range		33.00
Minimum		15.00
Maximum		48.00

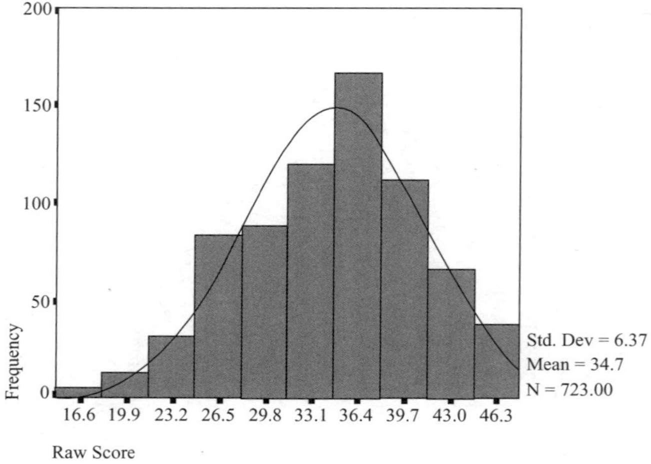

Figure 7.5 Distribution of Matrix Scores

Note further that the size and significance of the correlation coefficients between Matrices test raw score (*g*) and the number of brands recalled within the 60 timeframe displayed in Table 7.4 are entirely consistent with and supported by five previous studies on IQ*g* and RT*g* correlations. These five studies – namely Vernon, 1983; Vernon and Jensen, 1984; Vernon, Nador and Kantor, 1985; Vernon and Kantor, 1986; Vernon, 1989, – demonstrate absolute coefficient sizes in the order of .406, .206, .503, .446 and .673 respectively (Jensen, 1998).

Table 7.4 displays intercorrelations between product categories. Between product correlations demonstrate that if subjects were able to recall a large number of brands within one product category within the 60-second limited timeframe, they were likely to be able do so across all categories of products. The Pearson correlation coefficients between the product categories range from a low .451 between cars and fast foods to a high of .612 between drinks and this same product category. All correlation coefficients are highly significant at the .000 level. As a result, it can be seen the ability to recall a high number of brands within a specific product category can neither be restricted nor attributed to previous specific knowledge or learning that has occurred with respect to one of the product categories prior to the unaided recall test. Nevertheless, the table does demonstrate the correctness of declaring that soft drinks and fast foods be classified as low-involvement product categories and banks and automobiles as high involvement. The correlation coefficients of .509 between high-involvement products – banks and cars and .612 between low-involvement products – fast foods and soft drinks are the two highest coefficients within the table.

H1a: For highly learned items such as brand names, consumers with higher levels of *g* have ability to retrieve from long-term memory (LTM) and access in WM significantly more brand information than consumers with lower levels. Figure 7.6 supports H1a and provides further evidence for the proposition put forth in H1 that there is a positive direct relationship between total brand recall and *g*. The line graph depicted in Figure 7.6 details the number of brands respondents were able to recall for each of the four product categories varying by the actual Matrices test raw scores. The line graph demonstrates not only is there clearly a direct linear association between the cognitive ability of the subjects and the number of brands recalled in each product category, but that the relationship is strongly positive. Accordingly, individuals with higher levels of cognitive ability as represented by *g* and measured by the Matrices test raw scores are able to recall and enumerate more brands within a specified timeframe than individuals with lower abilities.

Operations performed in WM on brand names retrieved from LTM must occur before the information is lost. If the amount of new information incoming to WM exceeds its capacity, then transfer to and from LTM

Table 7.4 Matrices Test Raw Scores x No. of Brands Recalled (60-seconds) by Product Category

Correlations

		Matrix of Raw Score	No. of Soft Drink Brands Recalled in 60 Seconds	No. of Fast Food Brands Recalled in 60 Seconds	No. of Banks Recalled in 60 Seconds	No. of Automobile Brands Recalled in 60 Seconds
Matrix of Raw Score	Pearson Correlation					
	Sig. (2-tailed)					
	N					
No. of Soft Drink Brands Recalled in 60 Seconds	Pearson Correlation	.311*'				
	Sig. (2-tailed)	.000				
	N	330				
No. of Fast Food Brands Recalled in 60 Seconds	Pearson Correlation	.291*'	.612*'			
	Sig. (2-tailed)	.000	.000			
	N	327	327			
No. of Banks Recalled in 60 Seconds	Pearson Correlation	.381*'	.461*'	463*'		
	Sig. (2-tailed)	.000	.000	.000		
	N	329	329	327		
No. of Automobile Brand Recalled in 60 Seconds	Pearson Correlation	.345*'	.477*'	.451*'	.509*'	
	Sig. (2-tailed)	.000	.000	.000	.000	
	N	327	327	326	327	

** Correlation is significant at the 0.01 level (2-tailed).

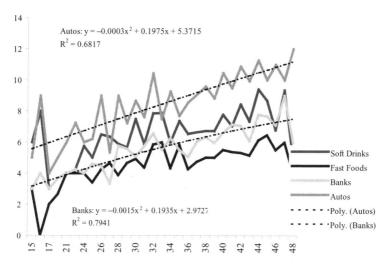

Mean Recall (y) by Matrices Test Raw Scores (x)

Autos: $y = -0.0003x^2 + 0.1975x + 5.3715$
$R^2 = 0.6817$

Banks: $y = -0.0015x^2 + 0.1935x + 2.9727$
$R^2 = 0.7941$

Soft Drinks
Fast Foods
Banks
Autos
·Poly. (Autos)
·Poly. (Banks)

Figure 7.6   No. Brands Recalled (60 seconds) Varying by Matrices Test Raw Scores

occurs in stages in order that all of it can be retrieved in WM for solving the problem or answering the query. Swapping occurs between processing and storage of information as transfers of information between LTM and WM and vice versa. This exchange alone takes up some WM capacity. Because the limited processing capacity of WM is a function of the speed and efficiency of information-procesing, individuals with greater ability are at an advantage insofar as they are able to process or store more information before it decays beyond retrieval. Table 7.5 demonstrates this clearly with respect to the total number of brand names recalled within the 60-second timed test and provides further support to H1a.

Matrices test raw scores were grouped into quartiles that range from a low of 15–33 correct test score items (mean 27.95) to a high of 42–48 items (mean of 44.17). Table 7.5 demonstrates both numerically and graphically in a more compact and concise form information presented in Figure 7.6. It is possible to observe in Table 7.5 the near perfect linear relationship between the number of soft drinks, fast foods, banks and automobiles recalled and *g* as delineated by quartiles of Matrices test raw scores. In every instance, subjects in the lowest quartiles of cognitive ability in the study find themselves at a disadvantage to those in the highest quartiles with respect to the absolute number of brands they are able to summon up within a limited amount of time.

Subjects were able to recall on average in ascending order, 5.13 brands overall for fast foods, 6.25 brands for banks, 7.20 for soft drinks and 9.25 for automobiles. Soft drink brand recall ranged from a low of 6.36 brands

Table 7.5 No. of Brands Recalled by Quartiles of Matrices Test Scores and Product Category

	Mean	Std Dev.
Soft Drinks		
15–33 (mean 27.95)	6.36	2.38
34–38 (mean 36.33)	6.78	2.29
39–41 (mean 39.97)	7.18	2.63
42–48 (mean 44.17)	8.40	2.95
Total (n = 326)	7.20	2.68
Fast Foods		
15–33 (mean 27.95)	4.51	2.01
34–38 (mean 36.33)	4.91	1.88
39–41 (mean 39.97)	5.29	2.11
42–48 (mean 44.17)	5.80	1.98
Total (n = 326)	5.13	2.03
Banks		
15–33 (mean 27.95)	5.15	1.98
34–38 (mean 36.33)	5.93	2.07
39–41 (mean 39.97)	6.56	2.37
42–48 (mean 44.17)	7.34	2.53
Total (n = 326)	6.25	2.38
Automobiles		
15–33 (mean 27.95)	7.76	3.35
34–38 (mean 36.33)	8.98	3.17
39–41 (mean 39.97)	9.58	3.14
42–48 (mean 44.17)	10.60	2.50
Total (n =326)	9.25	3.20

Recall (y) by Matrix Score (x)

in the lowest quartile to 8.40 in the highest while fast foods ranged from 4.51 to 5.80. Bank brand recall extended from a minimum of 5.14 in the 15–33 correct test item quartile to maximum of 7.34 brands called to mind by subjects in the highest quartile of 42–48 correct test items.

Automobile brand recall depicts strikingly similar results to those seen in the pilot study with girls. The number of automobile brands recalled not only exceeded counterpart high-involvement product bank brand recall at every level of cognitive ability, but that for each of the low-involvement products as well. The graph demonstrates that even in the lowest quartile of cognitive ability, subjects were not simply able to recall more brand names than in the other product categories, but were able to recall more than those in the highest quartiles for fast foods and banks. The question previously raised in the pilot study as to whether this can be attributed to the fact that in day-to-day life exposure to differing brands occurs frequently outside of any advertising medium as individuals come into contact with them in transportation is introduced again here.

The following Table 7.6 utilises the Tukey HSD test to examine the differences between the mean number of brands recalled for each quartile of cognitive ability and product category. The table demonstrates statistically significant differences between the means for the lowest quartiles and highest quartiles in each and every product category – soft drinks, fast foods, banks and automobiles. For soft drinks, members in the highest quartile of cognitive ability not only recall more brands within a 60-second recall test than those in the lowest, but also those in middle two quartiles. No significant differences in brand recall are observed within the lower three quartiles. Fast foods show a similar pattern, with the exception there is no statistically significant difference in the mean number of brands recalled for the two highest quartiles, specifically 42–48 and 38–41 correct test items. With respect to banks, the lowest quartiles of cognitive ability show no significant differences between each other, but do demonstrate significant differences for each between the upper two quartiles. No significant differences between the mean number of automobile brands recalled can be seen between the two upper quartiles of Matrices test scores. However, the lowest quartile exhibits significantly lower means than the remaining upper three and the uppermost quartile is significantly different from the lowest two.

Referencing Table 7.5 once again in the context of analysis presented in Table 7.6, it can be seen that not only are the differences in number of brands recalled for the upper and lower quartiles of cognitive ability statistically different, they are hugely so. For example, there is a 32 percent difference between subjects in the lowest quartile of cognitive ability and the highest with respect to the number of soft drink brands they are able to call upon in a 60-second unaided recall test (6.4 soft drink brands versus 8.4). This pattern repeats itself for each of the product categories. For fast foods

Table 7.6 Tukey HSD of No. of Brands Recalled by Quartiles of Matrices Test Scores and Product Category

Multiple Comparisons

Tukey HSD

Dependent Variable	(I) Quartiles of Cognitive Ability (Brand Study Only)	(J) Quartiles of Cognitive Ability (Brand Study Only)	Mean Difference (I-J)	Std. Error	Sig.	95% Confidence Interval	
						Lower Bound	Upper Bound
No. of Soft Drink Brands Recalled in 60 Seconds	15–33 (mean 27.95)	34–38 (mean 36.33)	-.42	.39	.714	-1.43	.59
		39–41 (mean 39.97)	-.82	-.43	.223	-1.93	.28
		42–48 (mean 44.17)	-2.04*	.40	.000	-3.07	-1.01
	34–38 (mean 36.33)	15–33 (mean 27.95)	.42	.39	.714	-.59	1.43
		39–41 (mean 39.97)	-.41	.41	.760	-1.47	.66
		42–48 (mean 44.17)	-1.62*	.38	.000	-2.60	-.64
	39–41 (mean 39.97)	15–33 (mean 27.95)	.82	.43	.223	-.28	1.93
		34–38 (mean 36.33)	.41	.41	.760	-.66	1.47
		42–48 (mean 44.17)	-1.22*	.42	.019	-2.29	-.14
	42–48 (mean 44.17)	15–33 (mean 27.95)	2.04*	.40	.000	1.01	3.07
		34–38 (mean 36.33)	1.62*	.38	.000	.64	2.60
		39–41 (mean 39.97)	1.22*	.42	.019	.14	2.29
No. of Fast Food Brands Recalled in 60 Seconds	15–33 (mean 27.95)	34–38 (mean 36.33)	-.40	.30	.549	-1.18	.38
		39–41 (mean 39.97)	-.78	.33	.091	-1.63	.08
		42–48 (mean 44.17)	-1.28*	.31	.000	-2.08	-.49
	34–38 (mean 36.33)	15–33 (mean 27.95)	.40	.30	.549	-.38	1.18
		39–41 (mean 39.97)	-.37	.32	.646	-1.19	.45
		42–48 (mean 44.17)	-.88*	.29	.015	-1.64	-.12

Table 7.6 Tukey HSD of No. of Brands Recalled by Quartiles of Matrices Test Scores and Product Category – *continued*

Tukey HSD

Multiple Comparisons

Dependent Variable	(I) Quartiles of Cognitive Ability (Brand Study Only)	(J) Quartiles of Cognitive Ability (Brand Study Only)	Mean Difference (I-J)	Std. Error	Sig.	95% Confidence Interval Lower Bound	95% Confidence Interval Upper Bound
	39–41 (mean 39.97)	15–33 (mean 27.95)	.78	.33	.091	–.08	1.63
		34–38 (mean 36.33)	.37	.32	.646	–.45	1.19
		42–48 (mean 44.17)	–.51	.32	.396	–1.34	.32
	42–48 (mean 44.17)	15–33 (mean 27.95)	1.28*	.31	.000	.49	2.08
		34–38 (mean 36.33)	.88*	.29	.015	.12	1.64
		39–41 (mean 39.97)	.51	.32	.396	–.32	1.34
No. of Banks Recalled in 60 Seconds	15–33 (mean 27.95)	34–38 (mean 36.33)	–.77	.34	.111	–1.65	.11
		39–41 (mean 39.97)	–1.41*	.38	.001	–2.37	–.44
		42–48 (mean 44.17)	–2.19*	.35	.000	–3.08	–1.29
	34–38 (mean 36.33)	15–33 (mean 27.95)	.77	.34	.111	–.11	1.65
		39–41 (mean 39.97)	–.64	.36	.292	–1.56	.29
		42–48 (mean 44.17)	–1.42*	.33	.000	–2.27	–.56
	39–41 (mean 39.97)	15–33 (mean 27.95)	1.41*	.38	.001	.44	2.37
		34–38 (mean 36.33)	.64	.36	.292	–.29	1.56
		42–48 (mean 44.17)	–.78	.37	.142	–1.72	.16
	42–48 (mean 44.17)	15–33 (mean 27.95)	2.19*	.35	.000	1.29	3.08
		34–38 (mean 36.33)	1.42*	.33	.000	.56	2.27
		39–41 (mean 39.97)	.78	.37	.142	–.16	1.72

Table 7.6 Tukey HSD of No. of Brands Recalled by Quartiles of Matrices Test Scores and Product Category – *continued*

Multiple Comparisons

Tukey HSD

Dependent Variable	(I) Quartiles of Cognitive Ability (Brand Study Only)	(J) Quartiles of Cognitive Ability (Brand Study Only)	Mean Difference (I-J)	Std. Error	Sig.	95% Confidence Interval	
						Lower Bound	Upper Bound
No. of Automobile Brands Recalled in 60 Seconds	15–33 (mean 27.95)	34–38 (mean 36.33)	-1.22*	.47	.044	-2.42	-.02
		39–41 (mean 39.97)	-1.82*	.51	.002	-3.13	-.51
		42–48 (mean 44.17)	-2.85*	.47	.000	-4.06	-1.63
	34–38 (mean 36.33)	15–33 (mean 27.95)	1.22*	.47	.044	.02	2.42
		39–41 (mean 39.97)	-.60	.49	.614	-1.85	.66
		42–48 (mean 44.17)	-1.62*	.45	.002	-2.78	-.46
	39–41 (mean 39.97)	15–33 (mean 27–95)	1.82*	.51	.002	.51	3.13
		34–38 (mean 36.33)	.60	.49	.614	-.66	1.85
		42–48 (mean 44.17)	-1.03	.50	.163	-2.30	.25
	42–48 (mean 44.17)	15–33 (mean 27.95)	2.85*	.47	.000	1.63	4.06
		34–38 (mean 36.33)	1.62*	.45	.002	.46	2.78
		39–41 (mean 39.97)	1.03	.50	.163	-.25	2.30

Based on observed means.
* The mean difference is significant at the .05 level.

the difference between the two groups is 29 percent (4.5 against 5.8), while for banks and automobiles the differences are 43 percent (5 versus 7) and 37 percent (7.8 and 10.6), respectively.

It can be seen in Table 7.7 that amongst high-involvement products, the combined number of brands recalled exhibit a 39 percent (13 opposed to 18) difference between the lowest and highest quartiles of Matrices test scores. Low-involvement products reveal a similar discrepancy – 30.54 percent difference between low and high Matrices test score quartiles. When all product categories are averaged, there is an overall 35 percent difference between low and high cognitive ability quartiles with respect to the absolute number of brands subjects are able to recall under limited time constraints.

Table 7.7 is worth further examination for additional meaning. Data displayed in the table show that across all quartiles of cognitive ability as measured by the quartiles of Matrices test scores, subjects were able to recall 25.71 percent more high-involvement products than low-involvement. This is an effect of the selection of automobiles for inclusion in this category. The issue previously raised with respect to generally high recall amongst all subjects automobiles applies here and obviously has a major impact on the between group (i.e., high- versus low-involvement) differences. Future research should take into account the disparity between the two products used for inclusion in the category [both from the recall and consumer product (auto) vs. consumer service (bank) levels]. Nevertheless, Tables 7.5, 7.6 and 7.7 offer substantial evidence to support both H1: for any given product category (soft drinks, fast foods, cars, banks) that there is a positive direct relationship between total unaided brand recall measured in a 60-second test and human cognitive ability – g and H1a: for highly learned items such as brand names, consumers with higher levels of g have ability to retrieve from long-term memory (LTM) and access in WM significantly more brand information than consumers with lower levels.

H2: Certain consumer behaviours, explicitly the number of hours of television viewing engaged in on a daily basis, will vary according to the individual's cognitive ability. New knowledge derived from measurement and assessment of g on individual levels can be seen in a recent research publication on teenagers originating from Halpern et al. (2000) of the University of North Carolina. Findings from this study prove, depending upon age and gender, that adolescents of average intelligence are up to five times more likely to have engaged in sex than teens with higher levels of cognitive ability. Surprisingly, the research established adolescents with the lowest levels of cognitive ability display similar behaviours to those with the highest and proposes parents and other guardians possibly shield them, particularly girls, from sexual relationships longer than others. The study which took age, physical maturity, economic status and other factors into

Table 7.7 High and Low Involvement Product Brand Recall Varying by Quartiles of Matrices Test Raw Score

	Mean	Std. Dev.
High Involvement Products		
15–33 (mean 27.95)	12.91	4.68
34–38 (mean 36.33)	14.90	4.47
39–41 (mean 39.97)	16.14	4.77
42–48 (mean 44.17)	17.94	4.23
Total	15.50	4.87
Low Involvement Products		
15–33 (mean 27.95)	10.87	3.97
34–38 (mean 36.33)	11.69	3.70
39–41 (mean 39.97)	12.47	4.34
42–48 (mean 44.17)	14.19	4.31
Total	12.33	4.24

n = 326

High and Low Involvement Products

Mean No. Brands Recalled

High Involvement Products
Low Involvement Products

15–33 (mean 27.95)   34–38 (mean 36.33)   39–41 (mean 39.97)   42–48 (mean 44.17)

account implies motivations for teenagers vary significantly across differing levels of intelligence.

Examples like the Halpern study which seek to understand the effects of human intelligence on behaviours are abundant in the field of cognitive psychology. Yet, though much research has been devoted to the role cognitive ability – *g* may play in human behaviour generally, no specific research in the marketing discipline has addressed this issue with respect to consumer behaviour or sought to understand its impact on brand recall.

H2 seeks to examine this issue by exploring a simple, everyday behaviour that most all consumers engage in on a daily basis – watching TV. H2 posits that this ordinary, daily consumer behaviour will vary according to an individual's cognitive ability and that he or she will tend to watch more or less according to where he or she may fall within that range. Inasmuch as a consequence of watching more TV increases exposure to brand advertising, it follows that increased exposure should lead to increased brand awareness across the full range of low- and high-involvement products. Later, H2a looks at this issue through the proposition that with respect to the ability to recall brands, cognitive ability matters more than exposure to advertising at any level of daily TV consumption.

Not only did subjects in the study complete the K-BIT Matrices test and 60-second timed brand recall test, but they were also required to answer additional behavioural, demographic, attitudinal and lifestyle questions. Though these questions varied from concert, theatre, art gallery, cinema, and museum attendance to books read, political party affiliations and the like, daily TV viewing, because of its obvious relation with brand recall issues, is the only question addressed in this study.

Table 7.8 following displays the mean number of hours TV watched daily for each level of Matrices test score result. Findings in Table 7.8 clearly indicate that subjects who score lowest on the Matrices test watch the most television while those who score the highest watch the least. Furthermore, the association between hours of TV consumption daily and Matrices test scores displayed in the scatterplot in Table 7.8 underscores just how orderly the relationhip is. Not only do subjects in lowest range of cognitive abilities as measured by Matrices test scores watch more TV per day than those in the highest, but they watch nearly four times as much.

The polynomial regression equation displayed in the graph pertains to the role that *g* as measured by the Matrices test scores (x axis) has in affecting consumer behaviour with respect to daily hours of TV consumption (y axis). Clearly the association is curvilinear, reaching a peak of approximately 5 to 6 hours daily at around 22 to 23 correct test items and then tapering off to about 1 hour daily for 48 correct Matrices test items. The adjusted R^2 on the polynomial regression equation is 0.65 and is highly significant and illustrates that in the TV viewing consumer behaviour subjects report to have engaged in, cognitive ability does matter.

Table 7.8 Daily TV Viewing Behavior and Matrices Test Raw Scores

How Many Hours of TV Would You Say You Watch Per Day?

Matrix Raw Score	Mean	Std.Error	95% Confidence Interval Lower Bound	95% Confidence Interval Upper Bound
15	3.67	1.06	1.58	5.76
16	4.00	1.84	0.38	7.62
17	5.00	1.84	1.38	8.62
20	3.33	0.75	1.86	4.81
21	3.17	1.06	1.08	5.26
22	6.00	1.30	3.44	8.56
23	5.58	0.53	4.54	6.63
24	2.60	0.58	1.46	3.74
25	3.60	0.82	1.98	5.22
26	4.47	0.43	3.62	5.33
27	3.50	0.53	2.46	4.54
28	4.74	0.38	3.99	5.49
29	4.79	0.42	3.96	5.62
30	3.14	0.37	2.42	3.86
31	3.88	0.41	3.07	4.68
32	3.37	0.35	2.67	4.07
33	3.98	0.36	3.27	4.69
34	3.73	0.31	3.12	4.34
35	3.05	0.41	2.24	3.86
36	2.91	0.34	2.24	3.59
37	2.29	0.32	1.66	2.92
38	2.78	0.31	2.18	3.38
39	2.55	0.33	1.91	3.19
40	2.50	0.32	1.87	3.13
41	2.44	0.30	1.85	3.03
42	1.42	0.43	0.56	2.27
43	2.47	0.45	1.59	3.35
44	2.07	0.39	1.30	2.84
45	2.42	0.42	1.59	3.25
46	2.00	0.58	0.86	3.14
47	1.50	0.75	0.02	2.98
48	1.00	1.84	-2.62	4.62

TV Viewing Hours by Matrix Raw Score

Legend: How Many Hours of TV Would You Say You Watch Per Day?
Poly. (How Many Hours of TV Would You Say You Watch Per Day?)

Hrs of TV: $y = 0.0002x^3 - 0.0145x^2 + 0.1686x + 3.7336$
$R^2 = 0.65$

X-axis: Matrix Raw Score
Y-axis: TV Hrs/Day

H2a: Total unaided brand recall is more dependent upon cognitive ability than advertising exposure. Basic support for H2 in the previous analysis provides strong cause to examine the postulate that unaided brand recall is affected less by media and advertising exposure as measured through subjects' self-reporting of TV viewing habits than it is by an objective measure of their cognitive ability. Correlation analysis demonstrates that the correlation coefficient between TV viewing hours engaged in daily and the total number of brands recalled by subjects across all categories is –0.233. For TV viewing hours engaged in daily and Matrices test scores, the coefficient between these two factors is –0.179. Coefficients for both test scores and brand recall with TV hours engaged in daily are highly significant (0.00).

The fact that increased TV viewing is negatively associated with increased brand recall is somewhat unexpected when viewed in isolation, but not when examined in the context of the cognitive ability of the subjects. The number of total brands recalled in the tests is highly associated with the Matrices test scores. The coefficient of 0.510 is significant at the 0.00 level and indicates a positive direct relationship between how many brands a subject is able to evoke in a timed test and how much ability is displayed with respect to processing information. The intercorrelations between these three variables – namely TV viewing hours engaged in daily, total brands recalled in a timed test, and cognitive ability demonstrate that persons with the lowest cognitive abilities are associated both with the highest levels of daily TV viewing and the lowest levels of brand recall. Inasmuch as at the opposite end of the continuum high cognitive ability is negatively associated with high levels of TV viewing and positively associated with total brand recall, the case can be made that when measuring the impact media exposure has on brand recall, it is not enough to simply say more is better.

Table 7.9 examines the issue raised in H2a in further detail by collapsing TV viewing hours engaged in on a daily basis into quartiles. Quartiles encompass ranges from 0–1 with a mean 0.814 hours of TV watched per day, to 1.5–2.0 (mean 1.949), 2.5–3.0 (mean 2.956) and 4.0–10.0 (mean 4.829) hours per day. Viewing the overall number of brands recalled for each TV viewing quartile reveals a mean of 28.71 for the first quartile, 29.41 for the second, 27.07 for the third and 25.42 for the fourth. With the exception of the second quartile recall of 29.41 total brands recalled across all product categories within the four minute test total (60-second test x each of four products), the mean number of brands recalled appears to display a basic linear trend at this fundamental level.

Closer examination of brand recall varying by TV viewing quartile is provided in the following Figure 7.8. This figure interposes Matrices test scores quartiles into the graph alongside TV viewing. Thus the x-axis in Figure 7.7 stands for both the previously delineated quartiles of TV viewing as well as Matrices test scores. The figure makes obvious the curvilinear relationship between the number of brands recalled and quartiles of TV viewing hours.

Table 7.9   Mean No. Brands Recalled Varying by Quartiles of Matrices Test Raw Scores and TV Viewing Quartiles

Quartiles of TV Viewing	Mean No. Brands Recalled	Std. Dev.	N
0–1.0 (mean .814)			
15–33 (mean 27.95)	27.77	9.23	13
34–38 (mean 36.33)	27.05	5.47	20
39–41 (mean 39.97)	27.38	9.27	21
42–48 (mean 44.17)	31.06	7.05	31
Total	28.71	7.77	85
1.5–2.0 (mean 1.949)			
15–33 (mean 27.95)	22.93	8.10	15
34–38 (mean 36.33)	27.12	6.60	33
39–41 (mean 39.97)	29.61	5.30	18
42–48 (mean 44.17)	34.55	7.12	33
Total	29.41	7.88	99
2.5–3.0 (mean 2.956)			
15–33 (mean 27.95)	23.64	7.65	22
34–38 (mean 36.33)	29.05	6.64	21
39–41 (mean 39.97)	26.38	9.24	13
42–48 (mean 44.17)	30.67	7.23	12
Total	27.07	7.93	68
4.0–10.0 (mean 4.829)			
15–33 (mean 27.95)	22.52	6.74	27
34–38 (mean 36.33)	22.70	7.66	20
39–41 (mean 39.97)	31.21	8.55	14
42–48 (mean 44.17)	29.75	9.16	12
Total	25.42	8.53	73

n = 325

The exception of 29.41 brands recalled previously noted for the second quartile brand brings the curvilinear function into relief and is reminiscent of the same relationship seen earlier in the analysis of TV viewing hours by the Matrices test raw scores scatterplot in Table 7.8.

The total number of brands recalled by Matrices test score quartiles is contrasted and juxtaposed in this same Figure 7.7 with brands by TV viewing quartiles. Apparent in the juxtaposition is the fact that while total brand recall diminishes as the intensity of the TV viewing behaviour increases, recall for brands as previously shown in H1 and H1a sets off in the opposite direction with increases in cognitive ability. As formerly noted, results depicted in this graph are due both to the fact that subjects with lowest cognitive ability are found in the highest quartiles of hours of daily TV viewing, and that total brand recall is strongly and positively associated with cognitive ability.

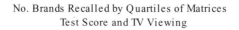

No. Brands Recalled by Quartiles of Matrices
Test Score and TV Viewing

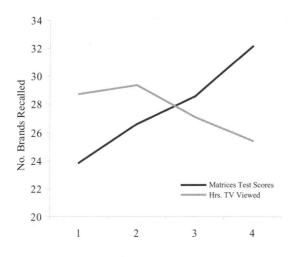

Figure 7.7   Brand Recall, Cognitive Ability and TV Viewing

Just how TV viewing quartiles differ with respect to total brand recall is set out in the Tukey HSD analysis following in Table 7.10. In the table it is apparent that at every level of media exposure represented by quartiles of TV viewing that when it comes to total unaided brand recall, subjects who engage in high levels of daily viewing are significantly different from those who engage in lower. Subjects in the lowest two quartiles of viewing are significantly dissimilar from those in the highest (mean differences of 3.2 and 3.9 respectively). With the exception of the third quartile, subjects in the highest quartile of TV viewing are unlike all other groups.

Figure 7.8 shows how the two factors, namely TV viewing and cognitive ability (*g*) interact. At each quartile of TV viewing, higher levels of cognitive ability correspond with higher levels of brand recall. Subjects in lowest quartile of daily TV viewing who fall within the highest quartiles for Matrices test scores are able to recall more brands in an unaided test than those subjects in the two highest quartiles of TV viewing.

Even subjects who watch lots of TV seem to benefit from higher levels of cognitive ability when it comes to unaided brand recall as the graph

Mean No. Brands Recalled by TV Viewing and
Matrices Test Score Quartiles

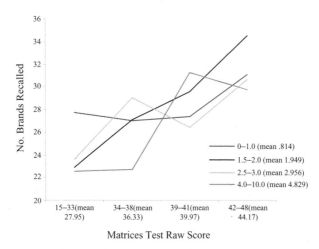

Figure 7.8   Interaction Effects of TV Viewing and Cognitive Ability – *g*

clearly depicts. Though it has previously been demonstrated that the
preponderance of subjects who fall within this quartile of heavy TV
viewing are most likely to score lowest on the Matrices test scores, data
nevertheless support the fact that more cognitive ability translates into
increased brand recall. Thus, individuals who score demonstrably and
significantly higher on the Matrices test for *g*, and who watch on average
nearly five hours (4.8) of TV per day, will always be able to recall
more brands than those whose cognitive abilities put them in the lower
quartiles.

Subjects who watch 1.5 to 2.0 hours of TV daily (second quartile; mean
1.94 hours) display clearly with respect to total brand recall, cognitive
ability has more of an impact on a subject's ability than TV media exposure. The data within this quartile represented by the colour blue in the
graph, depicts a near straight line relationship between *g* and unaided
recall. H2a is supported further by these findings. Were it not, each of the
lines in the graph representing TV viewing quartiles would display a similarly flat function with respect to Matrices test scores and brand recall.
Further, each of these flat lines should stack one on top the other with the
line repesenting the highest quartile of TV viewing on top and all other
below. This is clearly not the case and because this is so, findings in support
of H2a lead to some important implications for marketing strategists and
advertisers. These implications are discussed further in the concluding
section.

Table 7.10 Tukey HSD Test for Brand Recall Varying by TV Viewing and Matrices Test Scores

Multiple Comparisons

Dependent Variable: Quartiles of Brand Recall (Brands Only)

Tukey HSD

(I) Quartiles of TV Viewing (Brands Only)	(J) Quartiles of TV Viewing (Brands Only)	Mean Difference (I-J)	Std. Error	Sig.	95% Confidence Interval	
					Lower Bound	Upper Bound
0–1.0 (mean .814)	1.5–2.0 (mean 1.949)	-.7083	1.0999	.918	-3.5339	2.1174
	2.5–3.0 (mean 2.956)	1.6324	1.2102	.532	-1.4767	4.7414
	4.0–10.0 (mean 4.829)	3.2812*	1.1869	.029	.2319	6.3305
1.5–2.0 (mean 1.949)	0–1.0 (mean .814)	.7083	1.0999	.918	-2.1174	3.5339
	2.5–3.0 (mean 2.956)	2.3406	1.1715	.189	-.6691	5.3503
	4.0–10.0 (mean 4.829)	3.9895*	1.1475	.003	1.0415	6.9375
2.5–3.0 (mean 2.956)	0–1.0 (mean .814)	-1.6324	1.2102	.532	-4.7414	1.4767
	1.5–2.0 (mean 1.949)	-2.3406	1.1715	.189	-5.3503	.6691
	4.0–10.0 (mean 4.829)	1.6489	1.2536	.553	-1.5717	4.8695
4.0–10.0 (mean 4.829)	0–1.0 (mean .814)	-3.2812*	1.1869	.029	-6.3305	-.2319
	1.5–2.0 (mean 1.949)	-3.9895*	1.1475	.003	-6.9375	-1.0415
	2.5–3.0 (mean 2.956)	-1.6489	1.2536	.553	-4.8695	1.5717

Based on observed means.

* The mean difference is significant at the .05 level.

Discussion

Research presented in this chapter indicates that marketers, strategists, advertisers and even manufacturers need to consider the role human cognitive ability may play not only in brand recall but also in consumer attitudes towards brands, accessibility of brand attributes and corresponding attitudes, as well as other factors such as the attitude-to-behaviour process, brand choice behaviour, and media consumption as well as its effects.

Because WM has limited capacity, for any given product category (soft drinks, fast foods, cars, banks) there is a positive direct relationship between total unaided brand recall measured in a 60-second test and human cognitive ability – g. This relationship appears to strongest between high-involvement products where unaided recall response latency likely strains the limits of WM. Demonstrated further is the fact the consumers with higher levels of g have the ability to summon up from LTM and access in WM significantly more information with respect to highly learned items such as brand names than consumers with lower levels of cognitive ability. It has been previously established that this extra capacity for some individuals with higher levels of cognitive ability is both a function of the speed and efficiency with which they are able to process information. Thus it can be concluded that in the brand and advertising mêlée' of day-to-day life, given a normal distribution of cognitive abilities within the consumer population, some consumers will have more information available in WM during the automatic and strategic processing phases of brand choice decision making. This additional information, which some consumers are able to draw upon, is not so much a function of brand advertising exposure as its individual human cognitive ability.

Future research

Heretofore, the role that human cognitive ability may play in consumers' cognitive processes a propos brand choice and a host of other decisions and behaviours has been largely neglected in the marketing field. Previous research on brand recall, attitude, and behaviour towards the brand do not consider g as a possible source of response latency and TOMA variation. Studies by Cohen (1966), Fazio, Powell, and Herr (1983), Fazio, Powell, and Williams (1989), Grunert (1988, 1990), Woodside and Trappey (1992, 1996) and others, neglect both in the research method and in the analyses to account for individual differences in speed and efficiency of information processing and WM capacity.

Prior research has neglected a significant factor of variability in the brand problem-solving, selection and decision processes. Further, not only does the research fail to account for g with respect to RTs or response latencies and TOMA measures, but also whether subjects are being required to answer "Yes/No" or "Like/Dislike" or "True/False" when utilising the binary response console typically found in these experiments. Thus, the important 30 to 50 msec difference between a "No" answer and a "Yes" answer found in Jensen's (1987) work, introduces a reason for further and continued study into the impact of this source of variation. Future research in attitude-to-behaviour, attribute-to-brand evocations and other automatic and strategic processes with respect to consumer brand choice behaviour, should necessarily include or at a very minimum control for individual differences in cognitive ability.

Implications for marketers

This chapter demonstrates that at an elementary level, the recognition and recall of brand stimuli, the retrieval of information and provision of a heuristic for brand evaluation, and the ultimate relevance decision that determines further higher-level processing, are all ultimately governed by human cognitive ability or *g*.

Support in the pilot study that children's ability to recall brands may yield immediate benefits in terms of devising more effective communication strategies for marketers – particularly in light of recent European Union legislation restricting and in some cases banning conventional advertising to children. The notion that brand recall and information processing amongst children is conditioned primarily by cognitive ability levels, and less so by age, may call for a change in marketing communication practices. The findings here offer a proven basis for segmentation of the market that considers differing levels of cognitive abilities within the population. That being the case, children and consumers generally may be more respectfully addressed regardless of their place within the standard normal curve.

The realisation that *g* plays a central role in brand information processing implies that its role may also be central in other consumer behaviours hitherto unexplored. The role of *g* in brand loyalty and switching behaviour as well in customer satisfaction are topics worthy of further research. It may be that *g* plays a central role in communication messages and package designs that are considered misleading. The role cognitive ability may play in designing financial services, pension and annuities contracts and products is clearly an issue given the number of consumers in recent years who have been caught up in schemes for which claims of confusion and unethical selling abound.

Finally, amongst the major implications of this research for marketers is the number of uncovered questions that encourages further research into cognitive processing and cognitive ability when applied to both business and social activities at large. In effect, the issue calls for another look at, or in the extreme, a re-definition of a whole array of well-known business concepts such as brand loyalty, brand awareness, consumer attitudes, consumer benefits and satisfaction, consumer information, information overload, aims of advertising, etc. Viewed through the prism of individual human cognitive abilities, these notions acquire new meanings and connotations. Ultimately, there may be a call to redefine the mission and perspective of the marketing science: from excelling the powers of persuasion towards getting to know your consumers and respectfully co-operate with them.

References

www.dawson.cc.mt.us/faculty/Korpi/nervous system.htm.

Aaker, D. A., Bagozzi, R. P., Carman, J. M. and MacLachlan, J. M. "On Using Response Latency to Measure Preference," *Journal of Marketing Research*, 17 (1980): 237–244.

Alpert, M. "Identification of Determinant Attributes: A Comparison of Methods," *Journal of Marketing Research*, 8, 2 (1971): 184–91.

Anderson, J. "A Spreading Activation Theory of Memory," *Journal of Verbal Learning and Verbal Behaviour*, 22, 261–295 (1983).

Anderson, J. and Pirolli, P. "Spread of Activation," *Journal of Experimental Psychology: Learning, Memory & Cognition*, 10, 4 (1984).

Atkinson, R. C. and Shiffrin, R. M. "Human memory: a proposed system and its control process." in K. W. Spence and J. T. Spence (eds), *The Psychology of Learning and Motivation: Advances in Theory and Research*, Vol. 2. New York: Academic Press, 1968.

Axelrod, J. N. "Attitude Measures that Predict Purchase," *Journal of Advertising Research*, 8 (February/March 1968): 3–17.

Axelrod, J. N. "Minnie, Minnie Tickled the Parson," *Journal of Advertising Research*, 26 (February/March 1986): 89–96.

Balota, D. and Lorch, R. Depth of Automatic Spreading Activation: Mediated Priming Effects in Pronunciation but not in Lexical Decisions, *Journal of Experimental Psychology: Learning, Memory and Cognition*, 12, 3 (1986): 364–390.

Bouchard, T. J., Jr. "The Genetic Architecture of Human Intelligence," in P. A. Vernon (ed.), *Biological Approaches to the Study of Human Intelligence* (pp. 33–85), Norwood, NJ: Ablex, 1993.

Broadbent, D. E. "A mechanical model for human attention and immediate memory," *Psychological Review*, 64 (1957): 205–215.

Burke, W. L., and Schoeffler, S. *Brand Awareness as a Tool for Profitability*, Boston: Cahners Publishing Company, 1980.

Carroll, J. B. *Human Cognitive Abilities: A Survey of Factor-Analytic Studies*, Cambridge: Cambridge University Press, 1993.

Cohen, L. "The Level of Consciousness: A Dynamic Approach to the Recall Technique," *Journal of Marketing*, 3 (1966).

Collins, A. and Loftus, E. A Spreading Activation Theory of Semantic Processing, *Psychological Review*, 82 (1975): 407–428.

Corstjens, M. and Doyle, P. "Evaluating Alternative Retail Repositioning Strategies," *Marketing Science*, 8, 2 (1989): 170–80.

Craik, F. and Lockhart, L. "Levels of Processing: A Framework for Memory Research," *Journal of Verbal Learning and Verbal Behaviour*, 11 (1972): 671–684.

Craik, F. and Tulving, E. "Depth of Processing and the Retention of Word in Episodic Memory," *Journal of Experimental Psychology*, 14 (1975): 268–294.

Doyle, P. and Gidengil, B. Z. "A Review of In-Store Experiments," *Journal of Retailing*, 53, 2 (1977): 47–62.

Doyle, P. *Experimental Methods in Retailing, in Consumer and Industrial Buying Behaviour*, Arch G. Woodside, Jagdish N. Sheth, and Peter D. Bennett (eds), North-Holland, New York, 1977.

Duncan, J., Seitz, R. J., Kolodny, J., Bor, D., Herzog, H., Ahmed, A., Newell, F. N. and Emslie, H. "A Neural Basis for General Intelligence," *Science*, (2000), 289: 457–460.

Eysenck, H. J. "The Biological Basis of Intelligence", in P. A. Vernon (ed.), *Biological Approaches to the Study of Human Intelligence* (pp. 1–32), Norwood, NJ: Ablex, 1993.

Fazio, R. "How Do Attitudes Guide Behaviour?" In: Handbook of Motivation and Cognition (eds R. Sorentino and E. Higgins), New York: Guilford Press, 1986.

Fazio, R. H., Powell, M. C. and Herr, P. M. "Toward a Process Model of the Attitude-Behaviour Relation: Accessing One's Attitude Upon Mere Observation of the Attitude Object," *Journal of Personality and Social Psychology* 44, 6 (1983): 723–35.

Fazio, R., Powell, M. and Williams, C. "The Role of Attitude Accessibility in the Attitude-to-Behaviour Process," *Journal of Experimental Social Psychology*, Vol. 27 (1989).

Frearson, W. M. and Eysenck, H. J. "Intelligence, reaction time (RT) and a new 'odd-man-out' RT paradigm," *Personality and Individual Differences*, 7 (1986): 808–817.

Furnham, A. *Financial Times*, October 8, 1999.

Gruber, A. "Top-of-Mind Awareness and Share of Families: An Observation," *Journal of Marketing Research*, 6, 2 (1969): 227–31.

Grunert, K. "Research in Consumer Behaviour: Beyond Attitude and Decision Making," *Journal of the European Society for Opinion and Marketing Research*, Vol. 16, No. 5 (1988).

Grunert, K. "Automatic and Strategic Processes in the Perception of Advertising," Paper presented at the *22nd International Congress of Applied Psychology*, Kyoto, Japan (July 22–27, 1990).

Grunert, K. "Automatic and Strategic Processes in Advertising Effects," *Journal of Marketing*, Vol. 60, No. 4 (1996).

Hauser, J. R. "Agendas and Consumer Choice," *Journal of Marketing Research*, 23 (August 1986): 199–212.

Hilgard, E. R. "Consciousness in Contemporary Psychology," In: Annual Review of Psychology, 31 (1980): 1–26.

Horn, J. and Cattell, R. "Refinement and Test of the Theory of Fluid and Crystallised Intelligence," *Journal of Educational Psychology*, 57 (1966): 253–270.

Horn, J. "Intellectual ability concepts," in R. J. Sternberg (ed.), *Advances in the psychology of human intelligence*, Vol. 3 (pp. 35–77), Hillsdale, NJ: Erlbaum, 1986.

James, W. *The Principles of Psychology*, New York: Dover, 1950.

Jensen, A. R. "Psychometric g as a Focus of Concerted Research Effort," *Intelligence, 11* (1987): 193–198.

Jensen, A. R. "Speed of Information Processing and Population Differences," In S. H. Irvine and J. W. Berry (eds), *Human Abilities in Cultural Context*, pp. 105–145. Cambridge: Cambridge University Press, 1988.

Jensen, A. R. *The g Factor: The Science of Mental Ability*, Praeger, 1998.

Jensen, A. R. "The 'g' factor: the science of mental ability," Westport, CT: Praeger Publishers, pp. 531–534, 1999.

Johnston, E. and Dark "Selective Attention," *American Psychological Review*, 37, 43–75 (1986).

Kaufman, A. S. and Kaufman, N. L. *Interpretive Manual for the Kaufman Assessment Battery for Children*, Circle Pines, MN: American Guidance Service, 1983.

Kaufman, A. S. and Kaufman, N. L. *Manual for the Kaufman Brief Intelligence Test*, Circle Pines, MN: American Guidance Service, 1990.

Kline, P., Draycott, S. G. and McAndrew, V. M. "Reconstructing intelligence: a factor analytic study of the BIP," *Personality and Individual Differences*, 16 (1994): 529–536.

Kyllonen, P. C. and Christal, R. E. "Reasoning Ability is (Little More Than) Working Memory Capacity?" *Intelligence*, 14 (1990): 389–433.

Kyllonen, P. C. "Aptitude Testing Inspired by Information Processing: A Test of the Four-sources Model," *Journal of General Psychology*, 120 (1993): 375–405.

Lehrl, S. and Fischer, B. "The basic parameters of human information processing: Their role in the determination of intelligence," *Personality and Individual Differences*, 9 (1988): 883–896.

Lockhart, R., Craik, F. and Jacoby, L. Depth of Processing, Recognition and Recall. In J. Brown (ed.) *Recall and Recognition*, New York: John Wiley and Sons Inc, 1976.

MacLachlan, J. "Response Latency: New Measure of Advertising," New York: *Advertising Research Foundation*, 1977.

McClelland, J. and Rumelhart, D. "An Integrated Activation Model of Context Effects in Letter Perception," *Psychological Review*, 88 (1981).

McGue, M., Bouchard, T. J., Jr., Iacono, W. G. and Lykken, D. T. "Behavioural Genetics of Cognitive Ability: A Life-span Perspective". In R. Plomin and G. E. McClearn (eds), *Nature, Nurture and Psychology* (pp. 59–76). Washington, DC: American Psychological Association, 1993.

Neubauer, A. C. and Freudenthaler, H. H. "Reaction time in a sentence-picture verification test and intelligence: Individual strategies and effects of extended practice," *Intelligence*, 19 (1994): 193–218.

Newell, A. and Simon, H. A. *Human problem solving*, Englewood Cliffs, NJ: Prentice-Hall, 1972.

Peterson, L. and Peterson, M. "Short-term retention of individual verbal items," *Journal of Experimental Psychology*, 58 (1959): 193–8.

Piaget, J. *The Origins of Intelligence in Children*, NY: Publisher?, 1954.

Plomin, R., McClearn, G. E., Smith, D. L., Vignetti, S., Chorney, M. J., Corney, K., Venditti, C. P., Kasarda, S., Thompson, L. A., Detterman, D. K., Daniels, J., Owen, M. and McGuffin, P. "DNA Markers Associated with High versus Low IQ: The IQ Quantitative Trait Loci (QTL) Project," *Behaviour Genetics*, 24 (1994): 107–118.

Raven, J. "Guide to Using the Coloured Progressive Matrices Sets A, Ab, BC (1965)," London: H. K. Lewis.

Raven, J., Court, J., Raven, J. *Manual for Raven's Standard Progressive Matrices* (1996 edn.). Oxford, UK: Oxford Psychologists Press.

Richardson, J. T. E., Eysenck, M. W. and Piper, D. W. (eds) "Student learning: research in education and cognitive psychology," *Society for Research into Higher Education*, 1987.

Sternberg, S. "Memory-scanning: New findings and current controversies," *Quarterly Journal of Experimental Psychology*, Vol. 27 (1975): 1–32.

Sternberg, R. J. *Intelligence, information processing, and analogical reasoning: The componential analysis of human abilities*, Hillsdale, NJ: Erlbaum, 1977.

Sternberg, S. "High-speed scanning in human memory," *Science*, 153 (1996): 652–654.

Tigert, D. J. "Pushing the Hot Buttons for a Successful Retailing Strategy," In *Patronage Behaviour and Retail Management*, William R. Darden and Robert F. Lusch (eds), New York: Elsevier North-Holland, 1983.

Trappey III, R. J. and Woodside, A. G. "Attitude-Accessibility and Primary Store Choice," *Working Paper, Freeman School of Business,* Tulane University, New Orleans, LA. 1991.

Tulving, E. and Thomson, D. "Encoding specificity and retrieval processes in episodic memory," *Psychological Review,* 80 (1973): 79–82.

Tulving, E. and Schachter, D. "Priming and human memory systems," *Science,* 247 (1990): 301–6.

Vernon, P. A. "Speed of information processing and general intelligence," *Intelligence,* 5 (1983): 345–355.

Vernon, P. A. and Jensen, A. R. "Individual and group differences in intelligence and speed of information processing," *Personality and Individual Differences,* 5 (1984): 411–423.

Vernon, P. A., Nador, S., Kantor, L. "Reaction times and speed-of-processing: Their relationship to timed and untimed measures of intelligence," *Intelligence,* 9 (1985): 357–374.

Vernon, P. A. and Kantor, L. "Reaction time correlations with intelligence test scores obtained under either timed or untimed conditions," *Intelligence,* 10 (1986): 315–330.

Vernon, P. A. "The heritability of measures of speed of information processing," *Personality and Individual Differences,* 10 (1989): 573–576.

Ward, S., Wackman, D. and Wartella, E. *How Children Learn to Buy,* Place?: Sage, 1977.

Woodside, A. and Trappey, R. "Finding Out Why Customers Shop Your Store and Shop Your Brand: Automatic-unconscious Processing Models of Primary Choice," *Journal of Advertising Research,* Nov/Dec 1992.

Woodside, A. G. and Trappey, R.J. "Customer Portfolio Analysis Among Competing Retail Brands," *Journal of Business Research,* 35 (1996): 189–200.

8
Conclusions and Implications for Future Research and Marketing Strategy

Core propositions learned

Chapter 8 recapitulates the useful findings that each of the previous chapters covers. What is found here are the results that weave the body of work together into one structure. Though this text encompasses differing studies undertaken through the years – parts of which have been published previously, a common thread of research binds and advances the work as a unified whole.

Automatic processing of primary choice

Research on consumer automatic-unconscious processes in linking brand names with evaluative attributes is useful for learning the principal associations a store or brand holds in the minds of customers. A few of these links are likely to be associated with a store or brand being identified as the customer's primary store. Using research on customer automatic processing, advertising and marketing strategists also learn whether or not any customers retrieve their brand or store in association with important evaluative attributes or if their brand is inert in customers' minds.

For a given store or brand, marketing strategists may fall in the trap of advertising a link that their brand or store can not possibly "own," that is, be identified first as being the most, best, or lowest or a given evaluative attribute, because another brand dominates on this particular attribute. Or, such strategists may be advertising a feature or benefit that has little to do with their brand's or store's ability to gain primary customers. Unfortunately, too often strategists believe they know what their customers really are thinking without hard evidence of when their store or brand automatically comes to their customers' minds.

Customers can easily and quickly respond when asked to name a store or brand as first coming to mind for a given evaluative attribute. Their answers likely reflect an automatic-unconscious process that includes accessing an internal memory bank, retrieving a file of information, reviewing the file's contents, selecting and giving a response. A few such automatic associates are useful for predicting primary store choice or brand choice.

Research programs on customer automatic-unconscious processes will likely be useful for learning the "hot buttons" (Tigert, 1983) to use and to avoid for planning positioning strategies. Assuming that automatic associations of a store or brand with an evaluation are grounded in reality, then such research will likely be useful for improving product/service offerings to gain customers. For example, if substantial numbers of customers name store X for slowest checkout or highest prices, most likely checkout service needs to be improved and prices are indeed higher compared to competitors' prices.

The hypotheses developed and the results presented in this monograph extend previous consumer behaviour research on automatic-unconscious processing (cf. Fazio, 1986; 1989; Herr et al., 1990; Cohen, 1966; Axelrod, 1968; Gruber, 1969; MacLachlan, 1977; Aaker et al., 1980; Hoyer, 1984; Hoyer and Brown, 1990). This related body of work examines theoretically and empirically the effect on choice of the earliest accessibility from long-term memory of attitude to a global concept, for example, a brand name (Fazio et al., 1989) or the accessibility from long-term memory of brand awareness (Cohen, 1966; Hoyer and Brown, 1990).

The theoretical propositions of level of consciousness (Cohen, 1966), top-of-mind-awareness (Axelrod, 1968), affect referral (Wright, 1975), attitude-accessibility (Fazio, 1986), and unaided brand awareness (Hoyer and Brown, 1990) are likely to be most applicable for routine problem solving (Howard, 1989) for buying frequently purchased consumer products (e.g., candy bars, brands of peanut butter).

The attitude-accessibility of competing stores or brands as indicated by primacy of responses to evaluative attributes is useful for accurately predicting primary choice. Data on attitude-accessibility linking stores with evaluative beliefs are useful for building paramorphic models of consumer cognitive processes, especially cognitive processes involving bottom-up agendas. The empirical models described in the results section fits well with Howard's (1989) proposal of three key dimensions of store image affecting store choice for limited problem-solving situations. Supermarket store choice versus convenience store choice is assumed to represent more of the characteristics of limited problem-solving situations versus routine problem-solving, given that food stores represent one of the most complex elements of consumers' environments; food and beverage shopping are important activities representing 16 percent of the average U.S. household budget (Ambry, 1990), with expenditures likely to average more than $100 per visit to the shopper's primary supermarket.

Little loss in predictive accuracy is likely to be experienced from building primary store choice models from store attitude-accessibility data using the same evaluative attributes for competing stores. This speculation matches with another: not all food stores can claim effectively to be the one with the lowest overall food prices.

If a store is not believed by buyers to offer the lowest overall food prices and can not hope to change this evaluation, then the store's management may want to encourage shoppers to use hierarchical agendas that favor those store aspects that the store can dominate competing stores (cf. Hauser, 1986). Longitudinal research is recommended to assess the impact of such strategies, research that includes assessments of the images of competing stores using the described attitude- accessibility modeling approach. Before attempting to generalize the empirical results, research on store attitude-accessibility toward evaluative attributes held by customers needs to be extended to other retail store types, metropolitan areas, as well as through time.

While Corstjens and Doyle (1989) correctly assert that the most reliable means currently available of evaluating alternative store-image strategies is via experimentation and direct sales measures, field applications of such research methods are expensive and lengthy. More importantly, assessing store attitude-accessibility of evaluative attributes does appear to meet the requirements proposed by Axelrod (1986) for intermediate criteria that predict choice or purchase: sensitivity (discriminations between stores using small samples), stability (the same answers results from repeat testing), and predictive power (high explained variance). Attitude-accessibility, programmatic research on a monthly, quarterly, or annual basis to assess changes in store images is recommended as a useful method for auditing such consumer thinking.

Customer portfolio analysis

A store's attitude accessibility toward evaluative store attributes varies within a store's portfolio of customers. The attitude-accessibility of any given store, say Store X, toward evaluative attributes is likely to vary considerably among new, loyal, and defector Store X customer groups, as well as customers of competitors' stores. Information of the differences in store attitude and accessibility among these customer groups is likely to be very helpful in identifying competitive opportunities and vulnerabilities for a given store.

For example, a strong positive trend is found among several negative evaluative attributes being associated first with Winn-Dixie as some customers move from new to loyal to defector locations in Winn-Dixie's portfolio. The application of customer portfolio analysis to retail customers and store attitude-accessibility joins together two research literatures and extends the work of Tigert (1983) and Trappey and Woodside (1991). The moderately high levels of variance in primary store choice explained by the attitude- accessibility models indicates that additional research on attitude-accessibility and store choice is warranted. The survey results presented here are based on one cross-sectional study. Tigert (1983) demonstrates convincingly that store evaluative attributes do vary over time in the same market for the same retailer. Retailers do need to recognise that their customer portfolios are changing constantly. In fact, based on BehaviourScan, single-source data, Fulgoni and Eskin (1983) indicate that it might be more useful to conceptualise retail supermarket patronage in terms of store switching rather than store loyalty. The evidence from supermarket scanner-data linked to household information is that almost no household is 100 percent loyal to one store and about one-fifth of supermarket shoppers buy 70 percent of their groceries from one store over a 24-week period. Most customers switch their primary store choice among three or four stores within a two-year period (cf., Fulgoni and Eskin, 1983, pp. 270–271). Thus, understanding the amount and reasons for flows within a store's portfolio of customers and competitors' customers is important. Identifying key customer portfolio segments and these customers' attitude-accessibilities appears useful for developing such an understanding. Model building requires both analytic skills and theoretical foundation on the part of the researchers (Chakraborty et al., 1991).

Consequently, when using attitude-accessibility theory to model primary store choice it is recommend marketers begin with testing the hypotheses presented in this article. That is, customer portfolio analyses of major competing stores (resulting in tables similar to Tables 1, 2, and 3) are likely to indicate a logical set of likely independent variables affecting primary store choice. A few subsets of different independent variables are likely to include different variables that influence primary store choice significantly. Some variables may be excluded from entering forward stepwise regression models that have a profound influence on primary store choice, for example, the attitude-accessibility influencing primary store choice.

Store attitude-accessibility information may be useful for modelling customers' least favourite stores (i.e., "the store you don't like or rarely shop"). Such models indicate the evaluative attributes associated most with deciding actively not to shop at a particular store. From the data in the present study for example, the attitude-accessibility of Winn-Dixie first coming to mind for HOFP influences Winn-Dixie being selected as the respondents least favourite store. Customer portfolio analysis should include such research on what stores customers refuse to shop and why they refuse, as well as research for understanding and predicting primary store choice.

Understanding thinking among near and distant customers

The findings regarding the thinking of near and distant customers support the conclusion that supermarket shoppers can retrieve specific store names as "best" representing specific associative cues. A subset of such benefit-to-store retrievals is linked to the consumer's primary store choice. Some negatively worded associates may be associated with retrieval of a consumer's primary store choice, such as high overall food prices linked with Winn-Dixie among many of this chain's primary customers.

The associate-to-store retrievals among distant primary customers for a store are valuable especially for providing clues of why some consumers will shop primarily at less convenient stores. A few subtle, but strategically insightful, associate-to-store retrievals differences are likely to be observed by comparing nearby versus distant primary store customers.

The findings provide circumstantial evidence in support of the associate-to-cue proposition and choice sequence proposed by Holden (1993, p. 387): "By placing cues known to facilitate retrieval in the choice situation, the probability of brand evocation is increased, and thereby increases the probability of choice of the brand – without evocation, the probability of choice is zero."

Additional empirical evidence using experimental designs (Banks, 1965) with test and control groups is needed for confirming this proposition and the core proposition that the probability of brand choice is likely to increase as a function of the increase in the probability of evocation (Nedungadi, 1990).

Based on the findings described in this monograph, a corollary proposition is likely to be supportable: certain associate-to-store retrievals serve to decrease the likelihood of brand or store choice. Possibly, retailing strategists for Winn-Dixie may be causing more harm than good by communicating the message, "lowest overall food prices," given that the store chain is retrieved by a large share of this chain's primary customers as well as primary customers of competitors' stores.

Focusing on "lowest overall food prices" may result in a double-whammy. First, the lowest-price message is associated strongly with retrievals of "Superstore" and "Schwegmann's" among Winn-Dixie primary customers; consequently, more attention may be devoted to these competing stores resulting in their choice.

Second, by communicating an associate-to-store message, that is not held by target consumers, relatively less attention may be attended to a retrieval that is held which is helpful for building primary store choice. For example, Winn-Dixie might benefit more by focusing the store's strategy on positive associates known to result in high shares of retrievals for the store: most convenient location, best quality meats, and friendliest Personnel compared to trying to cause customers to reverse an associate known to be linked negatively for store retrieval.

Modelling bank loyalty

Previous research reported in earlier chapters confirms that brands mentioned in second or third place in unaided brand recall questions tend to be "switch-to" brands. Research reported herein provides added support for the theory that unaided brand recall can be an indicator of past or future switching behaviour. Moreover, expansion of this theory demonstrates other positions of unaided brand recall should not be overlooked for their information content when it comes to switching behaviour. Position of unaided bank brand recall will vary significantly between loyal (non-switcher) customers and those customers who have never been a bank customer and/or who have switched either to or from their main bank. Lower order positions of recall are highly associated both with respondents who have never been a customer of the bank and turncoat customers switching from the bank.

Evidence contained herein supports the fact that a positive brand image is associated with bank brand loyalty. In unaided attribute-to-brand recall questions, non-switching, loyal customers primarily evoke their own main bank or financial services institution when positive brand attributes are mentioned. Customers who have recently switched from a competitor to their current main bank are likely to evoke their new bank brand for positive attributes 2–3 times more often than loyal customers. The antithesis holds true for customers who have switched away from their main bank to a competitor. These customers are approximately 2–4 times more likely than loyal customers to evoke their previous bank brand when negative bank brand attributes are mentioned.

Non-switching bank customers demonstrate a willingness to remain loyal even though they may evoke their current bank brand for negatively worded bank attributes. High levels of unaided recall do not preclude unfavourable attitudes. Unfavourable attitudes may exist with high levels of bank brand recall. They possibly will also co-exist with favourable attitudes and might even be important in defining a given bank brand's loyal customer base. This does not suggest customers are indifferent to the brand. To the contrary, it implies customers are willing to accept and trade off some of the brand's negative attributes in favour of other positive attributes deemed more important. A zone of tolerance whereby customers accept certain shortfalls in the bank's expected delivery of services can be observed to varying degrees in each of the four banks. The evidence connects higher positions of unaided brand recall with a higher probability the bank brand will be evoked for a positive bank attribute in an attribute-to-brand question. Lower orders of brand mention are associated with higher levels of negative bank attribute-to-brand evocations.

Customers holding a positive image of the bank brand are less likely to switch banks and are therefore more likely to be loyal customers. The results indicate the more frequently a customer evokes a bank brand for positive attributes in an attribute-to-brand recall question, the more likely the customer is to be a loyal bank customer. This association does not hold for competitor customers, switchers, and/or new bank customers. The total number of negative attribute-to-brand evocations is uncorrelated with bank customer loyalty.

Customers who are highly committed in the choice of his or her financial services institution are more likely to engage in switching actions. Bank loyal customers also tend to be more lackadaisical and apathetic about their choice of a financial institution than are customers who engage in switching behaviour. Non-switching bank customers are more likely to state they do not feel "involved in choosing a bank," they "do not care" which bank they choose, and that they are "not at all concerned" about bank choice.

Customers with multiple versus single current accounts across various financial institutions engage in more switching behaviour. Customer satisfaction with the reliability of bank administration was shown to have a major influence on bank loyalty. When it comes to loyal customers' money, no amount of friendliness by bank staff can overcome administrative errors. The model demonstrates if a bank is to maintain loyal customers, there is no substitute for getting the details right.

Generally, loyal bank customers expect more problems to be associated with switching financial services institutions than do customers who have switched banks. A feeling of security and comfort with Internet technology is crucial if customers are to take up competing financial services' offerings. Willingness to conduct purchases routinely over the Internet can indicate how comfortable a consumer is with the technology. The proportion of bank-loyal customers can be seen to diminish significantly with ownership of an Internet bank account.

Not all customers with Internet bank accounts engage in switching behaviour. Some customers take up the electronic offerings of the bank with which they maintain their main account, while others switched – either before their main bank could make the offer, or notwithstanding it. Willingness to provide credit card information and purchase information through the world-wide-web and e-mail is a critical variable in the equation.

Linkage-advertising, brand knowledge and prior experience

The results provide strong support that the linkage-advertising program was a substantial influence on changing destination behaviours and increasing the expenditures of visitors to PEI. Previous studies have reported the use of formal quasi-experimental designs to measure the effects of marketing and advertising on customer behaviour variables (e.g., Ehrenberg, 1972; Lilien and Duxdic, 1982; Weinberg, 1960). Unfortunately, the vast majority of reported studies on the influence of advertising on customer expenditures and other customer behaviours do not include attempts to substantiate the interpretation of cause-and-effect relationships between advertising and customer behaviour. Advertising researchers and strategists need more knowledge about telling weaknesses of research designs that do not permit reasonable causal inferences of the effect of advertising on customer behaviour, such as the widely used one-group post-test-only design. The continued use of weak tests of causal hypotheses of the effects of advertising on sales likely perpetuates the low faith in advertising among many senior managers.

A substantial increase in the knowledge and application of these designs increases the credibility of the idea that advertising influences sales and profits; and, that marketers can usefully estimate sales and profit levels with and without advertising.

The results described for PEI support the view that the increases in customer expenditures and the resulting return on investment justifies the province's linkage-advertising program, even when the very conservative viewpoint is adopted that the program was not a factor in converting inquirers (persons requesting the linkage-advertising) into visitors.

The role of human cognitive ability

Research offered in this chapter points to the fact that marketers, strategists, advertisers, retailers and manufacturers could do with considering the role human cognitive ability plays not only in brand recall but also in consumer attitudes towards brands, accessibility of brand attributes and corresponding attitudes. Human cognitive ability may likely be found to influence other factors such as the attitude-to-behaviour process, brand choice behaviour, and media consumption as well as its effects.

The notion that brand recall and information processing amongst children is conditioned primarily by cognitive ability levels, and less so by age, may call for a change in marketing communication practices. The realisation that g plays a central role in brand information processing implies that its role may also be central in other consumer behaviours hitherto unexplored.

Evidence established in this chapter demonstrates that because WM has limited capacity, for any given product category (soft drinks, fast foods, cars, banks) there is a positive direct correlation between total unaided brand recall measured in a 60-second test and human cognitive ability – g. This relationship appears strongest between high-involvement products where unaided recall response latency likely strains the limits of WM. Demonstrated further is the fact the consumers with higher levels of g have the ability to summon up from LTM and access in WM significantly more information with respect to highly learned items such as brand names than consumers with lower levels of cognitive ability.

Extra capacity for some individuals with higher levels of cognitive ability is both a function of the speed and efficiency with which they are able to

process information. Thus it can be concluded that in the brand and advertising mêlée' of day-to-day life, given a normal distribution of cognitive
abilities within the consumer population, some consumers will have more
information available in WM during the automatic and strategic processing
phases of brand choice decision making. This additional information upon
which some consumers may draw is not so much a function of brand
advertising exposure as it is individual human cognitive ability.

Heretofore, the role that human cognitive ability may play in consumers'
cognitive processes in relation to brand choice and other evaluations
and behaviours has been neglected for the most part in the marketing
field. Prior research on brand recall, attitude, and behaviour towards the
brand do not take into account g as a possible basis of response latency
and TOMA variation. Future research in attitude-to-behaviour, attribute-
to-brand evocations and other automatic and strategic processes regarding
consumer brand choice behaviour, ought of necessity include or at least
take into account individual differences in cognitive ability.

Limitations

All of the work contained in this text relies upon large-scale surveys of
consumers. As such, it is subject to the same limitations a researcher would
stipulate for generalising the results of any sample to a population at large.
Extreme care has been taken in all the research studies comprising chapters
to assure proper marketing research methodology was carried out – from
survey design, testing, data collection and coding, to quality assurance and
analyses.

Each survey questionnaire was designed specifically with consideration
for the method by which it was to be executed. All surveys were first subjected to a pilot test. As a result, wording for questions in the surveys was
changed when subjects indicated they misunderstood or were confused in
their answers. When necessary, the order of questions was changed within
survey questionnaires to accommodate for any bias observed in the pilot
test. In some instances, questions were deliberately rotated from subject to
subject to prevent possible effects of order bias and rote response.

Telephone

Telephone surveys reported in chapters two, three and four utilised random
digit dialing of listed telephone numbers within the geographic area being
studied. Each number received a minimum of three callbacks before elimi-
nation from the sample. In the case where a subject was either unable to
participate because of time constraints or was not the appropriate person
within the household for the interview, a callback time was arranged.
Questionnaire length was kept to the minimum amount of time that would

both maximise the amount of information gathered and assure high co-operation and completion rates amongst the subjects studied. Response rates of seventy to seventy-five percent were targeted and successfully achieved for each of the telephone surveys.

In-person and intercept

In-person and intercept surveys utilised in chapters five, six and seven followed the same pilot test procedures as the telephone surveys with respect to the design and implementation of the final questionnaires. When subjects were required to choose from a multitude of possible purchase, behavioural or attitudinal responses (e.g., Which of the following best describes your attitude towards the Internet? as in chapter five), they were provided with cards listing the possibilities. This practice allowed the respondents who were working in less than ideal circumstances under constraint of both location and time to devote the maximum attention to choosing the best response, while at the same time freeing them from the chore of remembering all the alternatives.

Subjects were chosen at random at specifically designated locations within the geographic areas included in survey. Specifics of the geographic areas and selection methods have been previously discussed in the individual chapters. Every attempt was made to avoid interviewer bias in the selection process by stipulating an nth person procedure. Consequently, interviewers were instructed to choose every nth person and were allowed no discretion in these regards. Interviewers were further instructed no person in the company of a respondent should be allowed to assist in any way with answers or opinions rendered in the survey. When necessary and feasible, interviewers were instructed to lead subjects to a quiet area in the vicinity for the duration of the interview. The target of a seventy to seventy-five percent response rate was achieved for all the surveys.

Data entry and coding

Data for all surveys were entered by paid assistants. Assistants were trained in the use of SPSS statistical software and Microsoft Excel for entry of all data. Data entry assistants were allowed no discretion with respect to correction or coding of data, but were merely instructed to enter it precisely as it appeared on the questionnaire. In some cases, data entry assistants were the same assistants that had collected the data initially, and so had first-hand knowledge. Data entry assistants were required upon completion of the task to list the data file and check each record against individually numbered survey questionnaires. Frequency distributions were run on all previously coded variables to check further for number transpositions errors that may have gone unnoticed in the data listing verification phase.

SPSS "examine" statistical procedures were utilised by the author to further ascertain the verity and conformity of the data. Open-ended responses were recoded from alphanumeric string variables into nominal variables using SPSS "automatic recode" statistical procedures. These nominal variables in some cases were subjected to further recoding in an effort to reduce the number of redundant codes and categories that may have been created by the automatic feature of the software. Data were further examined for outliers and dealt with appropriately.

Data analyses

Data for all studies reported in this text were analysed using SPSS statistical software. Where appropriate and necessary, SPSS data files were exported for use with Microsoft Excel spreadsheet software for supplementary analyses and graphical presentation. Analyses used a variety of statistical procedures – from the most sophisticated (linear and nonlinear regression techniques, logit and multinomial logit, factor, cluster, loglinear, general linear models and multiple analyses of variance), to the most fundamental (frequency distributions, crosstabulations and descriptive statistics analyses).

Practical and strategic implications

Research presented in this text display a number of practical and strategic implications for researchers, marketers, strategists, advertisers, retailer, manufacturers and brand owners. Some of these have been previously noted in the conclusions of the individual chapters. What follows is a review and summary of some of the key points, with additional remarks.

The hypotheses developed and the results presented in this text are extensions of previous consumer behaviour research on automatic and strategic cognitive processing (cf. Fazio and his colleagues, 1986; 1989; Herr et al., 1990; Cohen, 1966; Axelrod, 1968; Gruber, 1969; MacLachlan, 1977; Aaker et al., 1980; Hoyer, 1984; Hoyer and Brown, 1990; Grunert, 1988, 1990, 1996; Woodside and Wilson, 1985; Woodside and Soni, 1991). The theoretical propositions of level of consciousness (Cohen, 1966), top-of-mind-awareness (Axelrod, 1968), affect referral (Wright, 1975), attitude-accessibility (Fazio, 1986), and unaided brand awareness (Hoyer and Brown, 1990) are likely to be most applicable for understanding routine problem (Howard, 1989) solving by consumers for buying frequently purchased consumer products like candy bars, soft drinks, personal care items and the like.

Understanding the amount and reasons for flows within a brand's portfolio of customers and competitors' customers is important. Monthly, quarterly, or annually programmed research on the attitude-accessibility of the firm's brands is recommended as a method to assess changes in brand image and as a means of auditing consumer thinking. A brand's attitude accessibility with respect to certain of the brand's evaluative attributes is likely to vary within a firm's portfolio of customers. Information concerning the differences in a brand's attitude and accessibility amongst these customer groups is very helpful in identifying competitive opportunities and vulnerabilities for the firm. The application of this type of customer portfolio analysis joins together two research literatures and extends the work of Tigert (1983) and Trappey and Woodside (1991). The moderately high levels of variance in primary brand choice behaviour explained by these attitude-accessibility models indicates that additional research is warranted.

Brand attitude-accessibility information may be utilised for modelling consumer's least favourite brand. Likewise, some negatively worded associates may be connected with retrieval of a consumer's primary store brand.

Previous research proves brands that are mentioned in second or third place in unaided brand recall questions tend to be "switch-to" brands. Research reported herein provides added support for the theory that unaided brand recall can be an indicator of past or future switching behaviour. Position of unaided bank brand recall will vary significantly between loyal (non-switcher) customers and those customers who have never been a bank customer and/or who have switched either to or from their main bank. Customers who have switched from a competitor bank to their current main bank will display a profile similar to loyal, non-switching customers. These customers are distinct however from the standpoint they are equally likely to recall the present main bank brand across first, second, and third positions. This reveals the strength of the enduring brand recall of the bank from which they switched.

In an unaided recall question of bank brands, defector bank customers are likely to not recall the brand at all. Results suggest that there is a very high likelihood that subjects who recall the bank brand in first position are either long time loyal customers or customers who have most recently switched to the bank. Lower order positions of recall are highly associated both with respondents who have never been a customer of the bank and turncoat customers switching from the bank.

A brand image relates positively with brand loyalty. In unaided attribute-to-brand recall questions, non-switching, loyal customers primarily evoke their own main bank or financial services institution when positive brand attributes are mentioned. Customers who have recently switched from a competitor to their current main bank are likely to evoke their new bank brand for positive attributes 2–3 times more often than loyal customers. The antithesis holds true for customers who have switched away from their main bank to a competitor. These customers are approximately 2–4 times more likely than loyal customers to evoke their previous bank brand when negative bank brand attributes are mentioned.

Non-switching bank customers demonstrate a willingness to remain loyal even though they may evoke their current bank brand for negatively worded bank attributes. Unfavourable attitudes may exist with high levels of bank brand recall. They possibly will also co-exist with favourable attitudes and might even be important in defining a given bank brand's loyal customer base.

The evidence connects higher positions of unaided brand recall with a higher probability the brand will be evoked for a positive attribute in an attribute-to-brand question. Lower orders of brand mention are associated with higher levels of negative attribute-to-brand evocations. If a brand has a low level of brand awareness or is unmentioned in an unaided brand recall question it is likely the brand will pop up later in a negatively worded attribute-to-brand question.

Results further demonstrates a strong association between loyal customers and first mention of the brand in an unaided recall test – thus early brand recall does imply brand loyalty. Customers who do not recall a brand at all in an unaided recall test are not likely to be loyal customers, though they may be competitor customers or new customers. There is a robust and significant negative association between brand loyal customers and no brand mention in an unaided recall test. Customers who cannot recall the name of the brand are therefore likely to be either customers who have switched recently, or loyal customers of competing brands. Loyal customers tend to think of their brand only in the prime recall position and in doing so relegate competing brands to lower order and no recall positions.

The results indicate the more frequently a customer evokes a brand for positive attributes in an attribute-to-brand recall question, the more likely the customer is to be a loyal customer. This association does not hold for competitor customers, switchers, and/or new customers. As one would expect, the total number of negative attribute-to-brand evocations is uncorrelated with customer loyalty.

Additional information, which some consumers are able to draw upon in the automatic and strategic processes associated with brand choice behaviour, is not so much a function of brand advertising exposure as its individual human cognitive ability. What is more, the notion that brand recall and information processing amongst children is conditioned primarily by cognitive ability levels, and less so by age, may call for a change in marketing communication practices. Thus, research presented in this text indicates that marketers, strategists, advertisers and even manufacturers need to consider the role human cognitive ability may play not only in brand recall but also in consumers' attitudes towards brands, accessibility of brand attributes and corresponding attitudes, as well as other factors such as the attitude-to-behaviour process, brand choice behaviour, and media consumption as well as its effects.

Heretofore, the role that human cognitive ability may play in consumers' cognitive processes a propos brand choice and a host of other decisions and behaviours has been largely neglected in the marketing field. Previous research on brand recall, attitude, and behaviour towards the brand do not consider g as a possible source of response latency and TOMA variation. The realisation that g plays a central role in brand information processing implies that its role may also be central in other consumer behaviours hitherto unexplored. The role of g in brand loyalty and switching behaviour as well in customer satisfaction are topics worthy of further research.

This chapter demonstrates that at an elementary level, the recognition and recall of brand stimuli, the retrieval of information and provision of a heuristic for brand evaluation, and the ultimate relevance decision that determines further higher-level processing, are all ultimately governed by human cognitive ability or g. Future research in attitude-to-behaviour, attribute-to-brand evocations and other automatic and strategic processes with respect to consumer brand choice behaviour, should necessarily include or at a very minimum control for individual differences in cognitive ability.

Avenues for further research

This text offers a number of opportunities for further research, but perhaps the most promising is the role that human cognitive ability may play in a whole range of consumer behaviours peripheral to brand choice. Recognition that human cognitive ability is measurable and that human beings differ individually with respect to this fundamental trait is a first step in addressing a whole host of issues in consumer behaviour. Many of these issues have profound ethical considerations for they bring not only a new dimension to the power of marketing, but also to the responsibilities of marketers.

One such issue worthy of ethical consideration and future research is the examination of the role that individual cognitive ability may play in consumer confusion, both with respect to susceptibility to dubious and/or misleading advertising, packaging and promotion. It may be also that human cognitive ability ultimately plays some role in consumer satisfaction, dissatisfaction and customer loyalty.

Cognitive ability relates with the consumption of some goods and not others. Compulsive behaviours and over-consumption of some products and services may have roots for some consumers in their inability to understand fully the consequences of engaging in the behaviours. With this in mind, future research may assist marketers in an appreciation of whether this is indeed the case, and if so, how to communicate warning messages and precautions for use effectively to consumers of their brands.

An understanding of the role that human cognitive ability plays in advertising response models and the effectiveness of media communications is certainly worth much future research. Issues surrounding the packaging and labeling of certain personal care, over-the-counter pharmaceuticals and prescription medicines pose new research questions for marketers.

Marketers for banks and financial services companies who sell pensions, unit trusts, mortgages and other products and services to consumers may wish to reexamine advertising, contracts and sales instruments through the lens of accommodating differences in the human population with regards to individual cognitive abilities. It may be in an increasingly complex world that some labeling, instructions for use, contracts, guarantees, and financial calculations are beyond the capacity for understanding by various segments of the population. If indeed such a fact can be proved to be the case, an argument can be made that the marketer is not relieved of the responsibility. In the future, such an argument may put forward significant ethical and legal questions and challenges for those firms who do not address the issue for fear of it being politically incorrect.

References

Aaker, D. A., Bagozzi, R. P., Carman, J. M. and MacLachlan, J. M. "On Using Response Latency to Measure Preference," *Journal of Marketing Research*, 17, 2 (1980): 237–44.

Ambry, M. "The Age of Spending," *American Demographics*, November 1990.

Axelrod, J. N. "Attitude Measures That Predict Purchase," *Journal of Advertising Research*, 8, 1 (1968): 3–17.

Axelrod, J. N. "Minnie, Minnie Tickled the Parson," *Journal of Advertising Research*, 26, 1 (1986): 89–96.

Banks, S. *Experimentation in Marketing*, New York: McGraw-Hill, 1965.

Chakraborty, G., Woodworth, G., Gaeth, G. J. and Ettenson, R. "Screening for Interactions between Design Factors and Demographics in Choice-based Conjoint Analysis," *Journal of Business Research*, 23 (1991).

Cohen, L. "The Level of Consciousness: A Dynamic Approach to the Recall Technique," *Journal of Marketing Research*, 3, 2 (1966).

Corstjens, M. and Doyle, P. "Evaluating Alternative Retail Repositioning Strategies," *Marketing Science*, 8 (Spring 1989): 170–180.

Ehrenberg, A. S. C. *Repeat-buying*, Amsterdam: North Holland: publisher?, 1972.

Fazio, R. "How Do Attitudes Guide Behaviour?" in: *Handbook of Motivation and Cognition* (eds R. Sorentino and E. Higgins), New York: Guilford Press, 1986.

Fazio, R. H. "On the Power of Functionality of Attitudes: The Role of Attitude Accessibility," in *Attitude Structure and Function*, Anthony R. Pratkanis et al., Lawrence Erlbaum Associates, NJ (1989): 153–179.

Fazio, R., Powell, M. and Williams, C. "The Role of Attitude Accessibility in the Attitude-to-Behaviour Process," *Journal of Experimental Social Psychology*, 27 (1989).

Fazio, R. H., Powell, M. C. and Williams, C. J. "The Role of Attitude Accessibility in the Attitude-to-Behaviour Process," *Journal of Consumer Research*, 16, 4 (1989): 280–88.

Fulgoni, G. and Eskin, G. J. "The BehaviourScan Research Facility for Studying Retail Shopping Patterns," in *Patronage Behaviour and Retail Management*, William R. Darden and Robert F. Lusch (eds), New York: North-Holland (1983): 261–274.

Gruber, A. "Top-of-Mind Awareness and Share of Families: An Observation," *Journal of Marketing Research*, 6, 2 (1969): 227–31.

Grunert, K. "Research in Consumer Behaviour: Beyond Attitude and Decision Making," *Journal of the European Society for Opinion and Marketing Research*, 16, 5 (1988)

Grunert, K. G. (1996). "Automatic and Strategic Processes in Advertising Effects," *Journal of Marketing*, 60 (1996): 88–101.

Grunert, K. "Automatic and Strategic Processes in perception of advertising," Proceedings *22nd International Congress of Applied Psychology*, Kyoto, Japan (July 22–27, 1990).

Hauser, J. R. "Agendas and Consumer Choice," *Journal of Marketing Research*, 23 (August 1986): 199–212.

Herr, P., Farquhar, P. H. and Fazio, R. H. "Extending Brand Equity to New Categories," *Working paper*, Graduate School of Business, Indiana University, 1990.

Holden, S. J. S. and Lutz, R. J. "Ask Not What the Brand Can Evoke: Ask What Can Evoke the Brand?," *Advances in Consumer Research*, 19 (eds) J. F. Sherry, Jr. and B. Sternthal, Provo, UT: Association for Consumer Research (1992): 101–107.

Holden, S. J. S. "Understanding Brand Awareness: Let Me Give You a C(l)ue!" in *Advances in Consumer Research*, 20, Provo, UT: Association for Consumer Research (1993): 383–388.

Howard, J. A. *Consumer Behaviour in Marketing Strategy*, Englewood Cliffs, NJ: Prentice-Hall, 1989.

Hoyer, W. D. and Brown, S. P. "Effects of Brand Awareness on Choice for a Common, Repeat-Purchase Product," *Journal of Consumer Research*, 17, 3 (1990): 41–48.

Hoyer, W. D. "An Examination of Consumer Decision Making for a Common Repeat Product," *Journal of Consumer Research*, 11, 4 (1984): 822–29.

Lilien, G. L. and Duxdic, A. A. "Analysing natural experiments in industrial markets," *TIMS/Studies in the Management Sciences*, 18 (1982): 241–269.

MacLachlan, J. "Response Latency: New Measure of Advertising," New York: *Advertising Research Foundation*, 1977.

Nedungadi, P. "Recall and Consumer Consideration Sets: Influencing Choice without Altering Brand Evaluations," *Journal of Consumer Research*, 17 (1990): 263–276.

Tigert, D. J. "Pushing the Hot Buttons for a Successful Retailing Strategy," in *Patronage Behavior and Retail Management*. William R. Darken and Robert F. Lusch (eds), New York: North-Holland, 1983.

Trappey III, R. J. and Woodside, A. G. "Attitude-Accessibility and Primary Store Choice," *Working Paper, Freeman School of Business*, Tulane University, New Orleans, LA, 1991.

Weinberg, R. S. *An Analytical Approach to Advertising Expenditure Strategy*, New York: Association of National Advertisers, 1960.

Woodside, A. G. and Wilson, E. J. "Effects of Consumer Awareness of Brand Advertising Preference," *Journal of Advertising Research*, 4 (August/September 1985): 41–48.

Woodside, A. G., and Soni, P. K. "Customer Portfolio Analysis for Strategy Development in Direct Marketing," *Journal of Direct Marketing* 4 (1991).

Wright, P. "Consumer Choice Strategies: Simplifying Vs. Optimizing," *Journal of Marketing Research*, 12, 1 (1975): 60–67.

Index